Bringing The Church Off The Slippery Slope

Recovery From Culture Wars

"If man searching for life, hope, direction, and meaning has only man to ask; if there is no revealed Word from outside man (Let's call that Word, God), then there is no answer to the question about man but man who is asking it."

Calling for World-Wise Christians
to be Subversive Agents for Christ
in a Seductive...Society

*Equipping His Bride to Display His Glory
Through World-View Studies*

Walter Puckett

Bringing The Church Off The Slippery Slope

Recovery From Culture Wars

Walter Puckett

Cover Design based on a concept from Patricia Puckett.

ISBN 0-916573-50-8

PUBLISHED BY
BRENTWOOD CHRISTIAN PRESS
4000 BEALLWOOD AVENUE
COLUMBUS, GA 31904

PUCKETT

12.95

Contents

86634

Foreword

Walter Puckett has done a great service for the people of God in writing this timely work. As we move rapidly towards the twenty-first century, only those who understand the times in which we live out the remainder of the twentieth century will be adequate leaders for this challenging time.

Dr. Puckett has read widely in the literature of the time; he has also comprehended a vast amount of details. We will fail to witness to the culture of dark shadows in which we all live if we do not respond positively to his type of criticism and response. The only other popular works of which I am aware that deal with Dr. Puckett's challenge are Russell Chandler's *Racing Toward 2001* (Zondervan, 1992) and Tom Sine's *Wild Hope* (Word Publishing, 1991). But I do him injustice if I affirm that his book is a mere rehearsal of their works.

Walter is first of all a disciple of Jesus Christ and a powerful preacher of The Word. His life's commitment is to bring The Gospel to bear on all dimensions of our world. As our culture has abandoned Christian presuppositions in every parameter of reality from mathematics to music, we cannot do greater service than to take a journey through Walter's work and apply it to our preaching and teaching programs in the local congregations. In our generation the Christian education programs have become the most expensive failures in the history of the church. Walter's work could reorder and redirect our absent vision.

In order to witness in the twenty-first century we must know the Word and the world if we are to cross-culturally communicate to the international mind set that has been on the slippery slope away from the Christian view of men and things for over two centuries. It is past time to address this demise and its consequences for the body of Christ. Walter's work addresses our "Dancing in The Dark."

Dr. Puckett's volume shows awareness of both the Word and

the world and gives constructive advice of how to address the greatest challenge in the history of the church—the culture shaping mind set of the last decade of the twentieth century. Thank you, Walter, for calling these crucial issues to our attention—hopefully in time.

Your fellow traveler
Dr. James S. Strauss
Professor of Philosophy, Doctrine, Theology
Lincoln Christian Seminary Lincoln, Illinois

About this book...

I am honored to be asked to review the material and have found it most edifying.

The subject matter is relevant, critical, and, therefore, much needed. The analysis of the present state of the church is very incisive, particularly for those becoming disillusioned with pragmatism. The call to let God be God and the church be the church rings a clear prophetic call.

You have approached the subject with scholarship, using respected resources for the material. The thrust is counter-culture, but that is the position to which God calls His people. I particularly appreciated the Christian world-view emphasis, largely overlooked by most contemporary church members.

This book is one that speaks to a contemporary need of the church and should be read by every minister, professor, and church leader. It is both scholarly and practical, which provides for the reader an insight into the posture of Christ's church in a world that is largely ignoring it. It also contains a prophetic quality that deserves consideration. It is my hope that you will proceed to publish this volume, and I would like to buy the first copy.

Your friend in Christ,
Marshall J. Leggett-President
Milligan College

Acknowledgements

"All writing is hard," says Paul Johnson. And, "creative writing is intellectual drudgery of the hardest kind." I do not think what I have written would be considered "creative", but it is imperative for the church to get off the slippery slope of a seductive society. Nevertheless Johnson's words still stand. That is why any writer is so dependent upon the kindness, generosity, and brilliance of others. I am grateful and dependent on a multitude of writers who helped me put together this primer about the imperative need of world-view studies in the congregations of Christ's Church.

When I was captured over two decades ago with the need to think Christianly by studying world-views and related issues, I began to graze through almost unlimited amounts of written and taped materials. Neither category was exhausted or could be by any one person. It is to this grazing I add my own thoughts, concerns and convictions, keeping in mind that there is really nothing original in most of us.

Greater minds than mine can be recognized in this production. The effort could not have been accomplished without them. I believe I have given credit to those for quoted material, and I trust that if something sounds familiar and is recognized as belonging to someone else, it is because no one can remember all that one reads. To all of those I give credit and acknowledge their expertise in their chosen fields of thought. I am grateful.

There is a large group of people who have contributed so much to my life and years of studies out of which this project has been birthed. To them I give my deepest appreciation.

There are those of smaller numbers that I do recognize as being so instrumental in my pilgrimage as a father, husband, Christian, pastor, and teacher at the congregational level. Next to the most important person in my life, my wife, there are my three children and ten grandchildren from whom I have learned and I am still learning so much. The most important person will be the one whom I shall recognize last.

I am indeed grateful for those of First Christian Church in Crown Point, Indiana, who have studied world-views and related issues with me. I am particularly grateful to the twenty-four people who helped me test an adult Christian education pilot project as part of my requirements for the Doctor of Ministry Degree from Trinity Evangelical Divinity School (TEDS).

In the same congregation there is another group of approximately seventy-five servants of Christ who have spent a one-year segment of their life in fifty-two one-hour sessions in the more technical study of world-views and related issues. I learned much from these two groups as to what was constantly pulling at their lifestyles trying to weaken their commitment to the theistic/Christian world-view and the Lord's Church. We all face that daily. Both of these groups have been gracious in their attempt to learn, and from their learning I have learned.

I would be labeled ungrateful if I failed to thank a particular pastor who influenced me greatly prior to my formal preparing for the local pastorate. This pastor, Dr. Marshall Leggett, is now President of Milligan College. In 1962 when I decided after four years of struggle to pull up sixteen years of roots in another avocation, Marshall was our family pastor. He helped us immensely. The one thing he said that I shall never forget, and I have passed it on to a son, a son-in-law, and numerous other young men who believed they were called to the pastoral ministry: "Walt, if you can be happy and satisfied by serving in the local congregation, don't enter into preparation for the pastoral ministry." At first, I thought that strange, but he did me a great service. He was saying, do not make the change wearing rose-colored glasses, for you will get hurt. That wise advice has seen me through pastoral situations when it would have been easy to quit. Thank you Marshall. Those with whom I have shared the same philosophy have also been grateful.

Two special professors helped me immensely in my first graduate program and my first thesis at Lincoln Christian

Seminary: Dr. James Strauss and Dr. Wayne Shaw. I have remained a student of serious study for thirty years because of their influence. There is another person who changed my life twenty-five years ago when I was ready to walk away from the Lord's church. It was Dr. D. Elton Trueblood who was used by the Lord to minister to me and encourage me to never give up. He has been a spiritual mentor and close friend to both me and my lovely wife in so many ways for all of these years. The first time I ever met him, he read me like a book and prayed intensely for me. Why? Because he loved me for who I was.

There is also the entire congregation who has heard the phrase "world-view" often in my sermons from the sacred desk. They may tire of this but are most gracious not to say so. There are also other adults from Bible School classes and the several Yokefellow Home Bible Study and Discovery Groups who have put up with this phrase. I believe they have learned much from it that is essential. Many of these people from all of the groupings have been my encouragers to attempt this book.

One of the greatest encouragers of the larger congregation during the birthing, genesis, and formation of this book has been a former Church secretary, Pam. Many times I would waver about continuing the project, but she would, in her own inimitable, very firm, but gracious loving manner, encourage me to go on. She worked laboriously as an editor reading and re-reading the manuscript always spotting mistakes and making astute suggestions. I am indebted to her.

There are two more individuals to whom I express my appreciation for their contribution to this work. They are Suelene Harrell and Lynn Cook.

The Star of all those who deserves the most credit is my wife, Pat, of forty-five plus years. It is not mere formality to say that without her this book would not exist. Her constant prayers, consistent smiling and loving encouragement, her incredible sacrifice in making my excellent library possible by working a career outside the home plus spending evenings and hours by herself while I was at the computer cannot, and will not, go unnoticed by me. She was also an editor for the work.

She has been my best friend and most faithful supporter for the forty-five plus years of our marriage and the mothering of the three best children God has ever given parents from whom we are blessed with ten grandchildren. She has been my best friend and faithful supporter from the start of our dating in high school a long time ago.

It was her radiant faith that broke through the stubborn rebellion against Christ in this person during the early years of our marital pilgrimage together. Christ was alive in her, and I knew it, but I did not want to admit it. She never nagged at me. I never felt that I was going to bed with Billy Graham quoting Scripture to me. It was her radiant faith that is still so alive that made her so magnetically different, and I had to go the same way. To say that I am so grateful to her seems like such empty words.

Through all of these years she has believed in me when at times I no longer believed in myself. When I was convinced of receiving God's call to the pastorate, it demanded that we pull up sixteen years of rooting down in a community and another growing and developing avocation. It was she and three small children who said, "let's do it." You see, God had answered her prayers that I would be called in order to find peace, joy, and purpose in life which our other avocation was not giving me and probably never would.

She has been the wind beneath my wings. If a star fell from God's cosmic universe every time I thought of Pat during the days and nights of our long journey together, there would be no more stars left for others to see.

To you, Pat my beloved, I dedicate this labor. Thank you for you who has been God's channel to get to me and bless me.

11

Preface

"Buried alive" in an "avalanche of change" is just one explosive significant truth throughout the writing of Tom Sine in *Wild Hope*. This truth is reinforced in Chandler's *Racing Toward 2001*.

These are just two of the proliferation of 90s materials perpetuating and reinforcing the truth that the church must be concerned with and involved in more than church growth methodology. The cacophony of Christian (and not so Christian) "pundits"—one pundit for whom "everything can be known, everything can be pronounced," centered professionally on the importance of marketing and methodological information alone—are almost drowning out the Word of God. Much of this methodology is building many larger religious institutions with "power religion." But is this building by conversions or by millions of Christians relocating in different fish-bowls for self-satisfaction? To raise this concern is disturbing to some, but as disturbing as that may be I think some out-spoken and disturbing convictions have to be shared in this book.

What is being revealed in the continued proliferation of 90s material like the two foregoing books, plus Hunter's *Culture Wars*, Wuthnow's *Rediscovering The Sacred*, Bennett's *The DeValuing of America* and many other productions, is that the church must be involved in world-view and trend analyzes studies. The imperative need of this discipline as part of Christian education is heating up, but too few pastors, church leaders, and local congregations are heeding the need as a crucial and critical part of evangelism and kingdom work to produce disciples beyond the success of "church growthism."

Shelly and Shelly's *Consumer Church*, another 90s book, know the danger of shallow church growth. Their concern is about the possibility of evangelicals winning the world while at the same time losing their souls. Furthermore, is to offer people the power and benefit of Christ without telling them the costs of following Christ false advertisement?

What about *Power Religion,* a 90s collection of essays edited by Michael Horton, author of *The Agony of Deceit?* These essays are about the evangelical church playing "me too" with the world's idea of power in psychology, sociology, and politics. The theme of the essays is that when the church replaces its unique message with power religion, it sacrifices biblical fidelity and public credibility. All of this concern relates to world-view issues, studies, and trends awareness.

World-view and trends studies are not a 70s issue. They are not studies just for the academic world. This is a 90s and 21st Century issue for Christian education at the local level, or the church will not understand what is going on in the world around it. We have waited so long to face this, and now much of the church is talking to itself.

What are world-views? This question is more fully answered in Part One. Brief definitive answers will suffice for now.

The most succinct definition is: "A world view is a set of presuppositions or assumptions which we hold consciously or subconsciously about the basic make-up of our world."[1] And every person has a world-view or a mix of world-views controlling life.

These "assumptions" are what people believe to be the final truths upon which life is based and lived out. A world-view is like a stability structure, a person's attempt to make sense out of the world of ideas and experiences. A world-view is one's philosophy of life. It is like glasses through which we see the world and the various dimensions of life around us. A valid world-view enables one to integrate all the parts into a meaningful, consistent, and coherent whole. My thesis is that the theistic/Christian world-view is the only one in the midst of many world-views able to accomplish that.

A world-view is Charles Kraft's "central control box," and whatever world-view is dominant in influence in the center of culture/society effecting every social parameter of culture/society is that "central control box." Until recent years the theistic/Christian world-view was the dominant influential world-view in this nation. No longer is that happening. We have to know why and reverse the trend.

If, in and through the Word of God, Jesus Christ meets each person and challenges each person to respond, then each believer has the extraordinary privilege and opportunity and the tremendous responsibility to think about this biblical Word in the context of cultural conditions and come to understand what it means for himself or herself and how it applies to daily life. The Christian world-view articulates truth that orients, challenges, and transforms as it opens new perspectives on life and the world.

Christian discipleship involves world-view understanding which is reading the signs of the times in order to discern where such transformation is needed and how to participate in the same.

I illustrate with one world-view running wild in society that demands the transforming power from the Christian world-view by the efforts of modern disciples. It is in both the liberal and conservative wings of the church. This world-view is "nihilism," an outlook on life that says there is not a thing in the universe to give meaning or lasting value to human life. This is only one world-view that Christians must understand and see what it's doing to society and many who claim to be Christian. It may be "more lethal to Christianity in the West" than other world-views.

John Castelein has insightful words about this world-view:

> Where is nihilism in our culture? I see it in the boredom of your youngsters. I don't mean the occasional tedium we all experience, but I mean the relentless disenchantment with life—the inability to enjoy anything for more than five minutes at a time (if at all). Even in our youth groups in church there are so many empty young people whose souls have already been "amused to death" so that everything except the most recent toy or fad is B-O-R-I-N-G!

14

I see nihilism in the even greater trivialization of the important things in life: life in all its richness, mystery, and tragedy is being reduced to simplistic caricatures of heroes and villains (World Wrestling Federation, Rambo, and many movies and TV programs). Where everything is "awesome," true awe is lost.[2]

Therefore more of what you can expect from this book as a primer for world-view studies in the local congregation is information, explanation, motivation, and more illustrative material to hopefully move Christians from this book's very introductory "why" world-view study is a rapidly growing imperative need and issue in local congregations of the church.

My desire is to help congregations move into necessary technical studies and fully realize why materials related to world-view concerns are still being produced in rapid-fire efforts. It must be said again: this is not just an academic concern. Indeed, it is that, and every person in any form of leadership/pastoral ministry preparation in Bible College or Seminary must become world-viewish.

But it must be pressed again that world-view studies at the congregational level are more imperative than ever before as our Western World continues to move through convulsion after convulsion in search of the meaning for life and the direction society must take or follow *The Fall of The Roman Empire!*

The future is already upon us when we consider the dynamics of change that are affecting and will effect much more in life, society, and church in the future. We are facing demographics that will change our country into being more elderly, Hispanic, black, and Asian. Revolutions in economics are now upon us. International politics are in constant ferment. An electronically connected community of the most powerful nations will, no doubt, bring forth challenges we have never faced. Then there is the new World Order. What will it bring? All of these dynamics involve world-views effecting every person, and these world-views will continue in different ways in the battle for the control of the modern mind.

There is also the growing tension of the global environment. How much of this is true? How much of it is false? How much of the issue is sheer politics on both sides? A world-view issue! The rise of ethical issues in the technological innovations of medicine that pictures someone "playing God" with human life is now a reality. Because of the power and growth of communications, the line between fantasy and reality will be even more blurred than now. All of this involves world-views.

Church and social historians believe that since most Christian leaders in the past failed to come to grips with changes taking place in the past such as "the 1950s (television), the 1960s (social unrest and anti-authoritarianism), the 1970s (the loss of idealism resulting from Vietnam and Watergate), and the 1980s (unbridled greed and increasing demands for rights),"[3] perhaps it is time the church prepare for the future before it gets here. After all, that is what some corporations and governments do. No wonder Jesus said in Luke 16:8. "For the people of this world are more shrewd in dealing with their kind than are the people of the light" (NIV). Is this still true in too much of the modern church, particularly older established congregations, where the leadership of elders and deacons is by and large just not cutting it in order to take on the 21st Century world for Christ's sake?

This is why Sine writes in Wild Hope: " . . . if we don't begin . . . to anticipate both the new challenges and the new opportunities the twenty-first century brings us, we will quite literally be buried alive in the onrushing avalanche of change."[4] It's all about world-views and trends, both of which the church must be able to handle and study.

In the future, if authentic Christianity flourishes, it will do so under greater pressures such as the growing height and thickness of the so-called constitutional law between church and state. This appears to be a continuing effort to take away from churches and Christian organization special tax privileges and as some think, the elimination of chaplaincies—all "an ongoing effort to remove any vestiges of religious advocacy from publicly funded institutions."[5]

Other pressures rapidly coming upon the church are the bitter fruit of the modern Christian and non-Christian dysfunctional families, substance abuse, various addictive patterns to life and living, and as Chandler correctly maintains, "an increased fuzzing of the lines between religion and transformational psychology and occultism," wherein "psychology as religion becomes an alternative altar."[6] It's all about world-views.

With all the tensions that will grow and mount their voice in present and coming years developing some of the most devastating human dilemmas modern man has ever had to face, who will supply the vision and values to guide and plot the way for this nation? The church? Sine insists that "only a church that is inspired, informed (world-views/trends), and forward-looking has any chance of being heard above the din of tomorrow's approaching hoofbeats."[7]

The church has not heeded the warning of the late Dr. Francis Schaeffer who cautioned the American society and the church about bowing their knees to "personal peace and affluence." That is a world-view issue. Even though many conservative Christian groups are growing numerically as stated in my opening remarks, I concur with Sine: "I don't believe they are always growing in their commitment to God and God's mission. To the contrary, many conservatives are finding all kinds of ways to use their faith to sanction their own private pursuit of prosperity, position, and power."[8] It's about world-views and the need of congregations to be world-viewish and aware of trends.

My intent for this book is to have it challenge, inform, and at times disturb if Christians will be open to its primary purpose of assisting local congregations develop not only a growing and ongoing Kingdom awareness but also a world awareness. This combination can develop authentic growth of Kingdom people in and for His church.

The future has already begun. The stage for the jarring and significant events of the coming decades has already been set by the past. Christians, Kingdom people, must use their brains, allow the Holy Spirit to inflame their will, and roll up their sleeves, realizing the survivors of the battles for the mind of modern man will be innovators bringing the live Word of God incarnated in Christ-followers into the marketplace of culture wars. It's about world-views!

The Lord's Church must be in a constant virtuous cycle: the informing and enlightening of the mind, the inflaming of the heart, that is, the totality of the person coming alive, and the subversive invading of and engaging in the world for Christ's sake, the world's sake, by His power, and moved by real hope!

All of this will require the kind of faith and hope of Abraham. Perhaps the future times will make this kind of faith and hope the last bastion of power to change the modern mind-set that is destroying so much in life and living. Paul writes about Abraham's faith: "Against all hope, Abraham in hope believed . . . " (Romans 4:18a).

What will the church do now in preparation for now and the future? Picture in your mind an idyllic, pastoral, wholesome, and pleasant-feeling picture of a community with the quaint, but beautiful, white church building with its majestic spire reaching off into the cosmos.

At the same time, consider the significant, but important, assumption that the culture/society or community around that majestic and reverent-looking building reminds us of the message of truth, hope, and life-transforming purpose found in the Person of Truth, Jesus Christ, flowing out from that setting. The imagined and assumed idea is, the church is not just an institution. It is a force of truth, hope, and purpose at the center of that culture/society. In that idyllic picture the church is assumed and recognized as a force with which culture/society had to reckon.

Along side that picture, see another. A picture with that white, quaint, reverent-looking church building setting on a slippery slope with its majestic spire reaching into the cosmos. It appears to be barely able to stay put. Will it slide off the slippery slope into oblivion? It sets there by itself away from culture/society. Few pay attention to it. To the masses it may be only a place to gather for a few minutes each Lord's Day, then, leaving the Lord there until they return, maybe, the next Lord's Day. To really expect that Christ and His Church has much of anything to do with the other six days of the week is not for multitudes including many believers.

Of course we know that the authentic church of the Living Lord, even though it may go through persecution, will ultimately never be toppled by anything or anyone in this world. But we are considering a contemporary situation in the present context of Christ, Church, and Culture/Society.

Again, put your imagination to work. In your mind look at the original idyllic picture, but see the picture with its quaint white church building and its majestic spire pointing off into the cosmos no longer there. It is gone! It's out on the slippery slope. Literally, there is a void in the center of the original picture. All that is growing, in the absence of that church building which at one time was the center of truth, hope, and transforming purpose for that culture/society, is weeds and rapid deterioration and disintegration all around.

This is no longer just imagination. It is now a fact. In the collision of world-views alien from and diametrically opposed to the theistic/Christian world-view, these world-views have overshadowed, outthought, and outpracticed those of the body of Christ, His church, who said they believed in and lived by the theistic world-view. The church as a bold force of true Truth and righteous Godly power of hope, joy, and purpose for life and culture/society has been repositioned by modern culture wars in our society to the slippery slope.

Now the church in its present position of crisis is being hammered on by the culture wars that are attacking the family, arts, sciences, humanities, education, law, politics, etc. The masses of the majority of the membership of the church in America, including my heritage to which I belong by choice, has little if any idea as to what has happened and is happening in this shifting, and why it has happened theologically, philosophically, and socially. It's all about world-views and related issues.

The remedy to reposition the church off the slippery slope

back into the center of culture/society is not the continued building of institutions of multi-million dollar facilities gathering in hordes of non-transformed people as exciting as that certainly can be. That is not necessarily evil. But the challenge is far greater. In the midst of a growing mega- and super-church mentality of "power religion," society continues to deteriorate. Why?

It is past time to recover the Christian mind! It seems that Christianity in America charges full-speed ahead in its "incessant activity, indomitable individualism, and irrepressible pragmatism."[9] Getting results and doing work seem to make-up the all-consuming objectives of most of the church leaving little room for tough-minded contemplation of the role of the theistic/Christian world-view being challenged and outdone by alien world-views.

But as historian Mark Noll quips, "Comprehensive and coherent Christian thinking has never been a major part of religious life in America."[10] I would think that if there is one Christian Movement that ought to set the pace in this needed thinking, it is the heritage to which I belong: Christian Church-Churches of Christ of The Restoration Movement. There was a time, according to history, when this same heritage did this, but not now. Therefore I pray that something from this book can recover the art of thinking by Christians who are really disciples of the Christ.

Introduction

Reading an introduction to a book is inviting some writer to break into my thought process to tell me something he deems important and essential. The material may be new, refreshing, disturbing, challenging, rewarding, or all of the foregoing, but I allow the writer into my mind .

I am asking readers to do the same. I believe my topic is one that most Christians and far too few pastors and other church leaders understand, therefore, missing a needed dimension in their development as disciples of and disciplers for the Lord Jesus Christ. The topic under consideration has much to do with the following:

> *What will the morrow bring/Will it me sorrow bring,*
> *Joy or dismay?*
> *"The future will be Christian, or it will not take place."*

The first two lines are from a German fraternity song that echoes, perhaps unconsciously, Jesus' words in the Sermon on the Mount: "Therefore do not worry about tomorrow, for tomorrow will worry about itself. Each day has enough trouble of its own" (Matthew 6:34). But the line after the song's words present the challenge that decides between "joy" or "dismay."

We are into the last tenth of the twentieth century labeled as the most bloodstained century since the world began. Pondering the dawning of the twenty-first century does not make it easy to share the carefree optimism of the fraternity. Those of us who take seriously Jesus' words and consider ourselves bound to heed them find it hard not to be anxious and worried.

The more we know and understand about the world now, the more difficult it is to be anything other than pessimistic and fearful in spite of the fact that we know God is faithful and sovereign. Harold O. J. Brown of Trinity Evangelical Divinity

School, in his paper: "Church, State, Society in Twenty-First Century America: Lessons That We Can Learn from Constantine the Great," gives the following observation by the Austrian systems analyst, Hans Millendorfer:

> Whoever follows the discussion about the future, as it is carried on above all by agnostics and atheists, is shaken at the hopelessness expressed, and at the deep longing for hope, which is seen as possible only if there is a transformation of values.[1]

Implicit in the observation is the suggestion that hope is possible—but only if a certain condition is fulfilled. Millendorfer expressed this condition orally: **"The future will be Christian, or it will not take place."** I apply that to our culture/society in this last decade of the twentieth century. Our society in its future will be Christian, or at least influenced by Christianity more than any other world-view, or it will not take place—and "if in some sense it does not take place," Dr. Brown insists, "that future will not be ours!"[2]

Everything that follows in this book is like an inspection tour of significant world-views and related issues/situations making the one-line foregoing statement significant.

If you are a lover of boating picture yourself in a canoe paddling down a lazy river when suddenly you come around a sharp bend and hear the roar of the rapids. I imagine that if you have been there you'll recall the mixture of fear and pleasure, the joyful anticipation mixed with a little dread. Our world, including this nation, of this last decade in the 20th century appears like that to me.

Perhaps we turned the bend in 1989 when the Berlin Wall fell. Now other walls have toppled, more may follow. Yet the world is filled with so many questions and concerns that don't seem to help the situation. When we scrutinize the world, particularly our own culture and society around us, we see religious explosions with Christian label. Yet with church membership at an all-time high, Christianity appears to have little effect on life and society. We have politics that few trust, economic fears and jitters, a judicial system held in suspicion by a growing number who have trouble trusting it, a public educational system that does not really teach or educate about life but trains youth in socialism and skills only for a job market, a quagmire of living and life that has little if any morality, plus other fractured and fragmented situations.

It has been, and continues to be, a time of revolutionary upheaval. Does the church, including my heritage, the Restoration Movement (Christian Church-Churches of Christ) have anything to say to this world? I am convinced that it does. But I fear that too much of the Restoration Movement, like much of the conservative church in America, has managed to sleep through the revolutions of thinking in and of the modern world and has survived only by the residue of our past strength of the plea for unity.

A defensive posture and an anti-intellectual attitude in so many has characterized much of the conservative church, including my heritage, and has caused a crystallization. That has prevented my heritage from translating the richness of its plea and legacy into a hopeful and powerful proclamation of the gospel. Removing the foregoing posture and attitude is the only way to encounter and engage the Gospel into the modern thought that came from the impact of a culture and society dominated by the assumptions of the Enlightenment. That is still not understood by much of my heritage and millions of other Christians.

Should it be understood? You decide. All that the Enlightenment did was to banish the Jewish-Christian God of the covenant community and enthroned a new king on the pedestal of the universe—the new king is the autonomous individual called "man" who was considered by Protagorus as ". . . the measure of all things." The time is late for my heritage and other Christians to come alive!

This failure to encounter the modern world under the cultural assumptions of the Enlightenment and a host of alien world-views has led to a kind of ghetto existence (a living away from the challenges of the modern world of thinking) for the Movement and a failure to let people in on our rich legacy.

I have studied in several institutions of higher-learning, and to this day when new friends understand the Restoration Plea, our history and purpose, the question is usually: "Where have you people been? You have so much to offer the world trapped in religious institutionalism who want to break out of denominational staleness."

My close friend and a spiritual mentor for 25 years, Dr. D. Elton Trueblood, still asks the foregoing question. He is appreciative of our legacy and purpose.

The Book's Direction

What I have attempted in this book can help the heritage that I cherish and other Christians to know the world in which we must minister. It can also develop a break out of a ghetto existence to encounter and engage the modern thought patterns of our world challenging every dimension of Christianity. Unless we know these thoughts as well as we are to know His Word, we will remain tucked away during the rest of the revolutionary times before us. At times the book may appear to be an angry book. There are reasons clearly stated for this.

We must understand that ideas have consequences. Armies do not control the world. Ideas do! The ideas called world-views controlling American culture, society, and much of the modern church have bypassed, ignored, or blatantly refused the wisdom of the ages and have brought us to a spiritual, moral, and cultural crisis wherein one wonders if survival is possible. Our culture and society is, as George Roche, President of Hillsdale College in Michigan, writes, "the modern tragedy"[3] of *A World Without Heroes*.

The only possible remedy is the recovery and assimilation of Judeo-Christian values translated into life through the ministry of the church. The present church as a whole, including the Christian Church-Church of Christ in its present state of shal-

24

low-thinking, "cheap grace," immaturity, and refusal to tackle the big ideas and their consequences, good and bad, is too ineffective to sufficiently bring God's saving power through transformed lives to all social parameters. This we are mandated to do even in the heartland of America as well as in the megacities where the major cultural and social decision-makers exist affecting each and every person, including the church, in this nation.

These problems did not crop up yesterday. *Time* magazine had this warning April 18, 1949:

> Communism is not the only threat to western civilization and perhaps not the greatest threat. The greatest threat to our civilization comes from within that civilization itself - our $64 euphemism for it is secularism. A much blunter word is godlessness. Our civilization, for all its churches and all its churchgoers, is predominantly a secular, godless civilization.[4]

I was not a believer then. I was just beginning to worship once in a while, but in 1958 when I surrendered to Christ I still heard nothing about the foregoing warning that is now in full fruition. This book is to challenge and hopefully disturb the Church enough to face the reality of the foregoing that has picked up steam since the quote. It is about the imperative need of Christians understanding world-views, related issues and their consequences from which comes the threat to our civilization and religious freedom. It is about survival. If the shape of the church in society is as George Barna says in *The Frog In The Kettle,* and I concur that he is correct, then this book in your hands is a possible tool leading to other more technical tools to help get the frog out while we still have time to bring new hope to the world.

It involves the work of pastors in the equipping ministry (Eph. 4:11-16—How strange this biblical description of the ministry for the entire congregation still is not accepted by churches locked into tradition and who harp about the clergy system.) to equip Christians—the priesthood of all believers—to sing the

Lord's song manifesting His glory in an alien land (Psalm 137:4); a contemporary society that is foreign and alienated from God and His grace and power. The world-view that has to be sung is the proven, time-tested, workable theistic/Christian world-view that the World needs now! Historically, its an old song, but it will always be more contemporary than tomorrows' news.

I have reasons for bringing in such a Psalm, a Psalm that is not on most people's list of favorite Psalms. It is one of the Psalms of negativity, the Psalms of complaints of various kinds, those Psalms that cry out for vengeance. At the same time, there is a profound penitence that is foundational to a life of faith in this particular Psalm.

Today much Christian piety and spirituality is romantic and unreal in its positiveness. "As children of the Enlightenment," Walter Brueggemann believes "we have censored and selected around the voice of darkness and disorientation, seeking to go from strength to strength, from victory to victory. But such a way," Brueggemann maintains, "not only ignores the Psalms; it is a lie in terms of our experience."

The Psalms as a canonical book is finally an act of hope. "But the hope," Brueggemann continues, "is rooted in the midst of loss and darkness where God is surprisingly present."[5] Psalm 137 is a voice of those who have lived longer and have learned with anguish that things would not immediately be righted. But the psalm does not despair. Hope is resilient. It draws its power and authority out of another vision marked by homecoming which seems remote, but it is not for one moment doubted. There is in the psalm a faithful tenacity to endure and an understanding of the costliness of resistant faith, all built on a passionate faith in Yahweh in an actual life situation.

In the singing of the Lord's song, it must be understood that the Dominion Mandate of Genesis 1:26-29 (This is not Reconstructionist Theology)[6] and the Commission of Christ to make disciples in the Witness Mandate of Matthew 28:16-20, a command that Jesus assumed would be carried out with His assurance by His disciples, demands world-view studies. The demand is not in order to be saved but in order to obey both mandates.

I believe that these two mandates need to be understood in this relationship. God made a covenant of His desire to have the lost world, man and the creation, reconciled to Himself (Mark 16:15-16). Therefore, the Great Commission (Matthew 28:16-20) is related to the covenant renewal of the Cultural or Dominion Mandate (Genesis 1:26-29). This context of creation and man involves reconciling the lost and equipping them to subdue and manage the earth. It restores the ability to man, through the power of Christ, to do what God originally told Adam and Eve to do. This view of the mandates means that the laos (people of God) who cannot spend all of their work hours trying to convert people, or they will be fired, can be just as faithful to the Great Commission by learning a skill and faithfully working on their jobs to express their relationship to God through their work carrying out the Great Commission and Cultural Mandates.

They can be disciples of the risen Christ, cleverly disguised as workers, career-people, professionals etc. working out their vocation of serving Christ in their avocation of wage-earning. This opens ways for disciples to witness to others on behalf of Christ, but they will have to know the world-views of those to whom they are witnessing.

The Bible is aware of world-view and world-views. What we find in the Scriptures are not bits and pieces of truths. It is a total cosmic world-view that encompasses the relationship of God to human beings and to the entire creation. It is when we learn to live in that total world, the strange new world of the Bible, that we have entered the realm of Christian truth. When we allow that total viewpoint to dominate our thought and action, when we live into it and participate in it, we, as Paul says, no longer consider anything or anyone from a human point of view (2 Cor. 5:16). The apostolic tradition becomes that which shapes the whole of our lives and world, and that leads to sound Biblical, Christian theology resulting in sound Biblical preaching and teaching.

Jesus had a world-view. He was fully God/fully man and as man He had perspectives on life that He shared with society including His enemies. His understandings and perspectives did not originate in His society. They came from God and were/are normative for all peoples for all times.

Therefore if Christianity is for all the world, and if Christianity is God's project, then to carry out God's project demands that Christians not only know God's Word, living and printed, but God's World of alien world-views. These alien world-views are spewing forth value systems diametrically opposed to all for which Jesus lived and died and arose to release resurrection power to make man new in order to carry out God's purpose.

How can we sing the Lord's song in a foreign (alien) land like our part of the Western world? The answer requires a realized preface related to the likeness of our time and that of the time of the Babylonian Blues of Psalm 137:4-5. The life of the one in exile is inexpressibly sad. The Babylonian lament has echoes for now. So, how do we sing the Lord's song that is the total message from God in Christ in our alien land?

There are two requirements. One is to know the Lord's Song which is Christianity. It is the only song for any new age, because it transforms people and transformed people can by Christ's power deeply affect and transform any culture/society. The song answers basic questions to which every world-view has to respond. The only song that answers those questions consistently, coherently, and logically is the theistic/Christian world-view.

The other requirement is to know the foreign (alien) land, a society that for the most part is foreign to and alienated from the theistic/Christian world-view of new life and hope. This is done by scouting out what is wrong with the alien land such as values, issues, fragmentation of life, etc. and the source of such. Christians become spies, subversive agents, finding out what

Satan and godless world-views have been doing, and then we set out to do something by action, even subversive action, through ideas that have good consequences on God's behalf and by His mandates about the situation within the principalities and powers. That requires world-view studies. These studies also keep the spy for God from forgetting our Jerusalem (the theistic/Christian world-view) and falling prey to the modern Babylon mindset. As George Herbert wrote: "The life of spies is to know, not to be known." Without world-view studies in this modern world, the church stumbles along like a blind man without his cane reaching a few people but making very little impact on culture/society.

You have a world-view. I have a world-view. Everyone has a world-view. The term "world-view" is really a poor English attempt at translating the German "weltanschaung." To add to previous definitive statements about world-view, it literally means "a philosophical orientation, a life perspective, or a life integrator."

And to add more to this, the Christian faith and world-view is not a blind faith. It is an attempt at a coherent view of life and society in all aspects to make sense of the totality of human experiences. It is to affirm the gospel as public truth which is to invite acceptance of a new starting point for thought for modern man, the truth of which will be proved in the course of a life of reflection and action which proves itself more adequate than any other world-view to the totality of human experience. It is presenting and commending what we believe to be a true and coherent view of the whole of life.

More definitive statements for world-view will be expanded.

Book's Purpose Expanded

This book is not a detailed study of various world-views per se, but various dimensions of certain world-views will be considered. It is not intended to be technical. It is a primer to assist Church leaders and all Christians. It is intended to raise a more conscious awareness of some ills and issues facing the Church;

ills and issues coming from world-views other than Christianity that are doing great damage to human life and our culture/society.

It is not intended to be controversial. But it is written from the standpoint of one who is děeply committed to the Christian faith and theistic/Christian world-view. It needs to be known that this commitment was not the first thirty years of my life.

The book's aim is not to present a defense of Christianity to all comers. Nevertheless, strong convictions for authentic Christianity are stated. Many of my thoughts are an apologetic. In the spirit of tolerance, it is my hope and desire that readers outside my circle of theological and personal convictions will think about and grasp the substance of my claims and apply them to their own context of thinking and living. I would hope that Christians would put the book in the hands of non-Christians who are willing to use their minds.

It is written with the conviction that there is one world-view which answers the basic questions of life in a cohesive and con-sistent logical manner that will be considered. It is written with the conviction that the loss of this one theistic/Christian world-view as the dominant influence in Western society has taken away a consensus on essential and absolute ethical and moral answers. From this has come a created society of grays and con-fusion.

I hope the efforts set forth will reveal some other weakness-es found in my heritage but less often in the camps of our allies. One of these weaknesses is a contrary proneness to anti-intellec-tualism and superspirituality. These traits too often lead to a disparagement of logical reasoning and to a failure to give prop-er attention to such things as philosophy, the arts, humanities, sciences plus other important aspects of our culture requiring intellectual thinking. It is time for pastors to understand that to be intellectual in order to face our world is not being an "egghead." That is only the slur of the uninformed who have shortchanged their witness.

The story goes that in some of the countries in Eastern Europe they have militiamen who go around in threes. The reason for this is that the first one knows how to read, the second knows how to write, and the third one is there to keep his eye on those other two intellectuals.

There are some settings and church leaders who can make one feel like the story's point if you speak intelligently for more than two minutes and with more than one thought in each. You are considered dangerously intellectual and unspiritual. The sad note is that too many pastors, some really good people who are missing so much by not being thinkers, in the entire Christian camp lead the pack in this kind of thinking. They have not realized that they must not only know God's Word but also God's world which is in shambles in almost every parameter of society. They have refused to accept the mandate of exegeting culture along with the Word of God. They have also shortchanged their own lives and ministries.

The fact is that the church must rise above such a level illustrated in the foregoing story and demand pastors to lead as thinkers. That's a heavy demand, but it's imperative! Thinking and struggling with the ideas that have consequences is not an evil thing to do. I believe the times in which we live will force pastors to decide about the following: they will either attempt with hard work to keep up and abreast of the intellectual fashions of our culture/society or labor as pastor and minister only on a devotional level. If they choose only the latter, that will be disastrous for the church.

Furthermore an arrogant superspirituality too often found in my heritage and other groups leads many conservative Christians to sit on their hands while various systems and spheres of our society such as education, politics, media, etc. rush pell-mell to weed out, permanently, the fact of God and the theistic/Christian world-view.

Because of "the great absence" of God's allowed presence, we are an era that has ushered in characteristics and attitudes that violently agitate like a convulsion. The current revolt against a supernaturally grounded God-ordained morality has created philosophical skepticism and doubt, and we have a societal moral relativity that has engulfed ever-widening reaches of modern life until a sweeping civilization crisis now overshadows the West. It is a state of being carried away in a cataclysmic time of change captured in the opening scene of *A Tale of Two Cities,* the riveting novel by Charles Dickens:

> It was the best of times, it was the worst of times, it was the age of wisdom, it was the age of foolishness, it was the epoch of incredulity, it was the season of Light, it was the season of Darkness, it was the spring of hope, it was the winter of despair, we had everything before us, we had nothing before us, we were all going direct to Heaven, we were all going direct the other way—in short, the period was so far like the present period, that some of its noisiest authorities insisted on its being received, for good or for evil, in the superlative degree of comparison only.[7]

The dichotomous nature of the era that Dickens describes and then applies was certainly the result of the dichotomous relationship of the eras' two great events: The 1776 American Revolution and the 1789 French Revolution.

Both revolutions were against European monarchs in the late eighteenth century. But America did not rush to the aid of the French Revolution in their struggling to be free of a monarchical tyrant. Why? What issue was involved in the differing tension between the two revolutions?

World-views. The American leaders recognized that the world-view of the French was rooted in the non-theistic atheistic humanistic mindset that was entirely incompatible with their own which was a theistic/Christian world-view; a covenantal Christian response to God's grace. The world-view of the French Revolution was a deliberate affront to Christianity giving rise to a horrifying reign of anarchy and terror that cost the lives of thousands of innocent citizens and burned itself out in blatant licentiousness and rabid activity of sexual desire.

The dichotomy between these two world-views plus other world-views in tension with the theistic/Christian world-view is present today in our society. The tension is growing resulting in terrible depersonalization and destruction of human life and meaning plus the continuing fragmentation of culture and society.

The theistic/Christian world-view yoked to any non-theistic world view like secular humanism and/or other world-views is an impossible marriage. No society survives this kind of attempted marriage that I find going on, even within some of the church, because no world-view other than the theistic/Christian world-view fully answers life's basic questions.

Because so many world-views of ideas are battling for the mind of modern man with some having a more dominant unhealthy influence than others, we are in so many ways a fragmented society marked with some deadly attitudes: a craving for more and more, a preoccupation with self, a bondage to various fears, a callous disregard for human life, an entertainment addiction, an obsession with physical gratification, and a create-your-own-God mentality.

Masses of the unchurched and the lost have this profile: no practical consideration of God or Jesus Christ in their lives, limited or no working knowledge of the Scriptures, and a denial of the validity of any divinely ordained moral and ethical absolutes. They also consider biblical ideals, values, and religious ideas as irrelevant or unbelievable, church or Christianity means little or nothing—many are turned off by any institutional forms of Christianity, and self is the primary frame of reference wherein the rational, scientific way of acting and explaining issues is their predominant philosophy of life. This is all about world-views and their dominant influence.

All of these mindsets are deeply embedded in a growing number of those who are churched at least in some kind of spurious membership syndrome. Some who worship regularly often trip themselves up and reveal some of these profiles.

Many modern people unaware of how they are controlled by some world-views appear to have life quite out of focus. Walker Percy asks in his book, *Lost In The Cosmos: The Last Self-Help Book*, "How can you survive in the Cosmos, about which you know more and more while knowing less and less about yourself, this despite ten thousand self-help books, one hundred psychotherapists, and one hundred million fundamentalist Christians?"[8]

Percy also suggests that we are more adept at scientifically penetrating the universe and less competent in understanding ourselves. We shoot space craft into the heavens, moving farther away from our world, as if we have despaired of ever being at home on our planet. Science and technology have brought us many wonders but have, in the process, retarded our ability to wonder. Lost in the cosmos, we wander as exiles, aliens in our own land, drifting, cut loose from traditional proven moorings, traveling from a place we have long ago forgotten, being carried along to we know not where. I call this the loss of a binding address such as Paul teaches Christ to be: "He is before all things, and in him all things hold together (Col. 1:17). In other words, Christ orders all things for a purpose. He is the binding address.

My prayer and hope is that this book will help those of any background, who care, to understand the significance of world-view studies and some of our dilemmas caused by so many world-views controlling so many people unknowingly in different ways.

Such studies remind us that Christians are mandated by Jesus to be wise in the ways of the world. We are not to adopt those ways, but be sensitive enough to them to penetrate the world with the gospel. We are to have a ready defense against opposition to the message of Christ. Christians have the responsibility to respond intelligently to the world around them (1 Pet. 3:15). This will only be done when Christians not only understand world-views but also know and understand identified trends affecting our society in order to become effective agents of change rather than change agents affected by the world.

I have alluded to this, but it needs emphasis again. The church as a whole needs to come to grips with the truth that it is meaningful and worthwhile to do such studies so that Christians and other caring people can labor together in the world in a more meaningful way. The church needs to be the pace-setter in such studies and get outside of its walls. W. A. Visser't Hooft stated the necessity of this:

> One reason why the churches have not helped the laity to see the Christian significance of their vocation in the world is that the churches had lost sight of the cosmic dimension of the gospel. This could only lead to a self-centered ecclesiasticism or pietism. When we realize again that Christ is the hope of the world, we see also that activity in the world is meaningful. It does not carry its meaning within itself, but it has a goal, an end: the kingdom. Christians are men and women who live toward the future and manifest this faith by acts which express their hope and expectation. At a time when—because of the collapse of the doctrine of progress—there is a great danger that all human effort is poisoned by a sense of futility, the Church has the great opportunity of re-creating a sense of the meaningfulness and worthwhileness of worldly vocation.[9]

When the church knows not only what its world-view is and why it is believed to be the only valid one for life and society, and also knows the world-views vying for modern man's minds and what they are doing to life and society, then the church will be ready to take on the world. The church will then be ready to dialogue with those controlled by other world views and reveal the good news of Christ and the difference He makes in life and this world now.

It's the proper time and opportunity to tackle this in view of some fine print below a headline in a *Good Housekeeping* magazine: "Welcome to the Decency Decade, the years when the good guys finally win," describing '90s marketing predictions. The final line of the ad was: "America is looking for something to believe in."[10]

I insist that the theistic/Christian world-view offers that. I maintain that the theistic/Christian world-view can be demonstrated to provide for life and culture/society that which no other world-view can. I believe Paul was saying in the Ephesian epistle that the church does not just have a message, but it is to be the message as God's new humanity. I am totally convinced that today the church is called to demonstrate that new humanity in an open way but also be subversive in a wholesome way in a seductive culture/society that has and is seducing Christianity.

This seduction has, through culture wars, repositioned the church on a slippery slope. Too few Christians really know intellectually what is going on around them. I have to agree with John MacArthur, Jr., in his assessment that the church, instead of offering the sufficiency of Christ, seems to be scrambling for acceptability in the world luring people with all kinds of worldliness instead of making disciples of the risen Lord.

Rodney Booth of the United Church of Canada said: "Our world is desperate for another Luther. For someone who has the courage to read the signs of the times, and the wisdom to discern therein a new window through which to view and understand God's activity in the world today."[11] That involves world-view studies.

In the context of carrying out the mandates already stated within the realm of world-view studies, Dr. James S. Strauss of Lincoln Christian Seminary insists:

> the commission cannot be fulfilled as long as 'God's frozen people' are merely passive attenders at church services. Christians are called to be salt, light, and leaven—terms which conquer alien belief systems and convert individuals, institutions, and cultures. In order to do this every Christian must grow and go and witness.[12]

George Barna is correct: "Charged by Christ Himself to be agents to change the world rather than agents changed by the world, we have been mesmerized by the lures of modern culture."[13] I concur! Modern Americans, Christian and non-Christian, have been lured by world-views diametrically opposed to the theistic/Christian world-view.

We are in a war! It has been suggested that the world is now being ruled from the grave by seven men whose battle for the mind of man was the ultimate effort. They are winning as gods in the Western world. The seven men are: Charles Darwin and the evolutionary hypothese; Karl Marx father of socialistic communism (this mindset may be breathing its last breath); Julius Wellhausen who espoused "higher criticism" of the Bible resulting in modernity (We are now in the post-modern age); John Dewey in public education; Sigmund Freud in psychology; John Maynard Keynes from where our current budget deficit comes; Soren Kierkegaard, the existentialist philosopher. Where is the church?

To give some final direction the book is taking, a brief synopsis of the following Parts is justified to encourage the reader not to allow some of the more technical material to halt reading all the material. Every major Part, some longer than desired, are essential to the topic and purpose.

All that is written is understandable by anyone who wants to make a difference. Any one Part could be read by itself and make a contribution, but reading all Parts is essential for the Kingdom person who wants to count for Christ's sake. The Table of Contents gives the flow of each part. Use it as you think about the following synopses.

Part One about Perceptions is the most technical part of the book giving significant foundation to all other Parts, but its greatest significance will be seen in Parts Four and Five. Part One is a definitive portion of the book examining various worldviews and their relation to some basic questions of life that every world-view has to answer. Only one world-view can fully answer the questions. These are necessary perceptions to know.

I can say without reservation that any person, including some junior-high and many high-school youth, who want to grapple and grasp the material in this Part can handle and understand the material. That has been demonstrated by my people. If youth really want to make a difference in their world, and go beyond the pampering and entertainment given them by the church and some contemporary youth pastoring that means well, but keeps up more with fads that often pushes the Word of God to the side, then they can understand this Part of the book. It's up to them. Youth can either take on the world for Christ's sake or set around whining about being bored.

Part Two is a Proposal about the imperative need of world-view studies in the Christian education efforts of the local congregation. This Part also contains a personal note along with the fact that there is at least one congregation that has proven my proposal and conviction of the need of world-view studies in the pew.

Part Three is about getting some perspective on the relation of world-view studies and the contemporary Church Growth movement. Some strengths and weaknesses of this movement must be considered in relation to the danger of a mindset in the church that ignores the world; that is, Jerusalem must go to Athens. Meaning? That will be explained. It is very important. The growth of the church for Kingdom work is much larger than developing super-churches numerically. If the world is not effected by the mega-church, perhaps gnosticism has become the major message of the church instead of the Word of God in all its fullness.

Part Four examines the Problem that moves the reader into the crises that results in a culture and society when the theistic/Christian world-view loses its dominant influence. That Problem creates all kinds of crises, more than can be considered in one book. There is a raging battle between peril and promise

Part Five about Particulars contains the horror stories because the church refused to be aware and study what has been going on around it for decades. There is in the American Church, particularly the conservative church, a gnosticism that continues to try to separate that which God never separated: the sacred from the secular. I'm a late bloomer in the Christian faith, but understanding this infuriates me. This part is illustrative in various areas of life and living and what happens when the church fails to take the Good News to the Marketplace affecting and effecting every social parameter of God's creation. Perhaps this Part could be read first to motivate the reader to see from where the crises have come by then studying the Preface, Introduction and the first four Parts.

If the church is going to rise in a new century to its possible magnificent purpose and place and hopefully be repositioned back into the center of culture/society, a new appreciation and demand for high-level Christian education as the hope of the world is a most pressing need. The church must be educated to be world-viewish and trends aware.

"If the gospel is to challenge the public life of our society," writes Lesslie Newbigin in *The Gospel in A Pluralist Society,*

> it will not be by forming a Christian political party, or by aggressive propaganda campaigns. . . . It will only be by movements that begin with the local congregation in which the reality of the new creation is present, known, and experienced, and from which men and women will go into every sector of public life to claim it for Christ.[14]

Now, please read on, even if you become upset by some criticism, but read on to learn, assimilate, and for His sake, and in His power, and by His grace touch the society in which you live. Take your time in reading. Some may say this is too academic. I think not. But if it is, perhaps it is past time for local church leadership to be more academic along with the practical and pragmatic. The practical without true theory is eventually futile. Just because something works does not always mean, from God's perspective, that it's true.

Part One: Perceptions Necessary

Can The West Be Converted

Much of the contemporary church is striving for success instead of a rigorous faithfulness to the Lordship of Christ. How involved or not involved in such different and somewhat demanding studies as described and defined in this somewhat technical Part will make a significant decision about the future.

Will there be left to our children and grandchildren a significantly new, strongly biblical, Mother Teresa-type faithfulness as a Christian legacy? Or will the contemporary church that is so much like the non-Christian world in visions of possibility and life leave the same contemporary dull Christian legacy that is built more on modern mindsets that are biblically questionable? Will there be left only a civilization with its death rattle already clearly noticeable? Someone in the church had best decide and do it rather quickly!

Such a large segment of today's church is the last to know the issues challenging Christianity. The church must realize that America is a foreign, alien culture/society as far as the life of the church is concerned. Our modern popular culture/society has baptized the churched and unchurched alike in media messages to the place where we cannot even attempt to state a case for faith without some knowledge of the nation's and world's marketplace. The same earnestness invested in missionary endeavor must be used in our approach to our modern popular culture/society.

But, what's our response? We watch and complain. What we do not do is to listen carefully and really study our opponent's world-views. It is past time to recover the Christian mind.

Such works as Michael Scott Horton's *Made In America,* the shaping of modern American evangelicalism must be known. It is a jarring, but true analysis of modern religious life in

41

America. Yet, mega-Christianity in America pushes full-speed ahead on a course of "incessant activity, indomitable individualism, and irrepressible pragmatism." Getting "results" captures and consumes the objectives of much of the church leaving little room for tough thinking about the role of the theistic/Christian world-view. Phillips and Brown wrote in *Making Sense of Your World*: "Quantifying the work of the ministry has resulted in sanctified versions of the Fortune 500 (the largest churches and ministries), the top forty (Christian pop music), and the Nielsen ratings (Christian television)." Their continued and true assessment is that the "feel good" religion that Christianity has become casts a "jaundiced eye" toward anything that smacks of "intellectual pursuit"[1] that I am advocating in this book.

The 1990 Van Dyke Mission Lectureship at Calvin Theological Seminary in Grand Rapids, Michigan, dealt with the issue of "The Gospel and Western Culture." Three topics were considered: (1) The Mission of the Church in North America; (2) The Content and Proclamation of the Gospel; (3) Can the West Be Converted?

The third question cannot be avoided by the church except by refusal. It is related to the fundamental shifting in historical thought during the past many decades. This shifting and the resultant convictions and values relates to world-views that have created and are creating lifeviews, therefore giving us a partial understanding of the ideas that shape culture and society today.

Understanding the shifting of historical thought is part of the task of realizing the importance of cultural awareness for the church's purpose and ministry. Biblical theism, the theistic/Christian world-view that once shaped our culture and society has given way to a pluralistic mindset in a culture and society captured by many world-views related to and resultant from the shifting history of thought. These non-theistic, against-God, world-views are casting a suffocating shadow over the biblical theistic/Christian world-view in this nation. It is critical!

The theistic/Christian world-view that has a suffocating shadow hanging over it can be stated in this manner: It is the proclamation of the Lordship of Christ over all life and creation as set forth in Scriptures including all social parameters of life (Col. 1:15-17). This world-view also sees the Lord's church as "the pillar and foundation of the truth" (1 Tim. 3:15). This church is a people who "take captive every thought to make it obedient to Christ" (2 Cor. 10:5) believing that the theistic/Christian world-view is the only authentic and workable alternative world-view in a pluralistic world of competing world-views. The credibility of the gospel is at stake and must be demonstrated, and can be demonstrated, as valid and authentic through this world-view.

Therefore the opening logo question for this Part has survival overtones: can the West be converted or at least influenced enough by the resurrecting and the renewing of the theistic/Christian world-view to the point of overriding alien and destructive world-views? The church is called to this ministry. This cannot happen without the church understanding the Word of God, the shifting of historical thought, and the plurality of world-views.

Of course some people will be reached and reconciled to God without bothering about all this imperative work of study for understanding our world and nation and how we have arrived in this cultural and societal mess. But our task as the church must include the responsibility of learning from where other people's values come in order to be able to communicate the Good News to them. That responsibility is integral to the reconciling of the lost. It is also integral to the dominion mandate in Genesis.Thus the biblical demand for world-view studies.

There is material in this book that will, perhaps, be disturbing but hopefully challenging. I do this for a reason stated in the words of a friend and scholar, Dr. D. Elton Trueblood. They are more relevant now than when given years ago.

> One of my greatest fears about our generation is the fear that we may not know what time it is. If we do not know the time, it is very likely that our efforts, however sincere, will be wasted. There is, for example, little value in trying to answer questions which people are not really asking.[2]

It is in Luke's Gospel that we find the keenest sense of the importance of knowing the times when he shared what Christ had pointedly said to Jerusalem, "You did not recognize God's moment when it came" (Luke 19:44 NEB). We have not seemed to grasp the fact that most of Christ's contemporaries did not recognize Him. How much has this really improved? Because of the failure to recognize and heed the Christ, every culture and society finds itself out of step with God's purpose for the world, and this creates chaos and havoc, because our "time" is not understood as to what has happened and is happening.

To consider the time in which we now live in the context of the following materials about world-views and related issues, there are two approaches both of which are dangerous and opposites. They are complacency and despair. Dr. Trueblood insists that "to conclude that our society is fundamentally so sound that we are bound to come out all right" is complacency and a serious mistake, because the assumptions giving this kind of decision are false and irresponsible. Likewise, "if sentimental optimism is mistaken, the mood of despair is equally so."[3] I have to concur.

Therefore, the following material making up the book will be a helpful tool to steer God's people down the middle by their being aware of the constancy of God and His Word and the dangers leaping out at this culture and society from various world-views opposed to and contradictory of the theistic/Christian world-view. As any person struggles to keep from being drowned in either blind optimism or destructive despair, one promise made in John 1:5 will help lead any person through the center: "The light still shines in the darkness and the darkness has never put it out." (J. B. Phillips)

Fundamental Shifting In Historical Thought

When historical thinking shifts, the results birthed are different convictions, values, philosophies, patterns for living, and the way one looks at life and society. From this shifting comes world-views that battle for the mind of man and for the controlling influence in culture and society. We find ourselves in culture wars. This affects the church to the point that right now there must be continual critical examinations of the affect that our culture and society has on our walk with the Lord. The contemporary church is affected more by culture/society right now than most want to admit. Yet, the church's influence is muted and waning.

The most sudden and sweeping upheaval in beliefs and values in our society from the shifting of historical thought has taken place in this century. No generation in the history of human thought has seen such swift and radical inversion of ideas and ideals as in our lifetime. The radical shift in thought has fomented problems never before faced in our Western world. This radical twentieth-century drift and shift can be summarized as follows. It is a long sentence. Read it carefully.

Instead of recognizing God, Creator and Sustainer of all and everything, as the source and stipulator of ultimate truth and the good, most contemporary thought reduces all reality considered by modern man as just the now of what we can understand by our senses. Reality is reduced to the present and to impersonal processes and events, therefore insisting that man himself and alone, not God, creatively imposes upon the cosmos and upon history the only values that they will ever bear. Read that again.

Surely no one can miss the impact of this shift. We had better not miss this, because every generation alive and generations to follow will bear the brutal results of this philosophical mindset that has overshadowed and almost removed the once most dominate and influential world-view: the theistic/Christian world view. Dr. Carl F. H. Henry states the critical situation.

> This dethronement of God and enthronement of man as lord of the universe, this eclipse of the supernatural and exaggeration of the natural, has precipitated an intellectual and moral crisis that escorts Western civilization despite its brilliant technological achievements ever nearer to anguished collapse and atheistic suffocation.[4]

This man-centered power is perpetuated in such a subtle way that most miss it in the latest and powerful present Disneyland production called "Fantasmic." It is a powerful production produced and presented by excellence from Mickey Mouse and fantasy land. The message says that man alone has the power to win the ultimate battle with good over evil. Thousands see this every night at Disneyland, but I doubt if very many understand the significance of its message. It's a striking world-view presentation.

By the late 1920s, a striking shift of perspective and thought had prevailed. References to deity as the God of Abraham, Isaac, and Jacob, the self-revelatory God of biblical theism moved to some kind of God-in-general, then to a John Doe-god and even to what was called the not-God. This led to something called a divine Cause, to a divine Designer, to a divine Lawgiver, and finally arguing from the mind of man as if man was the center of truth, God ended up as an Absolute Reason. From our One personal God there emerged varieties of gods, infinite and finite, personal and impersonal.

Naturalism, a world-view we will introduce, dismissed God entirely except as a convenient symbol for man's supreme social or private values. This would be like tipping one's hat to God in most Civic Clubs. Yet, "American educators," Dr. Henry reminds us, "abandoned the concept of God as the integrating factor in modern university learning."[5]

Therefore, our present problems just did not happen yesterday. Oh yes, university campuses continued for several years having what was called the annual "spiritual emphasis" week, a kind of "be kind to God" week. But why? I don't know. I have never figured that out except that it was a smoke-screen for phoniness. Stephen Miller, president of Johns Hopkins University said in the 1980s that the universities may be producing a generation of "highly skilled barbarians."[6]

But being a churchman I think that I have the right to ask this question: where was the church during all of the years of this shifting? Why did it seemingly sit idly by without challenging the shifting that was going on in historical thought?

I am a late bloomer into Christianity. I am convinced that Christ is the only hope to turn any society around via His people. I made my commitment to Christ and His church in 1958, and as a person in the pew for a few years after that I never heard anything in relation to this shifting and what it was doing to the cause of Christ as the church ignored it. To this day I do not hear or read little, really nothing, about the fundamental shifting in historical thought from a people—a historical Christian Movement—who ought to be on the cutting edge of the issues as a so-called People of the Book.

Where was the church during this shifting? Looking back, it was busy saving a person's "soul." But that word was basically misused according to the Old and New Testament meaning. It was understood as something separate from our physical body that had nothing to do with this world now. The word for "soul" in both testaments is not some immaterial part of the body. The word for "soul" in both testaments is about the total living being of the person. To handle the word "soul" in any other fashion is a form of gnostic dualism that is preeminent in the conservative church.

During this radical shifting of historical thought the church appeared to totally ignore scholarship and the Dominion Mandate of the Old Testament plus the Witnessing Mandate of the New Testament. These mandates are to bring the power of God through Christ in transformed people, His church, into the marketplace, allowing the theistic/Christian world-view to influence every social parameter of a society.

Understanding this purpose makes the evangelistic thrust of making disciples in the church even more exciting and meaningful. This is so much more than the gnostic effort of "winning souls." It is about the disciples of Christ, not "souls" void of both the Old and New Testament meaning, in the marketplace who make the intended and possible difference. This is so much more than non-biblical "souls" setting in some multi-million dollar shrine on the Lord's Day morning but never impacting the society with the power of God during the week. Where was the church during the shifting of historical thought? I would like an answer.

To better understand the mindsets leading to value-shifting that have come out of this massive shift of historical thought, there are studies from which I draw that reveal various world-views other than the theistic/Christian world-view. The studies also reveal some weaknesses of the people and institutions, including the church, that espouse the theistic/Christian world-view at the present time.

Allan Bloom wrote in *The Closing of The American Mind:*

"There is one thing a professor can be absolutely certain of: almost every student entering the university believes, or says he believes, that every truth is relative."[7] This is the issue of truth against contemporary moral relativism that even many in the church seem to believe. It is the mindset that says there is no truth. Everything is relative. Einstein believed that in reference to space, time, and the natural world. But he called moral relativism a malignant "disease."

Peter F. Drucker wrote in *The New Realities* that: "the 'next century' is already here . . . . We do not know the answers" about the "issues." Between "1965 and 1973 we passed over" and entered "the next century . . . a political terra incognita with few familiar Landmarks to guide us."[8] This is saying that past traditional and workable values are lost landmarks for most, and it appears there are no answers for modern man at this point. The goal-posts for the game of life from the Christian perspective have been knocked down.

In the *The Naked Square* Richard John Neuhaus writes that our society "is the result of political doctrine and practice that would exclude religion and religiously grounded values from the conduct of public business."[9] This is the issue that separates the sacred from the secular; a private faith with no public involvement. For most of this century that is where biblical conservatism stood. We are slowly and painfully breaking out of that.

James Turner wrote in *Without God, Without Creed*: "religious belief passively collapsed under the pressure of science and social change . . . . In trying to adapt their religious beliefs to socio-economic change, to new moral challenges, to novel problems of knowledge, to the tightening standards of science, the defenders of God slowly strangled Him."[10] The church adapted to other world-views instead of standing firm with the theistic/Christian world-view. This was the last warning of the late Dr. Francis Schaeffer who said "the greatest evangelical disaster was the church's accommodating the gospel to the culture." He was correct. It is still true in the hunger to be successful.

Wade C. Roof and William McKinney wrote in, *American Mainline Religion* that: "the place of the religious institutions in American society is indeed changing, and at a fairly rapid pace . . . . Since the 1960s, the realities of pluralism and privatism have done much to undermine old religious and cultural hegemonies."[11] The theistic/Christian world-view lost its influence because of the weakness of the church.

Stanley Hauerwas and Wm. H. Willimon in *Resident Aliens* maintains:

> Sometime between 1960 and 1989, an old inadequately conceived world ended, and a fresh, new world began . . . Church, home, and state (had) formed a national consortium that worked together to instill Christian values . . . . A few years ago, the two of us awoke and realized that, whether or not our parents were justified in believing this about the world and the Christian faith, nobody believed it today.[12]

There are serious problems in the church because of its weak understanding and application of the theistic/Christian world-view.

Lesslie Newbigin wrote in "The Enduring Validity of Cross-Cultural Mission," that "Western culture was once a coherent whole with the Christian vision at the center. It has disintegrated."[13] Other world-views have taken over. Their influence overshadows the theistic/Christian world-view.

In *Fragmented Gods* Reginald W. Bibby wrote that "For some time now, a highly specialized, consumer-oriented society has been remolding the gods. . . . The problem with all of this is that religion, instead of standing over against culture, has become a neatly packaged consumer item—-taking its place among other commodities that can be bought or bypassed according to one's consumptive whims."[14] Some church growth folk need to see if they are not advocating the same thing instead of standing firm with all of the theistic/Christian world-view.

Herbert Schlossberg wrote in *Idols for Destruction* that "expelling the biblical presuppositions that were the only ones that could provide a foundation for rationality, we unwittingly invited the irrational to join us."[15] Forgetting to bring biblical faith into our reasoning and just using reason alone does this.

In *Kingdoms in Conflict:* Charles Colson wrote:

> On the surface, a value-free society sounds liberal, progressive, and enlightened. It certainly sounded that way to the generations of the sixties and early seventies—probably many of the same people now wringing their hands on the pages of Time. But when the public square is naked, truth and values drift with the winds of public favor and there is nothing to govern how we are to live together. . . . Whether we like to hear it or not, we are reaping the consequences of the decades since World War II when we have, in Solzhenitsyn's words, 'forgotten God.' What we have left is the reign of relativism.[16]

The radical shift in historical thought forces this question: How then does America hear the gospel? Different than in the past? The only certain way to answer that question is to know the world-views controlling America. (See Appendix.)

To have the proper perspective on the topic of world-views that have surfaced in the modern and post-modern world from the assumptions of the Enlightenment and other historical shifts of thought, the following divisions of Part One give essential perceptions anyone unfamiliar with the topic of world-view needs to grasp. These perceptions will give insight, knowledge, and assistance in the rest of the book.

The need for knowing these perceptions is more widespread than just in our own society. Reverend H. D. Beeby, colleague and friend, of The Selly Oak Colleges in Birmingham, England, and Bishop Lesslie Newbigin also of Birmingham are developing a national program of world-view studies for the British Council of Churches. Their program is rapidly creating much interest in that part of the world. There is also a net-working group in this nation, led by Dr. George Hunsberger of Western Theological Seminary in Holland, Michigan, working with Newbiggin and Beeby. Why? The need is desperate and widespread to know world-views.

What Bishop Newbigin wrote about the British culture in relation to that developing educational program is too important to reduce.

> Enlightenment values have come to dominate wherever Western politics, education, economics, science, industry, technology etc. are influential. At a time when the West doubts itself and loses hope,its axioms and values triumph elsewhere. Religious faith along with many facets of the rich diversity of human cultures, is more and more confined to the private sphere while the public sphere, like public architecture, becomes more and more of the same: Western and modern and Godless. Wars even against the West are fought with Western weapons. The slogans current throughout the world are Western cries of equality and democracy, and the world divides between the Western ideologies of nationalism, capitalism and communism. A mission to the Western world-view and its fruits is perhaps the most important single undertaking in the world-wide Christian mission today.[17]

What Bishop Newbigin wrote can be said with almost equal force about our culture/society. The values of the Enlightenment will be introduced.

Therefore, such a program of study that does require some thinking and often some rearranging of values in a person's life has to do with an examination of how the Christian Church can effectively confess its faith within the public life of this culture/society and the entire world. That is a task larger than anything the Western Church has ever faced.

In the context of the entire book, my conviction is that Christians in this final decade of the 20th century must be equipped as never before to enter into this culture/society armed with the possibility of new hope as it hovers between peril and promise. It is very much about the legacy for future generations. Can the church provide the correct and meaningful legacy? Will it? Is the church willing to make some radical and mature efforts and changes to be able to do so; not changes in the wonderful biblical message, but changes in educational efforts to become abreast of the world in radical change so we can communicate to it? Will the conservative church move into the future tense?

This hope would be the result of a world-view about life that has an almost two thousand year track record of answering the basic questions to be stated later about existence and living that man has struggled with and pondered over for centuries. This world-view is of course the theistic/Christian world-view. This is a presuppositional approach, but I am convinced rationally and experientially that it is the only one world-view that can save a culture/society on a collision course with various world-views by which our society and people are trying to live, but they are failing, world-views are battling for the mind of modern man.

To pick up again the theme of a Psalmist, Christians as God's spies must be equipped to answer the question Israel was asking when their tormentors commanded them to sing the songs of Zion. The question was: "How can we sing the songs of the Lord while in a foreign (alien) land?" (Psalm 137:4) I repeat again what the alien concept means. Christians are living in a society that is by and large foreign to and alienated from the theistic/Christian world-view. Authentic Christians are resident aliens, subversive agents, and spies in a society that is reaching out for something that will work in life. Secular humanism, the most influential world-view, has failed. New age philosophy is trying to do what secular humanism could not. It too shall fail! Nevertheless, new age philosophy will continue to grow right into the year 2000 because of the weakened condition of the church as a whole in this nation. Its influence seemingly continues to wane.

Therefore, all Christians must learn in a new way how to "sing the songs of the Lord" in this alien land. Christians will only be equipped to adequately do this better when they know two things: first, what they really believe, and why, in the context of world-view thinking, they believe their theistic/Christian world-view is the only hope. The second thing that they must know is, what the people around them with whom they are to share this world-view believe and why they believe it. Otherwise, in our alien land there is little chance of real communication and less chance of leading others by conversion into the only world-view that works and answers the basic questions of life consistently and coherently. Yet, conversions seem a rare fact today.

The theistic/Christian world-view is valid not only when it changes and transforms people's lives but also when those lives affect and effect society in such a positive way that many of the world-views and resultant value-systems that are ripping this society to shreds cannot survive and continue their destructive ways. In this process Christians are "singing the Lord's song" in such meaningful ways that those who may not have any relationship with the Christ of the theistic/Christian world-view, but do have a real sense of caring, decency, and concern about our world, realize what the theistic/Christian world-view is and does to keep life, culture/society alive and meaningful. They too can become singers for the Lord, because they have found something new and fresh in the person of Christ to whom they can and must develop a personal relationship.

This fundamental shifting in historical thought has brought into life many world-views. Therefore world-view must be defined.

World-View Defined

The most succinct definition is: "A world view is a set of presuppositions or assumptions which we hold consciously or subconsciously about the basic make-up of our world."[18]

These presuppositions or assumptions which people believe to be final truths and upon which life is based and lived out "are more or less self-consistent, generally unquestioned by each person, rarely, if ever mentioned by" one's friends "and only brought to mind when challenged by"[19] some other world-view or assumption about life.

A world-view most dominant in a culture/society "is the central systematization of conceptions of reality to which the members of the culture assent (largely unconsciously) and from which stems their value system. The worldview," writes Kraft, "lies at the very heart of culture, touching, interacting with, and strongly influencing every other aspect of the culture."[20]

A world-view is also like a stability structure. That is, every person has a set of beliefs and values about the world, and a world-view becomes the guiding principle for living in the world. A world-view is also a tool for cultural analysis. In more contemporary jargon, a world-view is what makes people tick and act, good or bad, the way they do.

A world-view is a way people see or perceive the world and life around them; the way they know it to be. What people see is in part what is there. It is partly who we are. Whether we begin with the presupposition or assumption that reality is personal or impersonal is a large issue in world-view studies. Is God personal or impersonal? What decides that makes a world-view.

A world-view is a person's attempt to make sense out of the world around him such as the world of ideas and experience. It is one's philosophy of life. Most cannot articulate it, because they are not aware of having a world-view. Someone said that it is like a Chinese riddle: "If you want to know what water is, why is the fish the last one to know?" This captures the essential difficulty Christians have in becoming aware of their cultural context. Therefore we have happening what Os Guinness called "the sandman effect."[21] This effect is the matter of Christians falling asleep in the face of extreme danger. There are three factors involved. First, they have no feel for the social dimensions of believing. Second, they have no tool for what we call cultural analysis. Third, they have no skill in contemporary comment. To be world-viewish remedies all three factors.

A world-view is like a platform or a base of operations upon which we stand and from which we look at the world before us. From this platform we obtain what Frank Gaebelein calls "the Weltanschauung, the world-and-life view which frames and focuses our understanding of the cosmos and all its complexities."[22] For example, if I am a nihilist I see life and art as phantoms of meaninglessness, their reality to be scorned, and all belief in their permanence to be destroyed. Therefore my art and my critique of art will support the fundamental position I hold. All is nothing. Or if I am a hedonist I see life as a large playground intended for my pleasure-making. I will do anything to make pain absent. Likewise my art and critique of art will conform accordingly to my world-view. If I stand on the Word of God as my platform, and it becomes my base of operations, then I see life and art and the entire cosmic world in an altogether different picture.

A world-view is like glasses through which we see the world and the various dimensions of it around us. Learning to think in world-view terms gives us confidence that we can meet tough universal questions and issues with solid answers. Everyone has a world-view or an eclectic world-view (a mixed world-view made by self drawn from many world-views that will not work).

World-view is a way one views the whole world and one's world-view makes a world of difference. It is an interpretive framework. It is a frame of reference like the diagram of Figure One in Appendix. A world-view is like a pair of colored glasses. It enables one to integrate all the parts into a meaningful, consistent, and coherent whole. But all world-views other than the theistic/Christian world-view have difficulty in getting the parts to fit properly for consistency and coherence. These world-views make this impossible, and the life that adheres to that world-view is also fragmented and fractured without knowing the reason or reasons why, and their life is inconsistent and incoherent when compared to the only world-view that works: the theistic/Christian world-view.

A world-view is a general framework within which one can fit or attempt to fit all the facts. It is like a plot that holds the play of life together if it is a valid world-view. Of course I am writing from the position that the only workable and valid world-view which meets the criterion for validity is the theistic/Christian world-view. This becomes our starting point of reference such as the diagram of Figure One in Appendix 2.

Having stated the foregoing strong position, does this mean there is no truth in other world-views? No. There is some truth in every world-view as brilliantly pointed out by Richard Mouw in his *Distorted Truth*. New Age world-view even has some truth, and this world-view has surfaced so powerfully simply because of the weakness of today's church. But finding what truth there is in alien world-views provides common ground for dialogue. This common ground of dialogue makes it possible to show the validity of the theistic/Christian world-view's ability to integrate all parts of life into a consistent and coherent whole for all of life.

An overall workable world-view has certain characteristics. First, it has a wholistic goal trying to see every area of life and thought in an integrated fashion. Second, it is a perspectival approach coming at things from a previously adopted point of view which now provides an integrative framework. Third, it is an exploratory process probing the relationship of area after area leading hopefully to a unifying perspective. Fourth, it has action outcome, because what we think and what we value guide what we do. It is a furnisher of guidelines for being, thinking, acting, and doing.

What distinguishes a theistic/Christian world-view from its competitors is the basic framework of biblical thought within which it operates and within which every aspect of biblical drama is set. It is an ongoing relationship between God and His creation.

A world-view is never merely a vision *of* life. It is always a vision *for* life. Our world-view determines our values. It directs our life and relationships. It helps to interpret the world around us. It sorts out what is important from what is not; what is true from what is false; what is of highest value from what is least. It provides a model of the world which guides its adherents in the world. Cultural life is not only rooted in the dominant world-view a person holds; it also orients life in culture/society in terms of that world-view. Thus world-views are best understood as we see them incarnated in actual ways of life.

Conceptualizations form world-views. The world-view lies at the very heart of culture/society, touching, interacting with, and strongly influencing every other aspect of culture/society. That is the purpose of the illustrative diagram of Figure One in Appendix 2.

Consider for illustrative purposes how a world-view affects youth. A world-view is imposed upon the young of a society by means of familiar processes of teaching and learning through television, school, culture, heroes (if we have any left), books, and advertising. In this way each youngster reared in a given culture is conditioned to interpret reality in terms of the conceptual systems of that culture/society. Thus a world-view that is dominant in any culture/society functions like Charles Kraft's "central control box."[23]

An illustration of the "central control box" concept is found when one studies the *Humanist Manifesto II*. In this document one sees the non-theistic, anti-Christian, secular atheistic humanistic world-view in the raw. In banishing God from all discussion it has left no sufficient point of reference by which to identify man, because man becomes the measure of all things. It is useless to say "man is man is man." The question must be pressed. Without God, in and by what relationships shall man be defined? Man becomes the only point of reference for life's meaning. That has not worked, and it will not work. Moderns are well aware, perhaps, that our age has suggested several alternatives for defining man by various world-views. He is a cog in the industrial machine, a locked-in part of the cosmic universe, a pawn of the State, a bundle of glands, one among the many animals, a cosmic accident, or a product of a purposeless process. Is it any surprise that man is confused and depersonalized from such a "central control box" in control of much of the modern culture/society?

Consider how this works out in society if man is no more than the foregoing. If man is not personality then what is real to him? Just more impersonality, and that continues to lead to the question of the hour in society: "Who am I?" You see, if man searching for life, hope, direction, and meaning has only man to ask; if there is no revealed Word from outside man (Let's call that Word God), then there is no answer to the question about man but man who is asking it. Is it possible that the masses of our social problems may be deriving from the world-view of this "central control box?" Non-theistic secular atheistic humanism has become the dominant influential "central control box" in our society, but it did not work, has not worked, and will not work in giving man and society meaning, purpose, direction and spiritual/mental health. Now the new age world-view is attempting to fill in the blanks in which secular humanism failed. But will it work? I think not! It can't!

In this technical Part of the book, there is more to comprehend. The definition of world-view must be tied to function for complete understanding.

Functions of World-Views

The survival of any culture/society depends upon its maintenance of commonality—common language, traditions, values, interests, goals, and assumptions about human existence. What follows is another expanded definition of world-view explained in functions.

Charles H. Kraft states in *Christianity and Culture* five functions of world-views. First is the "explanation of how and why things got to be as they are and how and why they continue or change." The world-view gives form for a people, whether explicitly or implicitly, "the basic assumption" concerning ultimate things upon which they base their lives." If the world-view conditions people to believe that the universe is operated by a number of invisible personal forces largely beyond their control, "this will affect both their understanding of and their response to reality." However if a world-view explains that the universe operates by means of a large number of impersonal cause-and-effect operations which if learned by people can be employed by them to control the universe, "the attitude of these people toward reality will be much different. Or, if a world-view is centered in a personal God as ultimate Reality Who explains the reality of this world, then people's attitudes, values and lifestyles are radically different and meaningful from those whose world-view is one without a personal God. When this is understood, many questions about life are explained.

The second function of a world-view of a people is that it serves as an "evaluational" function. This involves judging and validating. "The basic institutions, values, and goals of a society are ethnocentrically valued as best, and therefore sanctioned by the world-view of their culture/society and subculture. It is by their God or gods that most people understand their world-view" and their culture/society "as a whole to be validated." All important and valued behavior, whether classified as economic, political, scientific, social, educational or whatever, "is judged in term's of a culture's world-view assumptions, beliefs, values, meanings and sanctions."

From this, one can understand why we have so much trouble with evaluating what is right, good, decent, and meaningful in a society like ours that is filled with and controlled by a plurality of world-views battling for modern man's mind. When Christianity in America was the dominant influential world-view, this matter of evaluation was not a problem. Even though not all people were Christian, there was a strong Christo-centric consensus that Christian standards and morals were what man in society had to live by. This consensus was evaluated as acceptable by most parameters of the society.

The third function of a world-view provides "psychological reinforcement" for the people and culture/society. "At points of anxiety or crisis in life it is to one's conceptual system that one turns for encouragement to continue or get the stimulus to take other actions." These times all tend to heighten anxiety or in some other way "require adjustments between behavior and belief," and each tends to be dealt in a reinforcing manner by the world-view of a culture/society. This reinforcement may take the form of ritual or ceremony in which many people show support for the behavior of the group in a world that appears to be filled with capricious uncontrollable forces. If one's needed "psychological" reinforcement cannot be found in one's present world-view, then there is conversion or change to another world-view. For instance, we live in a time of radical church shopping and church hopping by people looking for just the right church that fits "my" needs. But the truth is, most of those do not really want a church that is orthodox in doctrine and practice. These hoppers are into developing their own self-centered and self-serving world-view and theology to suit their personal "psychological" wants. Christ's world-view is really not what they want.

A fourth function of a world-view of a culture/society is the "integrating function. It systematizes and orders for them their perceptions of reality into an overall design." In these terms "a people conceptualizes what reality should be like and understands and interprets the multifarious events to which they are exposed." Thus in all of these functions, "world-view lies at the heart" of a culture/society providing the basic model for "bridging the gap between the objective reality outside people's heads and the culturally agreed upon perception of that reality inside their heads."

However after viewing the four functions of a world-view, awareness must be made that "a group's world-view does not completely determine the perception of all its members at all times. Though there is characteristically a very high degree of conservatism to such conceptualizations, there is change in this and in all other areas of culture/society." Over a period of time groups such as the ancient Hebrews moved from belief in many gods to a strong concept of monotheism led by Abraham who moved to monotheism by radical revelation. "Likewise large segments of Western culture have moved through the Renaissance, Enlightenment, Industrial Revolution and American Frontierism from a belief in the supremacy of the Judaeo-Christian God to a belief in the actual or potential all-sufficiency of the technological human." Ordinarily such conceptual change takes place slowly. At other times the pressure for rapid change is great. Participation in the face of such pressure finds us a fifth function of a people's world-view which relates directly to the more disintegrative aspects of cultural change. That function is "adaptational." People, by adjusting their world-views, devise means for resolving conflict and reducing cultural dissonance. If a society gets into ideological difficulty "it may be easier to reinterpret" and attempt to remake new values than "reorganize society."[24] But what if just reinterpretation creates more faction and fragmentation of life and culture/society?

History has revealed that if the adaptation or change is to another world-view that still does not integrate all major dimensions of human life together, that culture/society goes from bad to worse, sometimes to total disintegration.

Therefore we are forced into another perception of thought that is related to the foregoing perceptions.

Understanding And Holding To A World-View Mindset

After understanding the definitions and functions of world-views, a world-view mindset is perceived out of whatever world-view by which one lives. To illustrate this I use the theistic/Christian world-view mindset because of the needed cohesiveness and consistency that is possible by this world-view in our society.

Being aware of this mindset is imperative for Christians and informative for others who are concerned about the direction our culture/society is taking spiritually, morally, and mentally. Unless this theistic world-view mindset takes place and is put to

61

work quickly by the church in our part of the world, we may be talking only to ourselves by the end of this century.

This world-view mindset begins to take form when Christians commence to think cosmologically and comprehensively about the total cosmic world. This is done by keeping the spiritual and the material, the sacred and the secular, on the same coin. The theistic/Christian world-view has never separated the spiritual and material, the sacred and secular, except for definitive purposes.

However, much of the modern conservative church has separated them with rhetoric that has perpetuated a gnostic dualism that separates spirit from matter. Richard Mouw is correct: "The basic duality in the biblical scheme is not spirit and matter. In the biblical scheme of things the fundamental twoness that cannot be avoided is the crucial distinction between the Creator and the creation."[25] The gnostic dualism rhetoric used has been such terms as "soul-winning," or the "saving of souls." So what? So this.

The word for "soul" in the Old Testament (nephesh) and in the New Testament (psuche) has not been understood and correctly used. Christian revelation has been contaminated by the Greek idea of the immortality of the soul. But in Jewish thought death is total. There is no immortal soul, no division of body and soul. Paul's thinking is Jewish in this regard. The soul belongs to the "psychical" realm and is part of the flesh. The body is the whole being. In death, there is no separation of body and soul. The soul is as mortal as the body. But there will be a resurrection. Out of the nothingness that human life becomes in the grave, God creates anew the being that was dead.

But the perversion of this by Greek philosophy has led many believers to see their relationship to Jesus Christ only for the purpose of getting their "souls", some immaterial entity, to heaven. This has been considered by many, perhaps sub-consciously, but considered just the same as some kind of fire insurance program to keep their "souls" out of hell.

Thus a real tragedy is that Christians have not understood or have ignored that Christianity is to have an effect on this world via their transformed lives by bringing the theistic/Christian world-view's values into the marketplace proclaiming the Lordship of Christ over all creation including every social parameter of life and living. They have also missed the fact that heaven is an euphemism for the presence of God which starts now in a transformed life and continues with an obedient person on into eternity.

I grant the fact that many Christians want to keep all of this separate, because it is easier and safer. But it is not biblical or Christian. Yet too many pastors continue to preach and teach this gnostic dualism. It does satisfy the consumer mentality that has entered the modern church, because it usually bypasses the mandate of Jesus to make disciples (Matt. 28:16-20) so that transformed disciples can adhere to the dominion mandate of taking care of God's world (Genesis 1:26-29). This dominion over nature mandate that God has assigned to man entails human sensitivity to the Creator's moral and spiritual purpose for our planet.

But this gnostic dualism that continues to be preached and taught is an improper message. It misleads people. It keeps the theistic/Christian world-view out of the marketplace, and our society rushes pell-mell on a collision course of many world-views and their strange values. People remain puzzled as to what's going on in a society filled with terrible problems. Christianity is then considered as something for another era or only for spiritual matters when in reality it is the only workable world-view for this modern world for both spiritual and secular matters. Of course it has to start with the spiritual dimension of reconciling people to the Lordship of Christ, but discipleship does not stop there. To stop there short-circuits the world-view mindset to which we must hold.

A young Christian leader, Ron Boehme, in the presence of two lady historians was confronted with a question from one of them. Without pretense and with great grace she asked: "Ron, can you tell me why Christian mission work in Africa, though extensive in nature, has left the majority of Africans still living in poverty under the domination of authoritarian governments?" He was taken back in a struggle for an answer. Even though in some African countries we are told that Christians are the majority, there is so much still wrong with the lives who have become believers. So much is still wrong in that culture/society. He finally conceded that he had no answer.

With confidence and warmth she said, "The reason so many African Christians, and many other evangelized people of the world today are still living in poverty and under oppression is that the missionaries gave them an incomplete Gospel. They saved their souls and didn't teach them to apply their faith to make Jesus the Lord of all of life. So they left them to live under misery and cruelty."[26] She was correct. He was stunned. To develop the theistic/Christian world-view mindset, Christians must think in cosmic and total comprehensive ways about Christianity.

The theistic/Christian world-view mindset is cosmic thinking about the totality of life. Jesus is Lord. He is the Lord over the totality of all of life. Christian discipleship that is able to take this world-view into the marketplace demands a way of thinking about everything. We are to "take captive every thought to make it obedient to Christ" (2 Corinthians 10:5). That is a theistic/Christian world-view mindset which is the foundation to the development and holding of the same. In this the church is really "the pillar and foundation of the truth" (1 Tim. 3;15).

Only with this theistic/Christian world-view in place can we hammer out principles of social reform in the terms of God's Word. Only then can we develop political perspectives based upon God's commands. Only then can we construct standards of justice derived from the precepts of God. Only then can we pioneer ethics, morals, and values that are grounded in the theistic/Christian world-view. This world-view mindset is a mindset of thinking in cosmic, total, universal, comprehensive ways. The Bible becomes a virtual blueprint for every area of life—the totality of life. As George Grant writes:

Everything in every field, on every front, must be built on a fundamental rejection of the notion that there might be areas of intellectual, cultural, or spiritual neutrality. Every realm of human endeavor must flow from Biblical principles—because God has ordained that the Bible govern them all.[27]

Does this mean that we will create some utopian reality? Not at all. We will make mistakes with our inconsistency. But the development of this world-view mindset and putting this the-istic/Christian world-view into action in the marketplace through authentic Christians does mean that we have a positive, work-able, proven alternative for life in the midst of many world-views that are damaging and destroying, life and culture/society in every sphere and social parameter of our soci-ety. Ideas do have consequences. World-views make differences and do alter the course of society in history. A cultural consen-sus of right and wrong can be brought back with this mind-set even though masses might never become Christ-followers.

Cosmic, total, comprehensive thinking for the Christian in developing a world-view mindset is living out the stewardship of life in this world that rumbles with the engines of death in so many ways. Millions are starving; tension between nations who could destroy each other seems constant; nuclear destruction could still happen in spite of the weakening of Communism. In many ways the "engines of death" seem poised in manifold ways with which our world is flirting. "We are living in a world," Douglas John Hall writes, "that has made a covenant with death—both physical death, especially in nuclear politics, and spiritual death that is numb to the injustice, violence, and threat to creation itself that surrounds us." At the same time our society does not seem to know or believe that there is a cosmic center, a binding but freedom-giving address of a world-view that has Christ at and as the Center, because He orders all things for a purpose (Col. 1:17) that can bring it all together for the hope and good of the universe.

This cosmic world-view is the Christian message that can enhance life, heal creation, and bring into being justice and the love of God. This means, Hall continues, "that to be a (Christian) steward in the world today is a more critical task than at any time in the church's past, since what is entrusted to our stewardship is the life of the creation itself."[28]

A theistic/Christian world-view cosmic mindset that is imperative as a perceived necessity for Christians, God's spies and subversive agents, to be able to "sing the Lord's song" in this alien land is a Christian worldliness. That keeps us from over-spiritualizing the earthy vision and purpose of Christ which is to not only to reconcile man to God but also to bring healing to our fractured society in God's creation. It is also recovering the earthward orientation of the gospel of the incarnation and the cross that gnostic dualism has almost removed.

Such a wholistic and integrated world-view mindset will keep the church from having "spiritual anesthesia." For the Christian this implies confronting with fidelity whatever comes to God's cosmic order. While probably no one in this life enjoys a perfect understanding of this cosmic order, we can make ourselves so spiritually numb that we would not recognize the cosmic if it shouted at us. Therefore to be whole by understanding and holding to this integrated world-view mindset is to be able to respond properly to the cosmic, because we cannot respond to what we do not see.

Now, if one world-view is not doing what is needed in life and culture/society, what is the next step? Conversion from one world-view to another.

Conversion And World-Views

Conversion is a change or exchange from something to something else. For example, when traveling between certain countries one kind of money has to be converted to another kind.

Since our thoughts are based on the theistic/Christian world-view, conversion in the biblical context is the change from any one or many ways of life or world-views to the Christ-centered way of life and the theistic/Christian world-view by becoming a Christ-follower and disciple. Conversion in this sense involves the exchanging of world-views. Therefore in this biblical conversion the result is what is called a "new creation" in man, and that man thinks about life and life's relationships and purposes differently resulting in a different lifestyle. A different kind of thinking-cap is put on. Life is seen from a new and different perspective. All of life is seen from the theistic/Christian world-view. When we consider a synopsis of the theistic/Christian world-view and others we will see how they differ and how the difference affects human life and spheres in every social parameter of culture/society.

In conversion one is choosing another world-view over and against the world-view he or she presently has. The cause for this change of conversion is that one has realized that their present world-view inadequately explains what is known to be the case or what really is, or it is inconsistent with itself. Because of these inadequacies or inconsistencies a new world-view is adopted. This change is related to the functions of world-views.

The perception on conversion and world-views must be expanded to be totally clear.In the exchange from one eclectic non-Christian world-view to the theistic/Christian world-view, world-view is the change-center and the Kingdom (rule-reign) of God is the change-maker. This means that world-view is a deep-rooted map of reality ordinarily unquestioned by the culture/society. It is as Kraft says a "storage-shed" of presuppositions about the world and various aspects of it. Its value system is a bank vault by which people live. As a "central control box" of a culture/society, a world-view has functions which we have already considered. However, that "central control box" is changed by a sovereign God and the act of His grace when the theistic/Christian world-view (another "central control box") is presented as an alternative life-style by a witness and accepted by the person to whom you are witnessing. God in Christ is at work in this change-over to capture the "stronghold of change". When the divine work is initiated people begin to change their world-view. Conversion is at work.[29]

As Christ captures the stronghold there is, 1) "a change of

allegiance that issues in", 2) "a concomitant change in the evaluational principles within the person's/group's world-view", and, 3) "a resultant series of new habits of behavior". This is the open-ended process or "reevaluation, reinterpretation, and rehabituation" that theologians label conversion. This conversion must be seen as conversion to Christ and His Kingdom to be a total conversion. It is the Kingdom dimension of conversion that the Church must recover today.[30]

The Kingdom dimension of conversion calls for a total cosmic comprehensive approach to culture/society that has not been characteristic of evangelism/missions. This has set up a weakness, and I want to come down hard on the church at this point. The traditional fixation on only the personal dimension of salvation has hindered the Church from incorporating the power for cultural change into other related aspects of life and living. The diagram of Figure One must again be considered as an illustration for this issue.

This means that the impact of the positive radical Kingdom rule of Christ will do more than merely modify a world-view or accommodate itself to an existing world-view which may be detrimental to culture/society. If true transformational change is to take place, the change must occur not merely at the behavioral edges of the world-view's manifestations but at its center. Here begins the process of "reinterpretation, reevaluation, and rehabituation". Out of the world-view now Christ-possessed at its root which is more than just some other religious view, the convert starts the life-long pilgrimage of Christ-transformation as salt, light, and leaven in related areas of life and culture.[31] That is from the Christian position good news from the person to the culture, because the theistic/Christian world-view is time-tested. It is pragmatic which Americans like to hear. It works in life as life was intended by the Life-Giver Himself. Throughout the years I have seen and heard this concept: "You know, that stuff really works." Although that is not the primary reason for connecting life to the theistic/Christian world-view, it is a blessed result. One connects life to it because it is true-Truth. Its working out positively is the result of the Truth of it.

How does one better understand a workable world-view? What is the criterion for validity?

Well-Rounded Workable World-View: Valid Criterion

A well-rounded workable world-view for life and culture/society in its simplest form will have basic answers to key questions in the primary areas of life and society that man has wrestled with for aeons of time. Those questions are in the next division of this Part. But prior to the questions we need the broader dimensions of the characteristics of the criterion of validity for an adequate workable world-view. This is to assist one in deciding if conversion from one world-view to another is necessary for authentic life beyond and above what man alone can concock.

First, the world-view one adopts should possess an inner intellectual coherence. That is, the world-view must be logically consistent. If not then this world-view is inadequate. Second, the world-view one adopts must be able to comprehend and account for the data of reality. All the information we receive through whatever source must be answerable by our world-view. If not then the data is faulty or our world-view is. Third, the world-view one adopts should explain what it claims to explain. If a world-view claims that matter is all there is to reality then it must give an adequate explanation for this claim. If it cannot the world-view is questionable. Fourth, the world-view one adopts should be subjectively satisfactory. How can this be? It can satisfy both, our felt needs and our unfelt needs. Both of these met needs are the result of true Truth which goes beyond anything man can dream up. Truth is ultimately the only thing that can satisfy.[32]

An adequate world-view can also be stated as Earl Palmer does in the following.

> One way to test the worthiness of a world-view or religious claim is to ask the question: Does this world-view bring all of the parts of the puzzle of my life together? Are the separate

pieces that make up the normal existence integrated so that each is meaningful and in clear focus when seen through the lens of this world-view?[33]

Tested Valid World-View: Answers Basic Questions

James Sire, in *The Universe Next Door* and *Discipleship of the Mind*, is most helpful in identifying basic world-view questions and brief answers. In the more technical study that Sire offers, one would study various world-views in the context of these questions and consider what various world-views say about the nature and character of God, the nature of the universe, the nature of man, the question of what happens to man at death, the basis for ethics, and the meaning of history.

In the context of the purpose of this book as an introductory primer to illustrate the need of world-view studies, and drawing from Sire, I have listed the questions (Every quote in the context of the questions is from Sire), stated some related thoughts for each, given a brief answer from the theistic/Christian world-view, and then again stated a conviction about the only world-view that I believe is workable and imperative for modern life and culture/society today. The basic questions asked through the ages are:

1. "What is prime reality—the really real?" To this different people might answer: "God, or the gods", the material cosmos or cosmic mind. Is there Reality beyond the reality we see in this world? What world-view or views give an affirmative answer to this question? Answer: God is the prime Reality beyond the reality of now. He is our point of reference for all of life and the reality we know and see. He is the center of our world-view and is to affect every social parameter of life and society.

2. "What is the nature of external reality", that is, the cosmic world around us? Here different people's answers point to whether they "see the world as created or autonomous, as chaotic or orderly, or as matter or spirit". They also show whether they "emphasize a subjective, personal relationship to the world or its objectivity apart from us." Answer: The cosmic world is

created and ordered by God and has purpose, direction, and meaning.

3. "What is a human being?" Who is man? To this, different people might respond: "a highly complex electro-chemical machine" whom we do not understand, "a sleeping god", a person made in the image of God, or a "naked ape." What difference does it make in living out life? Answer: Man is made in the image of God. From that God who is personal and our central point of reference, we find out who man, the human creature, is and our purpose in life and society. This has never failed any person. This relates to a most current persistent question by modern man which is still, "Who am I?" That was the question of the classic play, "Death of A Salesman." Willie, the son of the dead salesman, said his father "never knew who he was."

4. "What happens to a person at death?" Does it make any difference in life and values not to know? Different people might reply: "personal extinction or transformation to a higher state or departure to a shadowy existence on the other side." Answer: Death for the Christian whose Lord is Jesus Christ is the door to eventual resurrection with a new body from the grave to everlasting life in the new heavens and new earth. When a person who is in Christ learns how to die, he then learns how to live a life that is joyfully different than most of the world knows and understands. Death understood is evangelistic to the hilt.

5. "Why is it possible to know anything at all?" Some answers include "the idea" that human beings "are made in the image of an all-knowing", transcendent and immanent, personal, sovereign, good God. Others might say "that consciousness and rationality developed under the contingencies of survival in a long process of evolution." Answer: We can know because of being made in the image of an all-knowing, transcendent and immanent, personal, sovereign, good God, who as our point of reference for life wants us to know Him and His world. He made it. He owns the farm. We are His tenants and He pays us well in blessings.

71

6. "How do we know what is right and wrong?" Is there a basis for morality and ethics? What difference does this make? "Perhaps we are made in the image of God whose character is good." Or "right and wrong are determined by human choice alone." Or the notions are "simply developed under an impetus toward cultural physical survival." Answer: God is our basis for knowing right and wrong. He is also the basis for morality and ethics given to us in His Word from outside. Jesus is the ethic of life. In a world of absolutes, we follow God in Christ as the one ultimate absolute. This has never failed, nor will it. Is this easy? Not at all. But there is nothing better. This is the best.

7. "What is the meaning of human history?" What direction is history going from various world-views? So what? Some would answer that history is "to realize the purposes of God or the gods, to make a paradise on earth, to prepare a people for life in community with a loving and holy God," etc. Answer: History for the theistic/Christian world-view has purpose because it is heading somewhere. It is not cyclical. History has purpose.

8. Within world-views other issues often arise: a) "Who is in charge of the world?" God! b) "Is man determined," locked in, or free to choose? Free to choose! c) "How can we know, and how can we know that we know?" God is how we know we know. He is our source of revelation and basic knowledge about life and its purpose! d) "Is man the maker of values?" No! If he is, on what basis does he build values? What difference does it make? There has to be ultimate truth beyond truths as a basis for values. e) "Is God really good?" Yes! f) "Is God personal or impersonal?" Personal! What difference does it make? There is Someone beyond man's finiteness to whom we relate. g) "Does God exist at all?" Absolutely!

"When stated in such sequence" and fully studied, all of "these questions boggle the mind." But our own personal answers to these questions reveal our world-view. They are the toughest questions of life. Either "the answers are too obvious to us, and we wonder why anyone would bother to ask such questions," or "we wonder how any of them can be answered with any certainty"[34] There is no other world-view known to man that can answer the previous questions in any kind of positive, cohesive, coherent, and satisfactory manner. Not one other world-view can answer the questions as the theistic/Christian world-view can.

Yet, many Christians are apt to say why worry about what other people are thinking. We have enough to worry about just for ourselves. That very attitude has created a society wherein the world and the Church have passed each other like two ships in the night, and much of the church today on the slippery slope is far removed from affecting the modern world with the great Good News so needed in hostile times.

Tony Campolo says, after praising all the various ministries the superchurches and mega-churches are able to provide, when compared to the medium-sized and small churches, and even though they have, hopefully, reached many for Christ, "however, this kind of religion will not bring about social change." The preachers of these super and mega-churches "preach a kind of religion that will enable people to enjoy a happy state of consciousness in a society that is dying." If America is to change . . . "something more is needed."[35] The theistic/Christian world views has to be taken to the marketplace and challenge every other world-view alien to Christianity.

James Sires comments on the previously stated questions demanding answers.

If we feel the answers are too obvious to consider, then we have a world view; but we have no idea that many others do not share it. We should realize that we live in a pluralistic world. What is obvious to us may be a lie from hell to our neighbor next door. If we do not recognize that, we are certainly naive and provincial, and we have much to learn about man in today's world. Alternatively, if we feel that one of the questions can be answered without cheating or committing intellectual suicide, we have already adopted a sort of world view—a form of skepticism which in its extreme form leads to nihilism.[36]

This must be stressed again. In our culture of pluralistic world-views, is there one world-view that answers these questions with a flair of confidence that can assist modern man to find a foundation for and direction of life? Is there a time-tested world-view which "sings the songs of the Lord" that gives new hope, purpose, stability, and life to modern man in our alien land?

To answer that, I again state my presuppositional conviction. I believe by study and experience that the theistic/Christian world-view does so with confidence. It claims the answers are true and consistent with each other. It fits the criterion of validity which no other contemporary and major world-view does. How is this possible in light of all the confusion regarding our stated questions? I quote Sire again.

> The world view itself explains why. God wants us to know these answers, and he has told us what the the answers are. The Christian world view's answer to the first question form the basis for the answers to all the other questions, for what the Christian world view takes to be really real is an infinite-personal God who intentionally made the universe and us in it. He wanted us around to freely know him, and so he built into us the capacity for knowledge.[37]

I have stated my convictions and will continue to do so in the confident understanding that they can withstand scrutiny. I recognize the inadequacy of our own understanding and the fact that we are sinners and still make mistakes. But I would invite any non-believer to investigate my position by entering into a more technical study of the topic of world-view. This is why I have included such an extensive bibliography. I continue to study this topic and my position still stands.

There is one more perception to understand in this Part of technical information.

Culture, Consensus, Pluralism

Culture is a term which is not easily susceptible of definition. In the broadest sense, it means simply the patterned way in which people do things together.

Expanded, culture means the total pattern of human behavior and its products embodied in thought, speech, and action. Culture is the sum total of ways of living developed by a group of human beings and handed down from generation to generation. Central to culture is language, as the language of a people provides the means by which they express their way of perceiving things and of coping with them. Around that center one would have to group their visual and musical arts, their technologies, their law, and their social and political organization. And one must also include in culture, and as fundamental to any culture, a set of beliefs, experiences, and practices that seek to grasp and express the ultimate nature of things, that which gives shape and meaning to life, that which claims final loyalty. That is the part religion plays in culture. Religion—including the Christian religion—is thus part of culture.

Culture is the activity of man in society. It is something that reveals man as either noble or vile depending upon whom man believes himself to be. Cultural activity of man reflects his values and arises from basic convictions, religious and moral, about life. This is what makes the published work by Adler so important: *The Difference In Man and The Difference It Makes.* Society and social order is the result that is the compilation of culture or cultures. That is why I use the combination of culture/society in the writing.

At the center of culture/society is a world-view or an eclectic of world-views. That is, there is a general acceptance of the nature of the universe and of one's place within it. This may be religious or secular, a Christian or non-Christian concept of reality. From this basic world-view, if there is one that is predominant, flows both standards of judgement or values (of what is good in the sense of the desirable, or what is acceptable as in accordance with the general will of the community) and standards of conduct such as relations between individuals, between the sexes, and the generations within the community.

What if there is not one predominant world-view that fits the criterion for validity, but only an eclectic of world-views? Or what if a predominant world-view or eclectic of world-views brings forth values that are destructive to life and culture/society? There is confusion, consternation, and chaos.

Cultures are seldom static. Unless one world-view is dominant in a culture/society, there is a continuous process of change from world-view to world-view causing many to keep asking why are so many people living so differently than they once did. In this context the question must be pressed again: Is there possibly a world-view that could be at the center of culture/society that has proven to be able to hold life and culture together in purpose, decency, direction, righteousness, hope, and life enriching better than what any other world-view that could be doing if it was in control? This is answered by running world-views through the grid of previous questions and seeing which world-view gives coherent, consistent, and logical answers that works out consistently, coherently, logically and constructively in life and culture/society. This is exposed more in Part Four.

The Christian has to struggle and think through these issues or be irresponsible in discipleship. The non-Christian who is concerned with the deterioration of culture must do the same thing or be irresponsible in an attempted escape from the Reality behind reality and Truth behind truths.

Culture. A strange and frightening phenomenon. Masses of Christians in this century feel as if they have settled in Sodom. A culture/society once dominated by Christian values is now one of the greatest spiritual challenges for American Christians.

There was that time when decency and order seemed to characterize the lives of individuals and communities. Institutions and traditions created and respected by them seemed to make the American culture/society more hospitable to Christianity than any other culture in history. Thus the American society was regarded as a somewhat "Christian" society. This did not mean that everyone was Christian. But it did mean that the Christian faith was strong enough to greatly influence our society with tested, proven Christian values that enhanced life instead of depersonalizing and destroying life as is seen now. "But today

76

most Christians" Kenneth Myers believes, "regard their culture itself as an implacable enemy, a constant threat to their own sanctity and to the stability and faith of their families."[38]

To compound this in our historical era we now have to struggle with what is called "popular culture" that puts traditional "folk culture" and "high culture" in the shadows. It is these last two categories that in the past gave America a partial base of stability, tradition, and values that brought the broad concept of a "Christian society" as stated above.

What is "popular culture" that has proven to be in past decades and is in the present becoming even more troubling to parents, teachers, pastors, and counselors? "Popular culture" is that which takes its cues from such idioms as television, rock 'n' roll, and other related secularized non-Christian values. It is a culture locked into present time and space without any transcendent Godly values.

To compound the problem more, many Christians respond to "popular culture" one of two ways: boycott it or take cues from the secular counterpart, sanitize and customize it with Jesus language or Jesus overlay. That which has contributed greatly to keep a once stable culture/society in tact is now absent. What is absent is the theistic/Christian world-view that was the dominant world-view influence.

It is here that the issue and concern of consensus enters. In our pluralistic culture there is no consensus as to one life-building, positive world-view holding sway over other world-views. But there is now the combination of secular humanism and the New Age movement which are bed-fellows. They are both destructive to life and culture/society as more and more give consent to them..

The world-view of secular humanism is now familiar to us as the most dominating and influential world-view in these modern times. This world-view sets God aside and man is center stage. In secular humanism "man is the measure of all things." (Protagorus) This is atheistic humanism as found in the Humanism Manifesto II.

This world-view and the adherents that extol its virtues is brilliantly described in detail and depth by the twentieth century's foremost historian, Paul Johnson in his classic book, *Intellectuals*.

When clerical religious power declined in the eighteenth century, the mentor that emerged "to fill the vacuum and capture the ear of society" was the secular intellectual. As a deist, skeptic, or atheist, this new mentor was just as ready as any pontiff or presbyter to pontificate telling mankind how to conduct its affairs. "He brought to this self-appointed task a far more radical approach than his clerical predecessors," and he was bound by "no corpus of revealed religion" such as Christianity. Wisdom of the past, the legacy of tradition, or the "prescriptive codes of ancestral experience" could be followed or wholly rejected entirely as man might decide. "For the first time in human history, and with growing confidence and audacity, men arose to assert that they could diagnose the ills of society and cure them with their own unaided intellects: more, that they could devise formulae whereby not merely the structure of society but the fundamental habits of human beings could be transformed for the better," by man's power alone. Man had pushed God out of life and moved himself center-stage as the point of reference and truth. Unlike their predecessors, "they were not servants and interpreters of the gods but the substitutes."[39]

It is this secular humanist world-view that is the controlling consensus holding our culture/society in bondage. It is the world-view that controls the dangerous ambition that the ACLU (American Civil Liberty Union) espouses and epitomizes. Since secular humanism cannot do the job, its bedfellow, the new age movement is trying but only wrecking life and culture/society. It has nothing to offer. But such world-views have not always been the consensus.

In the first half of this century there was a consensus of the importance and acceptance of the theistic/Christian world-view as the center of culture/society. This was held by many who had no relationship to Christ and Christianity or even knew their position on world-views. There was what is called "Christendom" defined as a region dominated by Christianity. Not all were Christians, but all were influenced by its teachings and all institutions had to contend with it. There was a consensus of right and wrong and goodness and evil. But now our culture/society lacking an authentic and wholesome Christian and moral consensus led the late Dr. Francis Schaeffer to say in his last published book prior to his death, "the continuing secularization of our society overtly and covertly is eventually going to extinguish the church and snuff out its effectiveness in terms of religious liberty we now take for granted."[40] If this happens in its fullest, non-Christians and even those who are hostile to Christianity will be as brutally affected as all Christians, because present world-views at the center of American culture/society are not putting life and culture/society together. Our culture/society is deteriorating even in the midst of all kinds of religious activity carrying Christian labels. What is wrong? Even much Western Christianity has been culturalized away from Christ.

Mixed up in all of the foregoing is pluralism which is a partial description of the culture/society in which we live. Everybody believes something and in a pluralistic culture everybody is right. All you have to do is believe something and you are right because you believe it. There is no ultimate Truth and according to pluralism no God-ordained absolutes. One position is as good as another. Therefore most aspects of life are decided only from a human point of view.

But if there is a God who has revealed Himself in Scripture and in history and in creation and in the Cross and in the resurrection then that is another matter, because the Christ of Scriptures says "no" to the saving power of all human efforts. In pluralism we have diversity but no ultimate unity to bring the diverse things of our experience together in a coherent whole. We are and have only particulars and no universals. That will ultimately destroy a culture/society. The result of this is spelled: Chaos.

But the theistic/Christian world-view, because of its source and ultimate Truth is sufficient to survive to bring life and culture/society together in a healing wholistic manner in the midst of a pluralistic culture/society regardless of other beliefs if Christians are willing and if the church will be the church.

A bottom line is that there are strong and clear biblical sanctions for world-view studies. Why has this needed dimension of Christian education been ignored?

Biblical Sanctions

Biblical sanctions for world-view studies are in the Old Testament (1 Chronicles 12:23-38). When David was anointed King at Hebron the word spread and men begin to attach themselves to him. They were special men raised up by God to install David King over Israel. There were three distinguishing qualities about these men that all of God's people need to have. One quality is clearly stated as related to the understanding of world-views.

The first quality is commitment. That is clear in verse thirty-three. The RSV says that the men had a "singleness of purpose." The NIV calls this "undivided loyalty." A second quality is courage that is stated in verse twenty-five. The RSV says "mighty men of valor," and the NIV says "warriors ready for battle." The third quality clearly related to world-view understanding is competence as stated in verse thirty-two. The RSV states the quality by saying "men who had understanding of the times," while the NIV says "understood the times."

In the New Testament, there are several texts to be considered as biblical sanction for world-view studies. Matthew 16:1-3 cannot be overlooked. Jesus upbraided the religious leaders regarding how much they knew about the weather, "but you cannot interpret the signs of the times." The last line in the text ought not be taken lightly. "Jesus then left them and went away."

In Luke 19:44 is the phrase ". . . because you did not recognize the time of God's coming to you." The RSV uses "the time of your visitation" which Jesus stated to Jerusalem signifying that they did not know the time of events related to His presence. I just have to say that most Christians in our era of superficial faith do not understand their culture/society's events as they are related to the need of Christ's presence. They do not know the times in which we live or how world-views are threatening the very existence of Christianity being allowed to transform life and change society in our part of the Western world. They do know something is terribly wrong, but they do not know why beyond just saying that the cause is "sin." That is true, but more must be understood today.

I do not think it is misuse of a familiar text in Ephesians 6:10-20 to relate it to world-view studies. Paul is saying in the midst of standing strong in Christ and putting on "the full armor of God," that Christians have to scout out the "authorities" and "powers of this dark world and stand against the spiritual forces of evil. . . ." World-view studies reveal these "authorities" and "powers."

In the midst of these complex times, not only must we know them, but also be prepared and ready to confront these times with Peter's admonition in 1 Peter 3:15. Peter exhorts every Christian to ". . . Always be prepared to give an answer to everyone who asks you to give the reason for the hope that you have." Christians have to know both the world and God's word. World-view studies and apologetics must be tied together.

The most important New Testament text for world-view sanction is in Acts 17:22-34. Many church growth people are incorrect when they see Paul as a failure in this text. In all reality he is a smashing success because of what he reveals. It is the picture of how imperative and essential it is for Christians to know not only their Christian world-view but also the world-view of those to whom they may be witnessing or having dialogue.

We need to work our way through this text. In verse two Paul is in the synagogue at Thessalonica where "he reasoned with them from the Scriptures." He tells about Christ, the Jews become hostile, but some believed. In verse ten Paul is in Berea in the synagogue. The Bereans like the message. The Jews are hostile again, but some believed. In verse sixteen Paul is in Athens. He is distressed at the idols seen. He reasoned to the Jews and "God-fearing Greeks" as he had in other places. He also taught in the marketplace.

In verse eighteen Paul is found in the midst of a group of Epicureans and Stoic philosophers. There is a dispute going on, because Paul's message about Christ was a strange idea to their ears. Then in verse twenty-two Paul is preaching in the Areopagus. Paul played out the two things every Christian witness must know minimally: what the witness believes and why and what the persons to whom the witness is witnessing believes and why.

Paul preaches about an unknown God. The people are religious but not Christian. Paul's preaching and teaching counters the characteristics of minds encountered. You see, he had to already know their world-views before he ever took the Scriptures to them. No one was crying to this preacher to just "be practical" as we hear over and over and over today in some settings. Some Bible Colleges may be reinforcing that mindset with a form of education that is little better than catechism. As the late Joe Dampier once said: "What is more practical than the New Testament and knowing it." I wish he would have said the whole Bible, because my heritage desperately needs a lot of Old Testament understanding and studies to make the New Testament even more lively. When Christians attempt to oppose this kind of study in the context of this text and others, they need to be confronted by this question: Are you representing God or the community, because if Christians would start really representing God, we would bring the community to its knees.

Paul knew that there were certain assumptions or presuppositions that controlled the minds of his audience in Athens. As Dr. James Strauss has said, "Paul never gave up thinking and just went to preaching as many have today." Paul's audience was made up of Naturalists—no God, Materialists—material is eternal and uncreated, Universalists—saved by knowledge and autonomous reason, Evolutionists—man evolved rather than being created by God (Paul's opening remarks seems to show this), and Pantheists—everything is God/God is everything.

Paul attacks these assumptions by preaching that God made the world, that He is personal, and the material is not eternal, because it was created by God. Paul clearly stated that God is not in everything, but is the transcendent, Lord of heaven and earth. He also let it be known that God is not in shrines and is not served because He needs to be served. Servanthood is our need and freedom. Man is not saved by knowledge and reason alone but also by faith that is obedient to the Lordship of Christ, His word as in the Bible, and a lifestyle that is beyond lip-service. Paul also grounds the unity of man in God and not in the unity of man, and Paul's grammar reveals that his audience will not find God in the world-view of their assumptions. In verse twenty-eight Paul reminds them again that God is personal and is the sustainer of His created universe.

Paul's sermon is a classic. It is not a failure. He knew his audience well enough to speak to them intelligently without knee-jerk teaching and preaching of moralisms too often heard today. In Paul's world of Athens and in our world of confusing and complex world-views, conversion by faith, repentance, and baptism is really only possible by the Holy Spirit and the authority of the Word when proper communication takes place. Even then it is difficult to see real conversions happen when most people just want to join the church and not have transformation by the risen Lord's power.

Once we know world-views and are better equipped to take on the world, we must realize that it will not be easy. Ours is a time when people are looking for signs and wonders instead of looking to the all sufficient Christ. The entire spirit of the 90s, especially in the West, is in opposition to Biblical, historical Christianity. As we take on this kind of world, we will need to latch onto the true and encouraging words of Paul Johnson, author of *Modern Times* and *Intellectuals*. "Christianity is a historical religion or it is nothing. It does not deal in myths or metaphors or symbols or in states-of-being cycles. It deals in fact and the evidence supports the facts."[41]

If Christians will be brutally honest, they will concede to the fact that we live in a cultural situation in which historical Christianity appears to be in an eclipse. We have a lot of religiosity. We have the problem of the Christian church withdrawn from the public scene into a kind of privatism of faith. The conservative church must be faulted in their glaring inability to discern the encroachment of foreign/alien values upon the church's domain to the point of possibly stopping the church's witness. Persecution, a strange kind of persecution, may be on the way to our times in this nation.

But if our perilous times bring the fall of modern civilization, then there is another way of getting some perspective about our time. I believe it was Dr. George Roche, brilliant but humble President of Hillsdale College in Michigan who gave me this perspective. This might be a time of celebration, because the possible collapse of Western civilization will never mean the end of the Lord's church. It could signify a period of new starts and beginnings. If we are going to find a brighter road ahead, then we had best decide tomorrow's agenda today.

Concluding Challenge

If some helpful perspective has been realized with the various perceptions of world-view, we must then come to grips with various problems and crises when world-views are clashing with one another in a culture/society as ours. When a tested and tried world-view that lives up to the criterion for validity is not the predominant world-view as to influence, then we have much to be concerned about and much to understand, for from these more broad crises come particular crises that we live amidst. In Parts Four and Five we will think together about this.

But in preparation for and transition to Parts Two and following, the insightful words of the late W. A. Visser't Hooft who is a brilliant mind from the past. His words are clearly related to our consideration of needed perceptions.

One reason why the churches have not helped the laity to see the Christian significance of their vocation in the world is that the churches had lost sight of the cosmic dimension of the gospel. This could only lead to self-centered ecclesiasticism or pietism. When we realize again that Christ is the hope of the world, we see also that activity in the world is meaningful. It does not carry its meaning within itself, but it has a goal, an end: the kingdom. Christians are men and women who live toward the future and manifest this faith by acts which express their hope and expectation. At a time when—because of the collapse of the doctrine of progress—there is a great danger that all human effort is poisoned by a sense of futility, the Church has the great opportunity of re-creating a sense of the meaningfulness and worthwhileness of worldly vocation.[42]

Our task as Christians is audacious! The question introduced at the beginning of this Part, "Can The West Be Converted?" will not go away. The quotes from the several books used in the shifting of historical thought still squarely face us. They reveal our serious situation of the kind of culture/society Christians face. My own imposed question is, will Western Christianity rise to the challenge and cost? Maybe the question needs to be, can Western Christianity rise to the challenge? Probably not in its present weakened condition. Someone asked: "Can Christianity survive the church?"

George Barna gives some honest warnings to us as we plummet towards the year 2000. ". . . we have begun to witness a decline in the religious attentiveness of adults. . . . The indications are that the window of opportunity for evangelism, which was wide open in the early and mid-'80s, is rapidly closing." He reminds us that the very name "Christian" has come to mean everything and almost nothing by being "bland and generic." Much of the spiritual dimension of the concept has been lost while the population has been immunized to the Christian faith." In our rough path in the decade ahead, "the trends suggest that the importance of religion in people's life will continue its slow decline." In the midst of his candid evaluation of the church as a whole he stands firm on the mandate of making disciples. "One of the glaring weaknesses of the Church has been in the area of discipling and accountability."[43]

Barna's insights makes this statement by Rodney Booth of the United Church of Canada crystal clear. "Our world is desperate for another Luther. For someone who has the courage to read the signs of the times, and the wisdom to discern therein a new window through which to view and understand God's activity in the world today."[44]

The church faces the 21st Century with world-views colliding therefore exposing humanity to the most dramatic and traumatic change in world history. All of this is creating confusion, consternation, and chaos. Is there any Word from the Lord that the Lord's people will sing boldly and intensely? Will God's spies get at it?

They can, but something is required. Local congregations must recognize the imperative need of world-view studies in their Christian education efforts. The bride of Christ must be equipped by world-view studies and the Word of God to display His glory in the marketplace.

Along with this educational need is the call to look at the relationship of world-view studies and the contemporary Church Growth Movement. Without these two efforts, the crises in Part Four will not be countered and the reflections of our society in Part Five will not change.

Part Two: Proposal — Christian Education's Imperative Need

Christian Education: Hope of The World—But

A conviction continues to grow: Christian education in the church via preaching and teaching can be, must be, the hope of the world. But this possible hope must come out of a level of Christian education with much more intense depth and thought than what is now happening in the contemporary conservative church.

This hope must be spoken, demonstrated, and applied by Christians who know both the Word of God and what is happening in His world. The latter is known and understood via world-view and related trends studies. The important, essential, and imperative need of world-view studies in congregations cannot be overstressed. But having said that, the study and application of the life-changing Word of God putting before us the Incarnate God must always have priority as the foundation for such studies. And the studies of the Word of God and world-views must also be bathed in personal and corporate prayer. This is imperative in the contemporary church. Assuming this balance is present, Christians must become culture-watchers learning how to manifest Christianity in our ever-changing culture/society battling for the mind of man via cultural wars.

I fear a looming crisis for the Christian Church in this nation. Research continues to conclude that there are few differences between the people in our society who regularly worship and sometimes study the Bible when compared to those who do not; those who do other things on the Lord's Day and live lives the rest of the week unrelated to Christ's Lordship. Consequences of this lack of differences between Christians and non-Christians are deadening. Non-Christians perceive that

Christianity makes no qualitative difference in life and conclude, so why bother? Many Christians seem to have little to offer beyond the invitation to a privatized, feeling-oriented, subjective faith-experience and some social contacts, but with no real cultural impact on society's ills and evils. The church's influence continues to wane. More and more American church members are shallow believers failing to link their faith to daily life.

A dangerous situation is being developed. It may be further along than most want to admit. In the not too distant past our culture was decidedly pro-Christian. This does not mean that everyone was Christian. But most were friendly to and supportive of Christianity. Public consensus was strong for Christianity and Judeao-Christian morality. In the present, many sectors of our society are simply passive to the faith. In the future we can expect more disregard for that which the church stands and an increasing anti-Christian bias toward the claims of Christ and toward those who hold firmly to the Lord's views.

It appears that the Christian community, in the midst of rapid and radical societal change and a possible growing hostile environment, is losing ground and many contemporary battles. Christians in large numbers have been mesmerized by modern culture's lures while rejoicing in past victories. The consequences are:

> ... America in the '90s is rotting from the inside out. We are suffering from constant, if not almost imperceptible, shifts in perspective and behavior. As our population matures in technological sophistication and material comfort, we are losing our spiritual edge. We have embraced the means rather than the ends. Service to God has been replaced by a thirst for exaltation of self.[1]

Every social parameter of our nation is in trouble. That reveals the deterioration of our own spiritual and moral foundations. Therefore this nation's superficial spirituality demands a rededication to the proclamation of the theistic/Christian worldview in biblical relevant ways to our culture/society. This book is to assist meeting that demand by helping Christians know in a broader spectrum the world in which the Christian message is to be proclaimed.

Followers of Christ must have the opportunity for world-view studies to understand the dynamics of what is happening around them in order to be more prepared than surprised at our growing dilemmas. This calls for a kind of quality, high-level, Christian education that has not been seen in the local Church. George Barna insists that in the history of Christianity in this nation, the '90s are a pivotal decade.

> It is a time in which the Church will either explode with new growth or quietly fade into a colorless thread in the fabric of our secular culture. The changing nature of our society has pushed us past the point of simply being able to mark time. In this decade, Christianity must prove itself to be real and viable, or become just another spiritual philosophy appearing in the history of mankind.[2]

The church must not be trapped in gradualism. Gradualism is the story of the frog and the kettle of water. Put a frog in a pan of boiling water, and it will jump out immediately. That hot water is a hostile environment. Put the same frog in a pan of room-temperature water and it will stay there content with its environment. Slowly increase the water temperature, and the frog does not leap out, because it is unaware of the changing environment. Continually turn up the heat and the frog will boil to death, perhaps quite content, but quite dead. Barna's *The Frog In The Kettle* is his picture of the modern church.

The frog story illustrates that the Christian community must constantly be aware of changes in the environment of the world around it. We must readily recognize that we live in a world that is becoming increasingly estranged from Christian values. Christians must take a resolute stand against many commonly accepted axioms of the world. If we do not do this, we have no right to carry the name "Christian."

Nevertheless it seems the church has been unaware of the

changes made by other world-views and has been content in its unresponsiveness to the radical changing world around it. As I write this, the news is that two seven year old boys attempted to rape a little baby. Whether that is physically possible or not, I don't know, but what has happened to the mindset that little boys seven years old even know anything about such matters? Where has the church been; where is it located now?

I believe the area where conservative Christians must be faulted the most is in their glaring inability or just plain refusal to discern by world-view studies the encroachment of the values of the technological society upon the domain of the church. *The Technological Bluff* by Jacques Ellul might jar Christians sufficiently to awaken them from their intellectual stupor.

Having stated my hope in Christian education, I am convinced that most of that discipline in the local church is ignoring, bypassing or refusing to face, study, and apply this world-view dimension of Christian education. This dimension is imperative if the church is to take on the world in a positive way by giving it change and hope. At the present time most Christian education is the most expensive failure in the history of the modern church in two ways. It has failed to equip the church with the Bible, and it has failed by ignoring world-view studies, therefore not delivering the understanding of the nature of the world to the church. This assists and allows the crises in life and society to perpetuate themselves.

I am not opposed to the Sunday Bible School, but that alone in its present state cannot enable Christians to get even a glimpse of our complex issues in this world in order to be able to deal with them. So much Bible School Curriculum will not cut it. I am a promoter of small group philosophy. Next to worship it is the most important effort for the modern church to pursue. But even small groups along with the too typical Sunday morning Bible School class will not cut it.

Much youth ministry in its present mode of operations in many settings will not even begin to unveil the complexity of the times and prepare youth to confront culture/society in spite of the work and time put into that ministry by good youth pastors. Some are trapped in the drive for institutional success. Some are working under undue pressure from elders to get large crowds of kids who really aren't interested in the church. Most youth leave the church as teen-agers with some factual knowledge but only a second-hand faith.

Much contemporary preaching is often done in a vacuum catering to people's wants and "felt needs." That fails to prepare God's servants for the marketplace. What about those "unfelt needs," man's greatest need, that most moderns are totally blind to—forgiveness and a relationship with God; that one "unfelt need" for transcendence? Too many sermons from our recent Christian convention were mostly moralisms, news reports, and jokes all failing to give the "why" we are in the mess that we are in. What an opportune time to bring in world-view thoughts giving people reasons for the church's weakness and then preach Christ and His world-view. In the 1991 Myron J. Taylor Lectures on Preaching, Ronald E. Osborn spoke:

> My impression is that there is a widespread tendency to assume Jesus Christ rather than proclaim him. Preachers commonly enough begin with a parable or saying from Jesus and unfold it as significant wisdom for living. We seem more at home with that approach than with preaching the life and person and death and continuing ministry of our Lord. . . .In the great ages of preaching, beginning with the apostolic era, Jesus Christ has been the heart of the proclamation.[3]

I raise this issue on preaching for this reason. Is it possible that these "unfelt needs" are surfacing in a growing number of people needing transcendence, and they are not even aware of it? Doug Dickey suggests that, "more and more people are beginning, because of the despair that surrounds them, to feel their spiritual needs, perhaps vaguely, and that we can, like Paul in Athens, speak to them of the UNKNOWN GOD?"[4] What a possibility for releasing again in society the theistic/Christian world-view. Perhaps there is another clue to people realizing the need of transcendence for these "unfelt needs." The clue may be Wuthnow's *Recovering The Sacred*. This is about a quest for something more than what modern life without God in Christ offers. If this is happening, it is imperative to have Christians who can as did St. Paul see, by world-view awareness and trends analysis, through the foolishness of our times and then speak the Gospel to this generation in the vocabulary of our times.

In this context I am perplexed and somewhat angry at many church growth efforts targeting people as consumers and then marketing the Gospel by capitulating too much to our culture. Too often this seems oblivious to the possible surfacing of "unfelt needs" that can only be satisfied by the making of disciples. That effort is far beyond much contemporary "church growthism." To continue some "church growthism" that skirts the command of making disciples for the sake of success is a disgrace to our risen Lord. Our culture/society/world is much too complex for continuing with that kind of business as usual.

Christian education has to move into the crucible—a forum of radical Christian studies. Since I believe the church is the last possible bastion of truth and hope for the Western world, this missing dimension is weakening this possibility.

If the local church is going to be able to chart a hope-filled course of vision fulfilling the Dominion Mandate of Genesis and the Witnessing Commission Mandate of Matthew, if new hope is going to be present for Christians who are to be change-agents for the Lord of the Universe in our seductive society, then the missing dimension of world-view study, understanding, and application must be put into the Christian education program of the local church. If contemporary disciples on the threshold of the 21st century, a century unlike any century before, are going to be able to sing the songs of the Lord while in a foreign (alien) land (Ps. 137:4), a contemporary society that is for the most part foreign to and alien from the theistic/Christian world-view, this dimension of Christian education is long overdo!

This theistic/Christian world-view is the proclamation of the Lordship of Christ over all creation including all social parameters of life (Col. 1:15-17). This world-view sees the Lord's church as "the pillar and foundation of the truth" (1 Tim. 3:15). This church is a people who "take captive every thought to make it obedient to Christ" (2 Cor. 10:5), believing that the theistic/Christian world-view to be the only authentic and workable alternative world-view in a pluralistic world of competing world-views. The credibility of the gospel is at stake and must be demonstrated, and can be, as valid, credible, and authentic through this world-view.

The large picture of major world-views such as theism, deism, naturalism, existentialism, nilhilism, new age, etc. must be understood. These will be surveyed. Studying these is a part of the stewardship responsibilities of Christians. Douglas John Hall insists that:

> A faith that is not equipped to express the theological principles (within the whirling vortex of other world-views and reveal the emptiness of other world-views) upon which its moral values and its practical goals are based is a house without foundations. . . .Given the realities of religious pluralism and secular skepticism, North American Christianity today finds itself compelled—where it is alive to the spirit of the times—to develop a theological rationale for its pragmatically oriented religion; and that rationale must grow out of its own experience, its own suffering, and its own hope.[5]

There is radical and imperative justification for our Christian Colleges and Seminaries to require pastors and other specialized leaders for the church to study the humanities—the many areas of humane learning such as the arts, sciences, history, philosophy, literature, English, etc.—for their degrees and pastoral work so they will know the world-views coming out of those disciplines (Not enough Christian Colleges are doing this). There is the same justification for the local congregation to know the world around them by studying in the local congregational educational programs the world-views coming out of these disciplines in society. It is a matter of knowing this world and not just knowing about this world. There is a difference, and that can make the difference in the church's overall effectiveness.

This humane learning of world-views reveal the sentiments, attitudes, values, feelings, etc. that people have toward life and society. From this, God's people learn to see, judge, and analyze how only one world-view, the theistic/Christian world-view, holds our hope and help for the malignancies of our society.

This kind of broad intense study can be done. It must be done. It is not too technical for any disciple who wants to be able to take on the world for Christ's sake. This book is a spin-off of doing this kind of study in a local congregation that is still proving to be affective and effective.

I know what such studies have accomplished in people who have spent themselves in this type of study and sharing effort. They found that their involvement gave them confidence, rein-forced and enriched their personal faith in the Lordship of Christ, and generated new concerns beyond anything they have ever studied. The learning motivated them to be marketplace disciples concerned about the fracture of every sphere and social parameter of society. They developed a new concern for this world. They realized that Christianity is not just other-worldly. They come to realize the half-truth of "this world is not my home, I'm just a passing through." This world is our home now, and Christians are responsible for it. Christianity is very much about now in this world.

The tingle of resurrection power surfaced in my world-viewish people. Their love for the church increased. They no longer are satisfied to play church and just be religious. In some cases their family life changed into a family of communication with each other.

Therefore this writing is an introductory primer tool to encourage pastors and Christian educators of local churches to expand their horizons of thinking and understanding of this missing dimension. The bibliography points to the major resources that any committed, caring, and competent church leader can use to lead followers of Christ and non-Christians through.

A More Personal Note

At this point I wish to focus upon some of my own pilgrimage into the church. This gives more clarity to my convictions and the direction from where I am coming.

I have great affection for authentic Christians within the church. They know they are imperfect, yet forgiven, but they also know that something is terribly wrong with both church and society. They are willing to be on the critical cutting edge of thinking, living, and acting with a desire to bring the possible change, new life, and hope into society by reconciling the lost to Christ. They are His salt and light in a darkening world. They take the mandates of the earth's Maker and their Redeémer seriously.

To focus on authentic Christians first is a result of my own experience in life. In my first thirty years of life my relationship to Christ and my appearance around and within Christianity and the church was mostly social. My wife has an authentic, beautiful, quiet, redeeming, joyous-like, non-nagging, unpretentious, visible faith that kept magnetizing me during those years. It still does. Like a "good" husband and father I respectfully showed up periodically at worship and listened in on what was going on and being said. At that time there was not much of anything significant going on or being said. However, a young single pastor, Bob Walther, showed up at a country church and caused me to begin to sit up and take note of what he was saying.

The short of this? I was eventually captured in a rational and experiential way by Christ, Christianity, and the Church. Then after fifteen years of one avocation for earning a living I, very much like a reluctant pilgrim, changed avocations and began the present thirty year vocation and pilgrimage as a pastor. I fought it, but I could not walk away from the compelling call to change avocations for the greater vocation of telling the Good News. This fight within myself is another story.

Did I find the church to be perfect? Not at all. I have been hurt by the church and carry some emotional scars. I have met some mean people in the church. But I believe without reservation that any hopeful change, new life, old time-tested values that will always be new and fresh, and any new direction for life and a culture/society hovering between peril and promise will have to, and can, come from that authentic remnant of the church.

I have been in both camps: my world without the trinity of Christ, Christianity, and the Church, and a world of political, economic, ethical screw-ups by modern man who still thinks he can do something about the mess we are in by his own volition and power. That never has worked. Why would we moderns think we are any better equipped to do so today?

Therefore, with all the frustration of a lover's quarrel that I still often have with the church, there is that willing core of the church—they really understand the trinity of Christ, Christianity, and Church as needed in this culture—whom I believe offers the best and only glimmer of change, truth, light, and hope plus a path for life that the world and our society can have. But the church at large has to get on the cutting edge in thinking and acting!

I think it is Western society's last option for a world-view value-system that has demonstrated its power throughout history to change people and society. This authentic core of the church who is not worrying about their "felt-needs" does know that there is a Word, a Reality from outside, and they are willing to enter into the reality of the now.

It is the foregoing kind of church that will speak to the decent, morally-concerned, who may be willing to get on the critical cutting edge of thinking with authentic Christians. These people are also imperfect, often difficult to love, somewhat and sometimes rebellious against Christ, Christianity and the Church. These who refuse forgiveness from Christ also know something is terribly wrong with culture/society. But many, perhaps most, of them do not know where to turn for help. Some of these are in the position where "unfelt needs" may be surfacing as real needs for new life. I would hope that cutting-edge

Christians would assist non-Christians by sharing this and other materials with them that could direct them to Christ.

If the church and pastors will give consideration to such convictions, who knows what results beyond helping to develop a more stable society might surface? How many in this non-Christian camp might become forgiven sinners like Christians finding what so many of us have found: joy, purpose, a Shaloam, direction, and a new appreciation for life itself. All because of Christ, author and perfector of what I believe to be the only valid world-view for modern man and society. I think history past and future will always prove and demonstrate that God's grace really is amazing as my wife states and lives out in her life.

This introductory work of the importance of world-view study hopefully leading to a more in-depth study of world-views is not a panacea for all of the challenges facing the Lord's church and modern society as we rush pell-mell into the 21st century, a new millennium. But it can be a giant step of bringing positive change and hope into an unknown future. But what kind of church?

A Significant Question

A question of the hour: What kind of church will there be in the year 2001? An optimistic, realistic, alive, risk-taking, world-aware, determined church on the march for the Lord Jesus knowing how to really communicate to our modern society, or one huddled in a corner not knowing what it believes and why? Jurgen Moltman has asked the question in *Creating a Just Future*, "Does Modern Society Have a Future?"[6] The answer will be up to the church. Will the church really be ready and willing to be transformed into new possibilities, and will the church be equipped and willing to pay the price to bring the transforming message of the theistic/Christian world-view into the marketplace?

Christians and non-Christians have already sailed into a radically new environment in society regardless of their choosing to do so, and we need our sea legs quickly. Joseph Sittler of the

University of Chicago spoke of a certain person's theological writings as a hypnotizing and mesmerizing fog of beautiful rhetoric which surrounded and captivated the readers. But when the fog lifted all the furniture in the room had been changed. Far too many Christians, plus millions of other people who may be concerned, have no idea of what has changed via the shifting of the furniture of historical thought. Even though they are living with their bodies in the final decade of the 20th century, their minds appear to be lagging behind a couple of decades or more.

Yogi Berra, a favorite folk philosopher for many, spoke an inadvertent mouthful when he said, "You can observe a lot just by watching." David McKenna shares in his book, *Mega Truth*, an event that happened to him when Harold Pepinsky, a professor at Ohio State University, appeared at his faculty office one morning wearing an "impish grin and a balloon-sized lapel pin." Emblazoned on the pin were these large blue letters: "T.O.C.S." McKenna satisfied the plea on Pepinskys face by asking the meaning of the letters. Like a satisfied child this professor, considered by McKenna as one of the smartest persons he knew, "finger-walked" his way across the letters announcing as he went: "Thoughtful Observer of The Contemporary Scene.'" Like Yogi he knew that you can observe a lot just by watching. The seemingly bumbling wisdom of Yogi Berra matched the perceptive insight of this professor.

Concerned Christians have no choice but to be "T.O.C.S." people. World-view studies put into Christian education will do this. That is a fact! It is about Christians in action, equipping the Saints, strengthening the church, and blowing the trumpet.

Someone has suggested that man is the riddle of the world. If we are, then who are we? How do we find out? Who will unravel the tangle of man as the world's riddle?

Blaise Pascal was the seventeenth-century philosopher who made the riddle generic and suggested an answer or solution.

What a chimera then is man! What a novelty! What a monster, what a chaos, what a contradiction, what a prodigy!

Judge of all things, imbecile worm of the earth; depository of truth, sink of uncertainty and error; the pride and refuse of the universe!

As he penned these lines of bitterness and darkness about man, he then mused.

Who will unravel this tangle? . . . Know then, proud man, what a paradox you are to yourself. Humble yourself, weak reason; be silent, foolish nature; learn that man infinitely transcends man, and learn from your Master your true condition, of which you are ignorant. Hear God.[8]

World-view studies sorts through what world-view or world-views gives modern man this God to listen to in order to unravel just who and what he really is all about. And the church has God-ordained sanctions for such studies.

A Standing Truth—Transitional Remarks

The church has been repositioned by culture wars to a slippery slope, thus world-view awareness, perspective, and perceptions plus trends analysis must be and remain a significant part of the church's educational program for decades to come.

There will be constant change in world-views from the constant change of historical thinking, making the charge for world-view study imperative for at least two major reasons: one is to be constantly aware of world-views destructive to life and society. The other reason is to make certain that the church in the temptation to be successful instead of faithful does not compromise the Christian message by living on the slippery slope of unawareness and poor preparation of disciples making it impossible to carry out Peter's mandate in 1 Peter 3:15. Otherwise the church will not be able to penetrate a society influenced by a pluralism of world-views. Every generation and every Christian must be world-viewish.

My final remarks for this Proposal is in relation to some key words to understand that you have encountered in Part One. To know them is part of high-level Christian Education. They are defined in the glossary. Do not shy away from these. Master them for His sake.

In recent years a significant phenomenon called the Church Growth Movement has surfacĕd. The genesis of this is noble, but has it been captivated more by culture than by Christ and biblical evangelism and the mandate from Christ to "make disciples? Furthermore does world-view concern and issues have any relation to this phenomenon? I maintain that world-view studies have everything to do with biblical evangelism, the making of disciples, and church growth that expands the kingdom of God to penetrate culture/society with the Good News of the Gospel!

Part Three: Perspective — Church Growth Movement/World-View

The Church Growth Movement

As a preface to this Part I must make two clarifications. First, my concerns about the Church Growth Movement is not about personalities. There are certainly committed Christians involved in the Church Growth Movement of evangelism and the planting of new congregations.

My concerns are about a mindset observed in the movement that may contain dangerous attitudes, philosophies, theology, and actions. It is possible that these may be overlooked in the desire for success and increased numerical growth. The mindset under scrutiny comes dangerously close to reflecting not the mind of Christ but the mind of the masses. The appeal to the mind of the masses is an appeal that borders on trimming requirements for discipleship. This appears to require the least change from carnal to spiritual aspirations in order to attract the greatest number for a large membership. Some church leaders waste no time in learning what the masses' mind wants therefore shaping their message to appeal to the masses.

I am bothered when Church Growth advice seems to cater to the wishes of church shoppers. The schemes are unashamedly self-described as marketing mechanisms. I see a reinforcement of selfish small-mindedness rather than the proclamation of the great biblical vision of the church that can shake a world.

There is appeal from the Church Growth Movement advocates to the mass conversions in the Acts of the Apostles, but are they overlooking the fact that New Testament believers were stumbling blocks and offenses when "Jesus in Lord" was confessed? When these early followers communicated their faith, jail, persecution, or being run out of town was their reward.

There was not the present "cheap grace" that captured those people, who when converted, crossed cultural barriers and reached unpopular people. It was the Word of God, not gimmickry or entertainment, that captured followers.

These concerns must be considered in the context of the Church Growth Movement and the topic of world-view studies needed in all segments of the life and purpose of the church today.

My second clarification is about numbers. I am not opposed to numbers if they are the result of sound theology that calls people to fill the requirements for discipleship by obedience to the Lordship of Christ for the purpose of developing a healthy community called church. The strong health of that community is often the matrix of reaching new people for Christ.

To think that I am opposed to numbers in the context of authentic discipleship misses my concerns and care. I would love to see the excellent worship center where I preach and teach each Lord's Day morning filled with warm bodies that are growing into disciples. That may happen, and it can happen. But numerical growth must never be at the expense of truth about God, His Word, sin, faith, repentance, baptism, reconciliation, and His call for transformation of life by conversion wherein Jesus is Lord of all of life. Numerical growth must never be the result of entertainment or "cheap grace" wherein what results is spectator Christianity. The gap between the Church Growth Movement and theological church growth may be wider than many want to face.

The Christian message must not be aimed at the masses but rather preached among the masses and aimed at those potential Christians among them who are looking for directions from God. Those who respond must realize that every person in Christ is called to servanthood. So much for clarifications as concerns about the Church Growth Movement are stated.

The Church Growth Movement is the uppermost thought on the minds of many churchmen today. It borders on a mania in some environments. Is it too shallow, and does it skirt too much in what is involved in making disciples and equipping them as His bride to display His glory as mature disciples? That question relates to the fact that in the context of a growing membership and unprecedented Christian activity, never has the modern church's effectiveness in society been so weak.

Church leadership needs to be sensitive to and understand both the strengths to praise and the dangerous weaknesses that could misrepresent what the church is really to be and do with its witness and purpose. The question being considered by a growing number of leaders is, has the church already been misrepresented too much from a biblical perspective?

As noble, and I am certain exciting in some aspects, as the Church Growth Movement must be, I have to state a conviction among many convictions and concerns. The issue, purpose, and topic of world-view studies demanded by our times in the education and preaching efforts of the local congregation is larger than church growth and desperately needed in much of the church growth mindset. Church growth strategy, methodology, and the science of marketing may work, but it is not clear to many that it will be the Church of Jesus Christ that has thereby grown.

I am concerned from observation that quite possibly biblical evangelism in its fullest and deepest meaning of initiating the lost into the Kingdom (rule/reign of God) has been traded off by too many for church growth methodology. Is conversion and transformation that is integral to the Lord's final mandate of making of disciples happening to those reached so that they can be and will be subversive agents in our seductive society?

In *Consumer Church*, the authors are proper in asking two astute questions. The first one: "Can evangelicals win the world without losing their souls?" The second question: "Are we risking false advertising if we offer people the power and benefits of Christ without the costs of following Him?"[1]

The American mystique of growthism makes growing the church larger numerically an end in itself. I think Donald McGavran was a godly and committed person. But I am not certain that his emphasis on growth, in the contemporary context

103

and mind-set, is the "primary" purpose of the church. Sometimes this appears almost more important than representing the Gospel in all its fullness including the reign of God in life and society via transformed believers. It is possible that many evangelical congregations involved in radical growthism are overwhelmingly shaped by popular demand to primarily meet people's "felt needs." From this comes the mind-set that "fantastic increase of churches is obviously the will of God." Is it? This question is asked in the context that much happening as the result of the Church Growth Movement is not necessarily evangelism, because the methods, by and large, attract only people already affiliated with other churches. It is a consumer mentality problem.

Is seeking to have "felt needs" met a biblical perspective, or have we turned Jesus into the Master Psychologist just for peoples "felt needs" therefore bypassing His call to discipleship and servanthood? To be aware that we are needy and are to reach out to others at levels of their authentic needs is what I call legitimate longings for something or Someone larger than oneself.

Related to this issue of "felt needs" is a significant question that must be posed. What about all those "unfelt needs," the God-ordained spiritual needs, of man that must allow the ministry of the Holy Spirit work through the Word of God to re-generate man into a "new creation" reconciling him to God for salvation?

Consumer Christians may see the church as simply existing to "meet their needs," thus having no claim on their commitment and loyalty, but the church's calling is to demonstrate how different its understanding of human existence is from that of the surrounding culture/society's structured consumerism of self-wants, self-assertion, and self-fulfillment. This consumer mentality among church shoppers makes it difficult for loyal bible-oriented congregations to thrive and serve.

Reginald Bibby, Canadian sociologist, maintains that churches seem to offer religion like consumer goods, and instead of teaching this is what religion is, the implication given to the consumer mind is, 'what do you want religion to be and do for you?' When faith is packaged, based on what the market will bear, the consequences include the fact that the consumer is in charge. We could change that old hymn, "Christ Is Our Cornerstone," to "Christ Is Our Cornerstore," suggests Bibby, because Jesus is transformed into a commodity.

This mindset may be reinforced by some of the contemporary "recovery movement" that can so easily skirt sin. After all who in our sophisticated society wants to face that? There is great danger in the "recovery movement" of putting self and not Christ at the center of life. This is part of the therapeutic revolution spawned by Freud. It's an effort to heal people's spiritual wounds by a god who has no wounds. This may be the most significant source of a form of Christian idolatry. This revolution may be revealing a new measure of Christian credulity believing "another gospel."

All of this relates to world-view study, understanding, and application. This is much larger and more serious than the popular mindset that implies: If our church grows numerically, the rightness of our faith is somehow verified. And if this mindset is in control you can be certain that you will ultimately be evaluated by two pervasive and all important questions. How large is your church? And how much has it grown, meaning, numerically? Unfortunately there are many churches with this mindset that may see themselves as competing for market shares of believers and will try whatever seems to work to make sure that they compete successfully. Pragmatism becomes their foundation for doing what they do.

Some marketing efforts have become a science that emphasizes shaping a product appealing to the "consumer-targeted" audience. Some marketing approaches develop a product to convince the consumer that he "needs" the product. Is that the purpose of the church or is the purpose to proclaim Christ and His worldview to transform persons into "new creations" wherein these "new creations" take the salt and light and the theistic/Christian world-view into the marketplace for His glory and service?

Did Jesus miss the point of His purpose and message by not turning the Good News into something that was "user-friendly" like a computer so He would be mega-successful? Jesus would have been quite successful if He had altered the gospel of His world-view (a product) to help people into easy believism (purchase the gospel on their terms). But what kind of success is this? Contrary to popular thought Jesus did not appeal to the masses. They flocked to Him at first, but when He presented the fine print they deserted Him in droves. Would it be any different today if persecution really hit our part of the world?

Here is one bottom line. There can be fantastic, exciting, and rewarding numerical growthism happening as a result of various strategies, but what if the world of social fragmentation is only superficially touched if at all, or penetrated little if at all with the power of God in the marketplace by this mega-super-church mindset? If society continues to deteriorate morally and spiritually in the midst of unprecedented religious activity with Christian labels, then has the salt lost its saltiness and the light become darkness? This is a world-view issue.

What is the situation, biblically, when a congregation can gather thousands for worship but only approximately one-third or less of those want to be a part of the Body of Christ, the church? Therefore membership is played down, because baby-boomers and baby-busters do not want to belong.

Does not the mania of "growthism" shoot holes in the old myth that may still be lurking in the hearts of many? The myth is that the more believers there are the better society will automatically become? If that were so, according to the numerical size of the modern church our nation should be a much healthier society spiritually and morally than it is. The myth is false for we are a nation of spiritual pigmies and moral perverts, because the wrong world-views are in control even in many Christian lives. And that is the fault of the modern church, because no alien world-view is powerful enough to override the theistic/Christian world-view if it is alive and authentic.

Church Growth alone without social influence as salt and

light will not cut it. Furthermore it is unbiblical. To have the imperative biblical social influence demands an awareness of how we as a society have arrived at the historical juncture in all social parameters spiritually, morally, mentally, politically, etc.

Therefore, this is a world-view awareness issue: an awareness of not only the contemporary and new world-views that keep surfacing, but also the older classical world-views opposed by Christianity that brought us to this point of serious national and world problems must be known. These are world-views that most in the church have never faced and still will not face in most Christian education.

Such works as Chandler's *Racing Toward 2001* is a classic. We do need to be aware of all "the major forces shaping America's religious future," but we still must know something about all the world-views and trends that brought us to this point. Part of the cure needed for kingdom work to be effective in the context of the Church Growth Movement is to know what world-views have been the source of the wrong values that have developed such fragmentations of thinking and acting in some of the church, culture/society, and the world. This is about recovering "foundations for the future" for *The Church In Ruins,* as one author recently published.

Tony Campolo has some strong words about this issue in his *Wake Up America.* I have to concur with his conclusions. After praising all of the various ministries and services that super-and mega-churches coming out of the Church Growth Movement can offer, and that truly is wonderful, he boldly and clearly states his convictions. I believe that regardless of whether other Christians have trouble with his aggressive boldness, he has to be taken with the utmost seriousness in this matter.

> ... this kind of religion will not bring about social change ... because its preachers are not prophets who will lead the American people to weep over what they have become. As a matter of fact, these preachers will leave the young upwardly mobile professionals in their congregations quite content with their BMWs, Reebok sneaks, and expensive weekends. ...

They preach a kind of religion that will enable people to enjoy
a happy state of consciousness in a society that is dying. . . .
they present an incomplete version of God[2]

This is a world-view issue and concern. What world-view or
world-views would gather crowds, great crowds, but the society
around remains ill, morally and spiritually destitute, and even
continues to deteriorate in the midst of the greatest resurgence of
spiritual activity with Christian labels in decades in this society,
perhaps in all of history?

Some contemporary church growth is not always synonymous with making disciples according to Jesus' last mandate.
Much of what is called evangelism today is not synonymous
with making disciples, but making disciples, as mandated, that
are being transformed by the Christ to take on the world always
includes evangelism. But this will probably thin the crowds.

In the context of this contemporary critical situational danger, *The Logic of Evangelism* by William J. Abraham is a
refreshing source that much church growth thinking needs to
assimilate. It would rearrange some thinking.

Bringing people into the presence of the Kingdom, the rule
and reign of God, is what is needed in church growth talk and
work. That is what the theistic/Christian world-view accomplishes. That is far beyond much church growth strategy and
methodology.

It is clear that so much of the Church Growth Movement
thrives on the cacophonys of information as if everything can
known and announced, or that production comes only from
designing and engineering, that consumer satisfaction is required
from the marketer, that management requires consultants, or
healing comes from something like a therapist, and there must
be impression by images. This develops a mixture almost totally
dependent on professionalism and expertise with much disregard
for the content of the professionalism and expertise. But the crying need in the church today is to be addressed by the Word of
God in order to drown out the growing excess of the cacophonys
of ideas almost replacing the Word of God.

108

Therefore this question is significant. Robert Woods of Florida Christian College, referring to "growthism" asks, "is it possible that a new 'ism' is developing in our congregations?"[3]

Praises And Dangers

The praises for and the dangers about the current Church Growth Movement are significant. To some degree the Church Growth Movement appears to be an effort of back to the basics. This movement shows some concern for Christian renewal and reform or desired reformation within the church. Components of this renewal effort involves the centrality of the church, mission priority, reaching outside, sometimes acknowledging culture and society, insistence on results, and the use of various managerial insights and technology.

The Church Growth Movement does represent a most influential movement in the American churches in the 1990s, as well as some expression of the search for the lost authority of faith. Past decades have seen the church in America move through all kinds of activism, special interest groups, political efforts for reform, etc. But most of the strength in and of these efforts are almost bankrupt.

This popular movement offers an initiative of adaptation and innovation by the church. Of course tension always comes between those with the urgent desire to change and adapt new ways and the unwillingness of those who are always afraid of change. When the church is afraid of new endeavors without compromise, perhaps then it needs to be done. But in the effort of innovations truth often has a darker side. The church is prone to compromise with the spirit of its age in the name of success. Nevertheless down through history and the various revivals, the historic faith has been determined to innovate and adapt for the sake of the Gospel.

New insights, valid managerial efforts, technologies, all hold much potential for getting the Gospel out to hopefully reposition the church back into the center of society by getting it off the slippery slope. However these insightful words are correct.

Whatever criticisms of the movement need to be raised, the point is beyond dispute. The church-growth movement is extraordinarily influential and significant within American churches today. At its best, it needs to be applauded. But where it is not at its best, it requires criticism so that it might be. The church of Christ concerned for the glory of Christ needs more - not less - of the best true church growth.[4]

There are other danger signals beyond what has already surfaced warning us about other possible weaknesses of the Church Growth Movement.

World-view concerns move into the fray. The Church Growth Movement is a mixture of things good, bad, and in-between. There are deficiencies in the Movement. One is superficial theology. This can't be missed in some seminars of these mega-church approaches. One unnamed church growth voice stated: "I don't deal with theology. I'm simply a methodologist." This needs no elaboration. Another deficiency is much of the Movement's lack of real awareness of history. This awareness is important, because it can put light on the dangerous pitfalls in the present Church Growth Movement mindset. Without strong historical awareness of mistakes from the past, the evangelical sea change continues today not just in theological changes but also runs the gamut from "theology to experience, from truth to technique, and from an emphasis on 'serving God' to an emphasis on 'serving the self' in serving God."[5]

There are also flaws tied in with the deficiencies. On one hand there is the application of a biblical principle of relevance. But relevance in overdoing the being "all things to all people" becomes more important than historical, biblical, doctrinal truth. Compromise has often moved in. Another warning danger in the Movement is the poor or partial understanding of "modernity" and the lack of critical thinking about its insights and tools. This is one place where world-view studies are larger than church growth and imperative in the efforts of church growth and kingdom development.

Our society is now beyond modernity. We are now a post-modern society where even the Enlightenment principles are losing their grip. What does that mean to the church and its opportunities in this 21st Century world? Everything in the possibilities for communication if this shifting in thought is understood. Or it means nothing, if all this sea change going on in theology, philosophy, sociology, and world-view studies is not understood in the context of church growth.

This is larger than church growth strategy and methodology. Truth is at stake! Again some keen insight.

> I would therefore be the last, either as a Christian or as some-one trained in the social sciences, to deny the illuminating helpfulness of the social sciences (modernity's insights and tools). At the same time, however, it is amazing to witness the lemming-like rush of church leaders who abandon theology and charge after the latest insights of sociology—regardless of where the ideas come from and where they lead to.[6]

The Church Growth Movement also carries potential dangers summed up in the words and phrases of "no God" and "no grandchildren." "No God," can mean that the insights, tools, and wisdom of theological modernity can be so effective in the way the world counts success that there appears no longer any need for God. As for "no grandchildren," all the modern tools for success in one generation may not be able to be used and sustained in the next generation.

> The success undermines the succession. In short, through its uncritical use of modernity, the church-growth movement is unleashing a deadly form of "practical atheism" in the church-es. The result is a contemporary testament to the extraordinary power of religion that has no need of God. Critical discern-ment is necessary for all who appreciate the promise and the peril of the church-growth movement.[7]

Again the plea for world-view studies in the context of king-dom growth that involves the strengthening of the church in both numbers and stature. World-view studies can keep Christians from falling into equal and opposite errors when thinking of new movements such as what I am examining. One error is to give total support, praise, and applaud it because it is new and it works as if nothing else matters from beginning to end. The other error is to dismiss it because it is modern and it works. World-view studies keeps these errors in tension for the good of the Kingdom for Christ's sake.

Without the people who are really into the Church Growth Movement knowing and understanding world-view phenomena and being aware of trends by analyzes, they will never understand how modernity and alien world-views pose the greatest problem for authentic church growth.

> When all is said and done, the church-growth movement will stand or fall by one question: In implementing its vision of church growth, is the church of Christ primarily guided and shaped by its own character of calling - or by considerations and circumstances alien to itself? Or, to put the question differently, is the church of Christ a social reality truly shaped by a theological cause, namely the Word and Spirit of God? Behind this question lies the fact that the church of God only "lets God be God," and is only the church, and is free when she lives and thrives by God's truths and God's resources. If the church makes anything else the principle of her existence, Christians risk living unauthorized lives of faith, exercising unauthorized ministries, and proclaiming an unauthorized Gospel.[8]

That is what alien world-views that creep into the church accomplish, and that is the temptation modernity offers—the power and brilliance of its wisdom, tools, and insights. That convinces modern man even within the church to believe that he can pull off God's work without God. "In today's convenient, climate-controlled spiritual world created by the managerial and therapeutic revolutions, nothing is easier than living apart from God."[9]

It is like this. An unnamed Christian advertising agent, who represented the Coca-Cola Corporation and also put together the "I Found It" campaign several years ago, stated the point arrogantly: "Back in Jerusalem where the church started, God performed a miracle there on the day of Pentecost. They didn't have the benefits of buttons and media, so God had to do a little supernatural work there. But today, with our technology, we have available to us the opportunity to create the same kind of interest in a secular society."[10]

That kind of arrogance created unknowingly by modernity's hold, and the other extreme of a superspiritual fallacy that says we will never go that far, when both are tied in with what some church growth gurus say: "the No. 1 rule of church growth is that a church will never get bigger than its parking lot,"[11] it smells of all kinds of dangers in the Church Growth Movement. Some of this looks like a modernity takeover that is most dangerous at its best.

What about the stated "No. 1 rule?" Is that more important than a growing faith, a growth in the Word of God empowered by the Spirit of God? Is that what it's all about? I hope not! Isn't what really matters, after the accumulated wisdom of modernity has been put to proper use, is that the authentic character of the church remains to be demonstrated, and the authentic growth of the church remains to be seen?

In relation to the praises and dangers of the Church Growth Movement that has captured the masses, is the charge leveled by rock star Michael Been of The Call true? "Everything that goes on in every major corporation goes on inside the church, except as a sideline the church teaches religion."[12]

Hans Kung writes some clear perceptions about growth.

Given that Jesus Christ is the head of the church and hence the origin and goal of its growth, growth is only possible in obedience to its head. If the church is disobedient to its head and His Word, it cannot grow however busy and active it may seem to be; it can only wither. Its development, no matter how spectacular, will prove basically misdirected; its progress, no matter how grandiose, will prove ultimately a disastrous retrogression. The valid movements in the church are those that are set in motion by God's grace.[13]

World-view study is larger than church growth. It is imperative in this era of religiosity and numerical striving that seems to be changing few lives by transformation for the glory of God and our Lord and Savior Jesus Christ. World-views studies are not only revealing what alien world-views are destroying personal life and society as a whole. They also keep the church on the right path as it pilgrimages through this world's marketplace in the work of harvesting the lost by His intended power and purity of the theistic/Christian world-view.

This must be stated again. Never can world-view studies have priority over consistent, in-depth, serious, and intense biblical studies. But biblical studies in the context of church growth without world-view studies will by and large keep the Word of God in a vacuum, and the illusionary tools of modernity will possibly continue being used by many church growth mindsets believing they are doing it all okay.

There is another dimension of the praises and dangers of the Church Growth Movement to consider. It is about success and growth, but at what price? Anyone in Christian ministry knows that seductions of the modern world are at times hard to resist. Their benefits are just as hard to refuse. How can one say "no" to any of the church growth efforts without people thinking a person is too spiritual when it is achieved through the best management and marketing? Only by looking honestly at some facts.

There is the fact that our secularized society exalts "numbers" and "technique." Both are prominent in the Church Growth Movement. But has fascination with stats and data taken over at the expense of truth? Perhaps more than most realize until one looks under the tent flap of the movement.

> Some people argue that the emphasis on quantifiable measures—on counting—is the central characteristic of a rationalized society. Thus the United States has government by polling, sports commentary by statistics, education by grade-point averages, and academic tenure by the number of publications. In such a world of number crunchers, bean counters, and computer analysts, the growth of churches as a measurable, "fact-based" business enterprise is utterly natural.

The problem with this mentality is that quantity does not measure quality. Numbers have little to do with truth, excellence, or character. . . . For church growth viewed in measurable terms, such as numbers, is trivial compared with growth in less measurable but more important terms, such as faith, character, and godliness. The latter, of course does not preclude the former. But nor does the former necessarily include the latter.[14]

Then we have "technique." This is not wrong or evil, but consider it in this context. It is clearly a preoccupation in the Church Growth Movement. Popular church growth manuals or programs are guaranteed to work numerically for the largest attendance in the neighborhood. The promotion argument is, this or that program worked at one place, therefore it has to work every place. It's a matter of "technique."

The assumption is that by "technique" "life can be viewed as a set of problems, each set having a rational solution, an identifiable expert, and therefore a practical mechanism to effect it."[15]

Now this situation. It is related to and comes out of the foregoing praises and dangers of some of the mindset of the Church Growth Movement that I have briefly dissected. Recent materials about the lack of strong preaching in the American church, including the conservative Evangelical church, is expressing the same shallow approach to kingdom work that we have viewed in some of the Church Growth Movement's mindset.

Various magazines written for pastors and church leaders examine every conceivable problem in the contemporary church. But most ignore anything about the desperate need of Scripture and the Word of God being preached, not to meet peoples' "felt needs," but to hear again what God has announced and is still announcing even to a society playing church and religious games of one-upmanship. These journals or magazines are "in the form of the imperialistic genius of managerial and therapeutic insights," but "galloping secularization left theology in the dust."[16]

There is also the changing of profiles for the pastor that gives us another clue of the secularization within the Church Growth Movement. In 1934 pastors were looked upon to have five basic and distinct roles: teacher, preacher, pastor, leader, and administrator. These five basics are "notable for being few in number and biblical in content." A 1980 study revealed that a pastor's profile had expanded but was more secular. Pastors were expected "to be open, affirming, able to foster relationships, experienced in facilitating discussion, and so on." The premium was on skills in "interpersonal relationships and conflict management. Biblical and spiritual criteria of ministry were notably optional."

Then a study in 1986:

> showed that the differences in expectations between liberals and evangelicals has almost disappeared, that secular expectations grew while the spiritual shrunk, and that the profile was largely dominated by two sets of considerations - those therapeutic and managerial.

> Anyone who doubts this shift has only to look at church-growth literature and check for such chapters as "Portraits of the Effective Pastor." In one such best-seller, theology and theological references are kept to a minimum—little more than a cursory reference to the pastor's "personal calling" and to "God's vision for the church." The bulk of the chapter is taken up with such themes as delegating, confidence, interaction, decision making, visibility, practicality, accountability, and discernment—the profile of the pastor as CEO.[17]

A major point in noting the changing profiles is that the foregoing leadership qualities could apply to a multitude of other organizations. It is no small wonder that when a pastor returned home from a church growth conference he was puzzled. There had been "literally no theology," and "in fact, there had been no serious reference to God at all."

Other concerns about contemporary church growth efforts in the context of world-view could be and should be perceived. Just two more dangers must be stated.

First, within the movement, is there a "recycling of the compromise of liberalism" wherein even the evangelical church is doing what the World Council of Churches decreed in 1966: "The world must set the agenda for the church?" This relates to the current church growth infatuation with marketing the church. Some of this moves into the conviction that "the audience, not the message is sovereign." Yet, the *New Yorker* laments the new "audience-driven" preaching of the day wherein the preacher has nothing to say to the world that "drifts blindly into the future,"[18] because the world has set the agenda for his preaching.

Second is the concern of "the cult of relevance and the management of need." Relevance has its place, but an overheated use of this vaporizes into trendiness and captures the celebrated line of Dean Inge: "He who marries the spirit of the age soon becomes a widower." What about the law of meeting peoples' "needs" as two great commandments of the mega-church mindset: "Find a need and meet it, find a hurt and heal it."

> In short, the exaggerated half-truth about the church's "needing to meet needs" once again breeds untended consequences. Just as church-growth's modern passion for "relevance" will become its road to irrelevance, so its modern passion for "felt needs" will turn the church into an echo chamber of fashionable needs that drown out the one voice that addresses real human need below all felt needs.[19]

The most objective, scholarly, and honest treatment of the Church Growth Movement is in a collection of essays written by Os Guinness for Ligonier Ministries' *Tabletalk* journal. His total assessment will be painful for many in the Church Growth Movement, but the material cannot be ignored or improved upon by anyone that I know. These essays were my major resource for much that I have said in the section about the praises and dangers of the Church Growth Movement. I am indebted to Os Guinness for his keen insightfulness.[20]

Soren Kierkegaard is not widely read, and for some he is too radical, but we need to heed his wisdom. Since I do not have a direct quote, the warning had to do with the church that triumphs in this world and becomes such a friend to the world that no one can tell the difference. When that happens, according to him, Christianity is done away with. The gates of hell have prevailed.

I hope it is becoming clear that there is serious need of world-view studies in the contemporary Church Growth Movement. The big discovery might reveal just how much or little the orthodox theistic/Christian world-view influences such a Movement. The following section of this Part of the book would result through the Church Growth Movement if the theistic/Christian world-view was fully understood and fully in control of the movement. Other alien world-views would also have to move over because of the real biblical power of the church.

The Imperative Eradication of A Mindset

Christianity is not just about spiritual matters. That is Greek philosophy rampant in conservative circles. This philosophy is like a spiritual living in the clouds ignoring the world of matter and the marketplace of God's creation that He has promised to penetrate with the metaphorical meaning of salt and light through transformed lives of Christ-followers.

The *Wild Hope* of biblical promise creates the church, not just to be larger and larger institutionally and numerically, but to be a transformed and living hope for society by first, reconciling man to God by God's grace. Then reconciled people are to be equipped and released to effect change in the market place with the salt and light of the Good News. That is a biblical command. It is not optional. It is far beyond some church growth talk and strategy. For the church to refuse or fail to equip people to take the gospel into the marketplace is to lead them to believe that the spiritual journey with Christ is a spiritual sauna.

It is about world-view! It is about high-level Christian education in the local congregation that does more than to make sure the parking lot is the "No. 1 rule" in church growth. It is about the mind redeemed to take on the world in thinking and dialogue. It is about an early Church father's famous question.

It was Tertullian who asked the famous question that has been asked over and over. I ask it again: "What does Athens have to do with Jerusalem?" By Athens he meant and means the intellectual culture, the life of the mind in the study of philosophy, literature, history, and theology, etc. By Jerusalem he meant and means redemption through the blood of Jesus, faith, hope, and charity.

The question is asking rhetorically: If you are a new creature in Christ, why do you need intellectual culture? That is, if you have found the "pearl of great price" why and how can you still have any concern or heart for the heritage of the Greeks and for the liberal arts? You will not be judged on the Last Day by how much pagan wisdom you have assimilated. Why then should it be of any concern of yours now when you are supposed to be living a life in preparation for the Last Judgement?

It is like the question is saying, leave the pagan wisdom to the pagans. You go on to lead a life hidden with Christ in God. Feed the hungry, preach the gospel to the poor, rescue those whose lives are endangered. But intellectual refinement, vast knowledge, well-developed powers of criticism and analysis, is this not just a kind of luxury, an intellectual and not a material luxury at that, but a luxury all the same? If you insist on leading the life of the mind, are you not just "fiddling while Rome burns?"

The rhetorical position of staying in Jerusalem is very familiar in conservative circles of the church. And much of the church, including some of the Church Growth Movement, has fallen prey to and perpetuates it by ignoring Athens. All of the time in recent years, the culture wars were at work repositioning the church onto the slippery slope of society. Keeping the Christian mindset "private", while all kinds of alien world-views are controlling the "public" world is the position that ignores Athens. The eradicating of this mindset is about the study of world-view and changing a mindset of church growth most of which appears to be preparing people for everlasting life which is fine, but they are not equipping them to take "Jerusalem" to "Athens."

Of course Christians pursue the reconciliation of the lost to God via the Christ all of which is pure grace and no work of their own, and certainly no natural result of some earthly development. This ministry of reconciliation must have first priority in Christian labors.

But Christians also have biblical reasons sprung from the mind/heart of their faith in the Incarnation to take earthly development seriously. They have reason to commit themselves to the world of drawing all parts of human nature, all regions of human existence, and all social parameters of culture to Christ (Col. 1:17), making them share in the redemption, and in this way if I might express myself boldly, of also "helping" Him to exercise His primacy in creation.

It is uniting the two mandates that most of the conservative church has not done, because much of the gospel that has been preached and is being preached is more Greek and gnostic than it is wholistically biblical. This is about world-views, because there are many world-views in this society that are not only destroying man, the crown of God's creation but also His earthly creation. The two mandates that again have to be exercised is the Dominion Mandate of Genesis 1:26-29 and the great Witness Mandate of our Lord in Matthew 28:16-20.

The question again: "What does Athens have to do with Jerusalem?" Everything! Therefore the danger is not so much failing to appreciate fully the mind, but failing to appreciate precisely the deep Christian significance of the life of the mind, failing to understand adequately what it means to say that the university of the mind is born in the heart of the church. Every great university in the world started in the heart of the church and brought Jerusalem into Athens in our analogical context. But the church pulled away from this with Greek thinking that separates spirit from matter and it is to blame almost wholly for the death of the mind in the church and the world today.

This is intensely so of my religious heritage. I am in it by theological choice, but we are still caught up in a certain dualism of faith here (Jerusalem) and study over there (Athens) and the Sunday School in our churches has been the most expensive failure in Kingdom work thus perpetuating this horrible dualism. That is a major reason why most Christian youth go through culture shock in their first year at the university, and the majority walk away from the church. To bring Jerusalem (the theistic/Christian world-view) to Athens (the society of many alien world-views destroying so much) is the spirituality that knows how to integrate our intellectual work into the mystery of Christ, and of His Kingship in creation, the marketplace, and His church. It is the restoration of biblical secularity—the sacred and the secular on the same coin—the sacred on one side, the secular on the other with the church's responsibility to bring the sacred into the secular.

Furthermore, it may be that "if Jerusalem refuses to have anything to do with Athens, and if she in general fails to do justice to the incarnational significance of revelation and encloses herself in a onesided eschatological understanding, she will remain under-developed precisely as Jerusalem."[21] Why? Because Athens also has something to do with Jerusalem and the complete separation of the two is un-Christian and fatal regardless of how successful we may be with the Church Growth Movement.

It is about world-view. And at this point-in-time of the culture wars, Athens is seducing the western culture and the western church. Christians can ignore Athens. They can withdraw from the world, its thought forms and lifestyle. They can enshrine themselves in a monastery mindset. But as Dr. Robert Fife has written in a brochure about the Westwood Christian Foundation, ". . . Satan has never had any difficulty climbing monastery walls. Nor can true Christian faith long exist unless it expends itself in mission to the world." Dr. Fife continues by reminding us that secularism, which is basically intolerant, declares for the moment, "Let Christians have their own little compounds! We have the world!" This withdrawal by Christ-followers perpetuates the secularism that holds many major western institutions, including education at the university and public school level, in bondage.

If Athens and Jerusalem really belong together, whence this chronic antagonism between the Christian commitment to Christ and the ignoring of the intellectual world that needs Christ? It is easier to be Platonic in thinking and separate the sacred from the secular; the spirit from the matter.

There is only one thing wrong with that approach. It is biblically wrong and unsound and is a strange phenomenon for a supposedly people of the Book in conservative circles. But unless the church does something about this separation and moves beyond just church growth strategy, the words of Yeats will grow more loud and clear: "the center will not hold." Why? There is no center there, because the church has pulled Christ out of the created order and the marketplace almost totally ignoring Colossians 1:17. It is easier to be interested only in spiritual matters and getting to heaven but that is only half of the story.

It is all about world-views, understanding them, knowing them, and doing something about this in high-level Christian education in the local congregation. And it can be done. As I have already stated elsewhere Freshmen in high school have been taught world-view material, and they latched onto it. Whether they allow what they know to effect their lives is their responsibility, but the congregation did its part.

There is a danger in taking world-view studies seriously and really examining life. We, in a very conservative congregation, realized via world-view studies that most of our high school youth at an earlier time than now, even though they had been baptized (believer's baptism), were more a combination of existential nihilism than they were Christian. It was and is no wonder that Jesus does not excite most of them. They may have known Him cognitively, but surely they had not allowed Him to be Lord of life or nihilism would not have gotten hold of most of them whose vocabulary hinged around "I'm bored." We believe that has changed now with some youth who have studied world-views and went through some serious self-examination.

The church has been repositioned by society to a slippery slope, because it was too ineffective to fight back during the time of culture wars between the private and public dimensions of existence. This happened in the midst of unprecedented religious activity labeled Christian. ...It's a world-view issue and concern.

The culture wars in which the church is captured is about who we are as a nation and who we will choose to become. It is about world-views. "The fissures that divide America can only grow deeper."[22] What will the church be able to do about that at its present stage of unpreparedness in thinking? Alasdair MacIntyre writes, "The barbarians are not waiting beyond the frontiers; they have been governing us for quite some time. And it is our lack of consciousness of this that constitutes part of our predicament."[23]

In a recent episode of "Reasonable Doubt" on television, the one playing the role of detective made the statement, "the world is falling apart." True! The point is this: Church Growth unrelated to the rest of life in the world (Athens) will not have much if any effect on it. It is too alienated from daily life in social context because of the old myth ("What does Athens have to do with Jerusalem?") that still lurks in the shadows of conservative Christian thinking.

This is not a plea for the old liberal social gospel. It is a plea for the social implications of the Gospel channeled through twice-born people who know both the Word of God and God's world via world-view studies. Let the church do all that it can in that context and see what can happen to a very fragmented and hopeless society and world!

Wake-Up Calls: Preaching/Teaching In The Movement

World-view studies in the context of church growth are wake-up calls in many ways. They wake up Christians by helping them read contemporary society in order to live in it without being subservient to it. Neither accommodating the Gospel nor hiding in the religious ghetto serves the cause of Christ. By waking up, Christians find their place between a limping liberalism that does not know God's map, the Word of God, and a galloping conservatism that does not know God's world.

World-view wake-up calls can rally Christians to take charge and live creatively in a changing world of crises facing the human community as we whirl into the 21st Century. In Sine's *Wild Hope*, we wake up to "an economic Tsunami, . . a changing parade of power, . . a church out of the running, . . a co-opted church in North America . . . that forgot to count the cost," and allowed a pluralization of religion to overshadow and almost blank out a privatized Christianity that does not go public, a kind of Christianity wrapped up in "the pursuit of prosperity, position, and power." There must be a wake-up call to "the captivity of the Christian mind,"[24] and a wake-up call from the twenty-first century to take the future seriously.

World-view studies are wake-up calls to prepare for facing five "Master Trends" facing us; trends unlike any previous age; five trends which are shaping society and which raise questions of world-view options. They are: "Global Economic Integration, Environmental Vulnerability and Awareness, Unlocking the Secrets of Matter, The Vanishing Line Between Mind and Machine, and The Moral, Political, and Economic Decline of the United States."

From these trends jump six new categories of world-views: "Quantum Mystery, The Gaian Hypothesis, Cosmic Soup, Divine Design, The Force of Fate, and New International Order."[25]

It is true that all these large words and phrases will frighten many Christians. On the other hand too many Christians will just want to ignore all of this. But any Christian who cares, can and will through world-view studies study these trends and changing world-views and realize that in all of this mess there is still only one world-view—the theistic/Christian world-view—that can solve the culture wars tearing the world to pieces. That has to be a challenge for Christians who really want to count. All of this world-view talk and study is about what Sine calls: "Shifting The Church Into The Future Tense."[26]

What does this have to do with the preaching and teaching in the Church Growth Movement and all of the church? World-view studies reveal and reinforce that there is only one world-view that works for life and society, and that reinforces any pastor's or church leader's conviction and confidence in preaching and teaching. Wake-up calls via world-view studies in relation to preaching and teaching can release the "wild hope" of C. S. Lewis in his book, *The Last Battle*. It is the theistic/Christian world-view in all aspects of the work of the church including the Church Growth Movement that brings forth the biblical promise that unleashes a possible "wild hope" from the power and presence of God that effects life and society through transformed lives.

Therefore my perspective on world-view studies are not related only to the Church Growth Movement but also to the work of the church in all aspects. "The church of Jesus Christ has a unique opportunity to participate with God in the divine engagement of tomorrow's world."[27] Unless we do this with serious studies of Word and world we will rush pell-mell into the year 2001 with *The Church In Ruins*.

Part Four is about crises that result and remain when Perceptions (Part One) about world-views in general and the theistic/Christian world-view in particular are not studied and understood as a major part of Christian Education (Part Two) and then carried out by making disciples in authentic church growth efforts (Part Three) that reconciles the lost to God and prepares them to effect the marketplace with the Good News. The ultimate hope would be, and the possibility is always there because with God all things are possible, that the church would become strong enough through all of this wherein it would be repositioned back into the center of society as a force of truth and hope with which society has to reckon. Then so many of the crises we are facing that are illustrated in Part Five could be reversed.

Part Four: Problem Develops Crises

Theology: Imperative And Good—Not Evil

Christian theology is more than theory. It is the study of the living God as found in the living Word revealing His purposes for humanity living in various situations in our kind of a fragmented world. Theology is essential to assist in reinforcing the need for world-view studies for the laos (people of God). Theology also generates strength and validity for all that follows in this Part.

Theology involves the primacy of Scripture in any Christian life that attempts to live, interact, and witness to Christ's spiritual and real presence in this world. The books of the Bible are not theological documents to be read and understood in a vacuum. They were all written in specific historic and socio-cultural contexts to inform the people of God of their covenant responsibilities to Him as His witnesses in every culture/society of the world. This biblical witness functions through the church of Jesus Christ utilizing the theistic/Christian world-view as the lens through which to view and interpret the world around us that is in desperate need of that witness.

This means that the world—the situation in which the church exists and witnesses—has to be constantly interpreted or deciphered via world-view studies, or biblical studies are done in a vacuum without proper application to life in our convoluted and convulsion-like world environment. This means that questions must always be faced. What is really going on in the world by all appearances? What is the character and nature of the value-systems of this age? What are the times in which we live? Unless Christ's community of disciples risk in attempting to answer such questions plus others, its rendition of God's Word is probably less than the full Gospel, because the gospel is effective good news only in relation to its acceptance and application to what is transpiring in the life of the world to which it is addressed.

I believe that is a fundamental reason for the words of Jesus when He berated His hearers for their failure to interpret the time in which they lived.

> When you see a cloud rising in the west, immediately you say, 'It's going to rain,' and it does. And when the south wind blows, you say, 'It's going to be hot,' and it is. Hypocrites! You know how to interpret the appearance of the earth and the sky. How is it that you don't know how to interpret this present time? (Luke 12:54-56)

This same indictment could be laid before most of the American church including evangelicals and my heritage that I believe has much to offer the cosmic world. If it would just mature and move its mindset from the fifties to the 21st century by world-view and trends studies that involve more than church-growth methodology plus keeping a solid biblical and theological position during its maturing, the heritage could move to the front row in kingdom work and develop a cutting edge in social parameters that really does the work of the church instead of just church work. There is a radical difference!

Therefore world-view studies have everything to do with the Word of God and theology. The witnessing community must have two interfacing efforts of concentration and/or orientation all of the time. There must be:

> an ongoing struggle to comprehend the Scriptures and the long tradition of those who in the past have done the same thing; and a continuous attempt to decipher the worldly context in which the community is to make its witness. Theology is what happens when these two orientations intersect—that is, when the biblical testimony of the Word encounters the spirit of the age, and when the Word encounters that spirit (Zeitgeist—the trend of thought and feeling in a period of history).[1]

My persistent calling for world-view studies is that this is as much about being a steward of God in all matters as it is in the grace of giving or any dimension of stewardship privileges and responsibilities. This concept of human stewardship is pertinent to articulating and proclaiming the gospel in today's world. When one begins to understand the Gospel and the world of now, we are impelled to believe that ours is a world in which human beings are required to find a new way of conceiving their identity and vocation. I believe that can be found only in the Lord's new song of the Gospel. If that does not happen, there can be no averting the catastrophic future that appears to be courted by modern man.

This is why certain mandates of God in Scripture must always be kept before the people of God: the Dominion Mandate of Genesis 1:26-29 and the various witnessing and disciple-making mandates in several commission passages such as Matthew 28:16-20; Mark 16:15-16; Luke 24:47-49; John 20:21; Acts 1:8; and Romans 16:26.

The Larger Picture—Major Problem/Resultant Crises

The major problem in the midst of unprecedented Christian activity is that the theistic/Christian world-view is not the dominant influence in our culture/society as it once was. World-views that are dominant are in opposition to the theistic/Christian world-view. Collisions of world-views battling for modern man's mind are in full force, and world-views opposing Christianity are winning too easily resulting in many crises. They are winning through culture wars that has caused the radical social dislocation of the church out of the center of society. The church must be alerted.

A major crisis, perhaps the major crisis, in contemporary Western culture/society because of the stated major problem is a crisis of ascertained and authentic faith in something or Someone larger than man and society. In what or whom or which world-view does one put his or her faith, obedience, trust, and life for living? In the collision of world-views, can one world-view be ascertained to give coherence, consistence, and direction for culture/society as well as personal life? The short answer and my conviction already stated several times is "yes." But the short answer is not simple to come by. In the effort to keep the good news of Christ so simple and almost so simplistic to be nauseating, much of its force and possibility has been negated.

Someone said, "civilization does not crumble all at once. It falls by chunks." But how many falling chunks can we stand in our culture/society? Are we living on the edge of total chaos? Do we stand on the brink of a new dark age? IS there "the smell of sunset" as the dean of evangelical thinkers, Dr. Carl F. H. Henry, warns? Charles Colson of Watergate fame says "yes" to all three answers in his book, *Against The Night*.

Four or more decades ago Dr. Henry wrote on the subject that "the barbarians are coming, the Lord Jesus Christ is coming, and the church is here." He has written again on the same theme but in a different context. The barbarians are here. Charles Colson agrees with that perception. They both still believe that the Lord Jesus Christ is coming, and Henry says "let the church that is here come now with good news, the only durable good news, and come in time."[2] But he also says that "Christians are here now: do they know whether they are coming or going?"[3]

Colson writes:

> The barbarians of the new dark age are pleasant and articulate men and women. They carry briefcases, not spears. But their assault on culture is every bit as devastating as the barbarian invasion of Rome. We have bred them in our families and trained them in our schools. Their ideas are persuasive and subtle, and very often they undermine the pillars upon which our civilization was founded. Can the tide be turned?[4]

Colson's assessment is a world-view issue. What is the world-view or world-views of the "barbarians?"

My certain answer to Colson's question is a "yes." But at the same time I have to admit that in the midst of epochal trends and mindsets straight out of the Enlightenment that have been and are so dominant in our culture/society (Enlightenment mindsets appear to be crumbling in our post-modern world) plus the related strains of paganism that have come out of these trends, the influence from Christianity is rapidly dimming and waning in our culture/society of this Western world. Added to this dimming influence of Christianity in our own society is the mindset that now questions the possibility of any kind of "truth" let alone anything such as the true Truth of Christianity. From this comes the epistemological crisis of our time: the doubt that Christianity is even worth considering as a serious alternative to any other current preference about truth, life, and values. We have certainly arrived at the warning from Os Guinness a long time ago: The modern church has a serious "plausibility crisis." This is a serious world-view issue of a major problem causing crises after crises.

To enhance our understanding of Christianity's dimming influence and the genesis of our contemporary major problem, some elaboration about the Enlightenment is necessary.

From the journey into a look at the Enlightenment and the paganistic strains, we therefore have to face the unhealthy nature and the cause of the same of the evangelical church.

The Enlightenment-Epochal Trends/Strains

Our modern lostness plus the shaking foundation and edifice of Western culture/society finds its source in certain epochal trends and mindsets out of the Enlightenment. This was the philosophical era of the 18th century (1600-1780) labeled the "age of reason." Man was certain that all of the problems of the world would be solved by his autonomous reasoning. That is, he would need no word or help from outside such as God and His Word. That Enlightenment mindset was and is a world-view.

It is now commonplace that the pervasive faith that has shaped our modern world since the Enlightenment is that set of presuppositions or assumptions that we call modernity (the mindset of modern man who discounts the reality, presence or need of a personal God, for man is his own god). Doug Dickey says, "what is interesting and crucial about our current crisis is that our culture is disintegrating around us, and there is growing disillusionment with the faith that underlies this disintegration."[5]

That "faith" is the Enlightenment that is the root/roots of modernity. The results of this has been that in religion God is omitted. Likewise, commitment to the Christian faith as the source of morals and values is cut off. In human knowledge we have facts empty of meaning because of no overarching truth. In the social sciences and humanities human beings are destroyed by cold logic void of any transcendent dimension of hope outside of man. All of this has shaped our society into modernity. We have now moved into a post-modern mindset. Some are calling our time a post-post-modern world.

It has been suggested that Enlightenment is a conversion word, not of the experience of an individual but of entire cultures. In the Enlightenment there was a major paradigm shift in the way men viewed reality. Their vision shifted from heaven to earth, from God to man, from religious and ecclesiastical authority to human autonomy, and from dogma (a Word from outside) to inductive search. Lesslie Newbigin suggests that "if you want to grasp the essential elements in what we call modern Western culture, the best place to begin is with that exhilarating feeling that light (created in the Enlightenment) has come into the world and banished darkness."[6] That was the conviction of the Enlightenment. But results from that world-view demonstrate its failure as a workable world-view as our Western world tumbles from crisis to crisis into what appears to be more and more chaos looking for a centering place found only in the theistic/Christian world-view.

There are five categories of thought from the Enlightenment mindset that helps to capture and understand the current trends in culture/society. After stating and elaborating on each category I will put them together for an overview understanding.

Epochal Trends • Technical Reason

This means human transcendence and not the Transcendence of God over nature wherein human reason is able to grasp the causal connections of nature's phenomena. The application of this is that man has increased his understanding of the basic workings of nature but with that comes the capacity for increased control and power. Robert Benne, from whom I draw heavily for the five categories says: "The upshot of this application of technical reason to the world has been the magnification and intensification of human powers."[7] Think about that in the context of culture/society right now as man continues to blunder in life and society, because he believes that he alone will be the solver of life's problems and social issues.

Of course there have been fantastic discoveries, realizations, and blessings from technology. Wondrous things have happened. Consider the breakthroughs (and costs) in the field of medicine. How fantastic the discoveries. This technology has wrestled from nature a level of living that transcends the pressures of mere physical survival. The affluence produced by this triumph has enabled the masses in our Western world to live in relative security and comfort. What was once limited to the privileged few is now the privilege of the many. True, there are still some in our society who cannot participate fully in this triumph of the "achievements of technology," yet "the benefits are widely dispersed."[8] But the irony of this is the suicidal mindset and the hectic pace people keep just to try and keep up with the affluence and other results of so many discoveries and breakthroughs.

Nevertheless in spite of the many benefits, there are more ambiguities. There is social change, increased mobility, parochial identities overshadowed, tightly knit communities are affected, and old means of production and lifestyle are shattered. When man believes he has all of this power to seemingly control nature there is lost some solid reason and value for living life other than what man can devise. What becomes the level and meaning and value for life? Only what man accomplishes. It seems that all this responsibility we have assumed has caused more pressure. "The magnification of human powers," Benne believes "means that we can more easily destroy ourselves and our natural environment. The affluence generated by technical capacities tempts us to reject necessary restraints and pursue our

132

limitless desires."[9] One only has to look around to see the human carnage to understand this. In so many technical advances, issues are raised that we did not have to face before; issues raised in an environment void of little, if any, consensus at the spiritual and moral levels. It's a world-view concern.

The kind of power in this category reminds one of the story of the Greek god Prometheus. He became concerned about the plight of man and at the same time angry with Zeus the chief of the gods. Prometheus took upon himself to do something about the human condition for the better. He did three things believing they would make the difference. First, he caused mortals to cease foreseeing doom. He took away the knowledge of the day of death, the sense of limits, the awareness of mortality. Freed from this, humans could now attempt anything. Second, he placed in them blind hopes. He instilled incentive in men and women to be more than they were, to reach out, to stretch themselves, to be ambitious. But the incentives were blind and directionless and unrelated to any Reality outside of man. Third, Prometheus stole fire from the gods and gave it to humanity. With this gift the people were able to cook food, make weapons, fire pottery, etc. The entire world of technology opened up.

Extreme technical reason today carries the idea to the point that as in the day of Prometheus man attempts to live and act out illusions of divinity. The story is a tragic bordering on being a horror story. Our time is tragic because a world-view, the New Age Movement (NAM), is reinforcing this mindset with the teaching that man and God are equal. This is the story of Western civilization now: incredible progress in things, defiantly unmindful of the nature of our humanity, unimaginable suffering of persons. This is the way life is now. This Promethean myth is the greatest expression of the tragedy of our own nature. Our age is Promethean even though earlier generations posited warnings. Is it then any accident that the most technically advanced societies are in some sense also the ones most worried about their spiritual and moral foundations?

Don't ever forget the tale of three nations: Israel, Germany, and . . . America. Israel ignored God and fell. Germany was very religious but Godless, and from that most technological advanced nation at that time came the worst savagery and suffering ever known to man outside of nuclear power. Now America? Millions of babies have been murdered since 1973 and the church's voice in the midst of unprecedented activity appears to be too weak in faith and influence to touch this cancer. Are we becoming desensitized to this horror? The Promethean spirit is very much alive for Christians to confront and bring the only hope to this epochal tragedy of technical reason as stated.

It would be time well spent for Christians to read *The Technological Bluff* by Jacques Ellul. Geoffrey W. Bromiley wrote in the Translator's Preface:

> As Ellul sees it, either technology as a whole or individual technologies are hurrying us into a situation of catastrophe. Lulled by the bluff of technological discourse, we sleepily fail to perceive the perils that confront us. Ellul's purpose, therefore, is to jolt us awake before we pass the point of no return (If we have not already done so). A special concern, perhaps, is to awaken the timid churches that are paralyzed by their fear of being derided as old-fashioned and outdated.[10]

Historical Reason

There is overlap in the two categories of the technical and historical. If technical reason gives man illusionary divine transcending power over natural processes, historical reason demonstrates our radical immersion in time and space in a way that we have no certain way to transcend our relativity and our nowness to time and space.

This mindset makes the Christian's simple claim to absolute truth and morality difficult at best, because according to this category of historical reason there is no direct access to historical and absolute truth outside of the now or outside of autonomous man and reason. There is from this view no clear universal viewpoint of true Truth outside our present history from which to draw so man can unerringly judge concerning truth and moral rightness. Moral principles come only from human reason. Historical reason debunked the claim to Godly absolutes that gives strength to our spiritual life. Of course the theistic/Christian world-view challenges that.

Historical reason is a way of saying God is out and faith in and obedience to Him is only a personal and private preference for you but not for me. Therefore keep it private. That is very American right now. Don't bring God and His Truth into the now, because the only history is the now of time and space.

Triumph of The Liberal Spirit

"The dominant mark of the Enlightenment," maintains Benne, "was its confidence in the capacity of unencumbered Reason to ascertain the good, the true, and the beautiful."[11] This was making man even more powerful and God-like.

Prior to considering the dark side of the liberal spirit from the theological perspective, the non-theological meaning of "liberal" must be understood. Keep in mind that "liberal" means "generous." Therefore the non-theological meaning of a "liberal" spirit is the spirit of inquiry and searching with a reaching out to help man find larger dimensions for life and living that has made many enduring contributions to Western achievements. That is generous. We would be considerably poorer without it. We might still be living under the dark hand of superstition in religion and other aspects of life. We must keep this in mind.

> The liberal spirit was healthy and positive as long as it had the substance of the Western Judaeo-Christian civilization to criticize, alter, reform, and "enlighten." It was not really Reason that was guiding things, but rather it was the deposit of those faith communities, enriched by classical traditions, that was being revised by the critical and liberal capacities of humankind to be a fit instrument for Western instrumentality. As that deposit was increasingly qualified by the spirit of the Enlightenment, relativized by historical reason, and made increasingly problematic by scientific and technical reason, the liberal spirit became markedly impoverished. Without the

substance of tradition to reform, it becomes increasingly empty and impotent to guide either personal or public life.

Therefore, our politics become the clash of interest groups rather than the subject of rational debate. Liberal education loses its coherent base and degenerates into the competition of disciplines. Liberal economics abstracts "economic man" from the restraints of culture, assuming untrammeled self-interest as the spring of motivation. Liberal religion becomes a congeries of debating societies devoted to further liberation from tradition, unable to replenish itself. Rational ethics continues its elusive search for a universal and abstract ground, but is frustrated by an ongoing disagreement within its own ranks that enables it to say more forcefully what we should not do than what we should.[12]

Do we then abandon the good side of the liberal spirit? No. But we must clearly see that without living traditions carried by historical communities that the liberal spirit can constructively assist, it becomes empty and compounds our present confusion in culture/society which increasingly turns aimlessly in life when liberated from that theistic/Christian world-view which can and does give identity and direction.

This is the dark side of the liberal spirit: a theological mind-set that dissolves by the cool light of man's autonomous reasoning powers the suprarational (outside help such as God for man's reasoning and thinking in the development of life and culture/society), the supernatural (God as the One in charge of nature), and the traditional biblical teachings on God-ordained absolutes which give, not bondage, but authentic freedom that is unexhaustible and abundantly meaning-filled. It was and is a way of saying to God, 'hands off. We have it all figured out and we will do it all very well thank you.' True or false in the current context of an ill culture/society?

I believe it is clearly seen at this point the picture that is going to flash out as one ponders the compounding of these first three categories of Enlightenment trends. The key scene is that of moving man center stage on the stage of history and edging out God more and more until He is completely edged out and ignored. The next category enters the setting.

The Ethic of Self-Enhancement

Here comes our "predicament of modern man." This will not be properly understood by most moderns and much of the contemporary church until the church demonstrates and speaks clearly and boldly to the source of the issues of life and culture/society that has us in such a morass of problems. Albert Camus, the existentialist, gave a direct challenge to the church about doing this, and he was not a churchman. He insisted that if the church had anything to say, it ought to do it loudly and boldly.

Dr. D. Elton Trueblood's book, *The Predicament of Modern Man* published in 1944, could be dated today and be a best-seller. It was in that classic production he gave the picture of the "cut-flower civilization"[13] that was then already evident. Nevertheless the warning was not heeded and it is really not heeded now. The "cut-flower civilization" is one severed from its roots. It is in our case severed from the Judaeo-Christian world-view. It is a civilization living only on the residues of the past which will eventually run out.

What then will give direction to this kind of civilization confused and fragmented by the three previous categorical trends from the Enlightenment? By now anyone reading this will know my answer. I see it clearly. It is the returning to, recovering of, and assimilating by modern man the theistic/Christian world-view. Or putting it another way, it is allowing God to have His farm back wherein we as his subjects begin living for His pleasure by His freedom-giving absolutes of truth and righteousness. This is not the answer given by the affluent society of the West that is challenging the church like never before in this nation. I am not at all certain how much of the modern church is really saying this in its drive for success as the mega-church. Imagine the influence the mega-church could have if it was a disciplined body of believers dealing, not with "felt needs," but with serious study of both the Word and the world.

The dominant answer for life and living from our Western world is to enhance yourself. "I am entitled to my rights." This is the cry of 25-30 year-old adolescents called "Baby Busters" as they live in the shadow of the "Baby Boomers." Determine your direction and wants in life by your own desires. Make your relation to your environment painless and pleasurable. Our popular culture suggests to look out for number one. Do what feels good. Pursue your own interests. But what if my desires clash with another's desires? So what. Do your own thing. Enhance what you want. The "Imperial Self" is in control. I see this as a phenomena beginning to surface within some of the church.

Again we are face to face with NAM (New Age Movement). What's wrong with this ethic? Nothing except more divorce, abortion, sexual exploitation, political apathy, narrow careerism, etc. In the context of much of the modern church cheap grace will be given for those who shop from church to church for their own ego-centered wants instead of looking for the true Truth from God about life. The sad part of this is that many modern churches gear up for this to satisfy people's wants and spurious self-manufactured wants of self-enhancement. In the interest of "self" significant ministries within the local church are canceled during the summer months, because there are so many other good things to do. How odd of God to expect His people to serve the year-round. A dominant dangerous theology found in much of the modern church, my heritage included, is a theology of needs and Jesus becomes one's need-meter instead of Lord. Yet churchmen trapped in this cheap grace still ponder why the church is weak in effectiveness on the world's destructive value systems.

Of course none of this self-enhancement ethic is really new. It is as old as the garden of Eden, but now it is epidemic and has a Western culture/society in bondage. How could this happen in a country filled with religious activities called Christianity? The church has been successful in getting crowds by the dispensing of cheap grace but I fear fewer and fewer true conversions.

The capacities for affluent people to support their self-enhancement ethic is combined with the waning certainties of traditional religious and moral claims. . . . The capability for moral self-government, which is indispensable to political and civil liberty, is eroded by the license that accompanies widespread affluence. Confusion is inevitable in such a situation. A cultural war is going on between moral sensibilities and self-enhancement. It is not that there are no moral commitments left; it is rather that they are so mixed with the egoist impulses that are encouraged by the surrounding culture. It is never certain which directives will win out. Little can be counted on.[14]

In a culture/society which says everything is true or nothing is true, Jesus gives a beautiful directive to this which is the start of erasing chaos out of a confused culture/society. He said it would work and nearly two thousands years has proven Him right in the lives of those who took Him at His Word. He said, "Seek first the kingdom (His rule and reign) of God, and then . . . ." (Matthew 6:33). That is true, powerful, and beautiful.

Secularization

This is the cumulative effect of the first four categorical Enlightenment trends. The overall picture can begin to surface. Technical reason took the mystery out of natural processes. Man took on more divine-like power. Historical reason debunked the claims of theological absolutes of right and wrong that makes Christianity workable to free man. The theological liberal spirit dissolved the suprarational and the supernatural by cool reason. The ethic of self-enhancement and self-fulfilling by any means one chooses "flowed over and obliterated the fragile demarcations of religious and moral practice."

As these claims weakened, so did the church. In a way the church became part of the problem as it was pushed off the "center of the society's stage." Christian thought was pushed "out of the center of the intellectual"[15] life. It would be more fair to say that Christian thought was pushed out of the intellectual center, because the church allowed it to happen with its anti-intellectual stance. As a result we have what Richard John Neuhaus labels "the naked public square."[16]

The results in this category are like the results of the other four. They are highly ambiguous. Nevertheless it is surely safe to say that man has little left but himself, and this secularization (God completely out of the picture) flattens out any real and lasting meaning to one's self. When this is all that culture/society has left, and when culture/society cannot stand this aloneness, what happens? I use youth to illustrate this. Suicide is epidemic in youth and the age range is getting younger. Even youth who wear a Christian label whine about being bored, and that surely means that they are as empty of real life as the non-Christian. This factor can contribute to the suicidal mindset. Boredom in Christian youth is something that I do not understand unless it means that they are Christian in name only.

Our culture/society and sub-cultures in our society are like one big emotional fallout, and since man cannot stand just by himself alone surely another drink, a new woman, or drugs, or a better and bigger job with more money will suffice and solve the horror of just seeing nothing but self in the mirror. Our confusion is like that of Babel. We think that we can do more with what we have than we actually can, and when we fail we become confused and then wrongly aggressive or despondent.

We stand as 20th century humans on the verge of a new century near the start of a new millennium in the year 2001. That millennium will no doubt be unlike anything that we have ever known in matters of change, perhaps repeating the idolatries of our forebearers but in different guise and form. Thus society casts around for its bearings and ends up with what Barbara Walters labeled "cultural barbarians" in her jarring program on public education.

It is of concern to me that the largest lobby group overtly and covertly for most of the epochal trends we have listed is the NEA (National Educational Association). This is one of the largest, if not the largest, trojan horse of destruction to what

Christians hold to be true and dear. Yet few parents have any idea as to what their children are being taught in public education. I state that as one who is still trying to be pro-public education. Christians must be the salt of public education that demands salty Christians (Matthew 5:13).

The overarching summary picture of these epochal trends reveal that the trends were hardly triumphs at all.

> The triumph of technical reason brings along with its dominance of nature a rapid technological change that threatens the natural environment itself as well as stable human communities. Historical reason, with its deeper and wider capacities to understand our place in history and society, brings with it a debilitating sense of relativism and rudderlessness. The liberal spirit, with its confidence in Reason to supply direction to a world of historical and social relativity, finds that the moral air becomes distressingly thin as it climbs the mountains of rational enlightenment and leaves particular communities in the valley far below. Affluence carries with its promise of a better life the distinct possibility of existence characterized by chaotic desire. Secularization flattens out our existence.[17]

The power of five categorical epochal trends straight out of the Enlightenment Era from over two centuries ago is unsettling. People discarded the God-hypothesis (God exists) and believed that through human reason they could develop sound moral principles and policies. That took root in this nation in the 1960s, and now far too much of America is controlled by that right across the board of culture/society. This is being done by living as if God did not exist or was a remnant thought of the past by simple-minded people who did and do not know any better.

That is what Nietzsche meant when he said that God would be dead in the 20th century. Of course God has not literally died and never will, but secularized people and weak Christians have also disallowed His presence and control to the point that God is not alive in their life and our society. I have asked the question before: where was the church when all this mind-boggling transition in thinking was happening? What is the church and those morally concerned solid non-Christians really doing about it today? Charles Colson said in an interview that this Enlightenment thinking being accepted today accounts for the "diminishing influence of the Judaeo-Christian heritage in our society."[18] From these categories of Enlightenment thought the following has surfaced in our culture/society.

Related Paganistic Strains

Mike Yaconelli wrote in *The Wittenburg Door* suggesting that:

> Americans are in the process of nibbling (Like cows nibbling through pastures without fences) their way to lostness. Americans are not deliberately turning their back on God. It is not that the American culture is obsessed with sin or determined to reject Christianity. What is more accurate is that millions of us are just nibbling our way to lostness.[19]

Whether there is just a "nibbling" or an out and out rejection of Christianity resulting in more and more "lostness" and paganism could be debated endlessly. The fact is that it is becoming increasingly difficult to find authentic Christianity as defined by the Apostle Paul that impresses the world or causes our culture/society to notice (2 Corinthians 2:12-6:13; 1 Thessalonians 2:1-13). Masses want to change Christianity to fit today, but they still want to be called "Christians." It is just as difficult to find the kind of moral and stable non-Christians who have a sense of authenticity.

There are strains of paganism stated by Yaconelli that are clearly the result of the near total secularization from the Enlightenment and other non-theistic world-views of the controlling mind-set of the American culture/society.

First is "the legitimization of self-interest." This is when one no longer believes that Jesus is to be first in life. He is only first as long as He benefits "me." Others are second as long as they make my personal situation better. Also this self-controlled person may be willing to put himself last if that guarantees him to be first. For Christians trapped in this strain, self-interest for

142

them is no longer contradictory to serving Christ. This is related to the health, wealth, and feeling-good gospel. Any talk of losing oneself for His sake is meaningless and disturbing for this person. Some have "nibbled" their way so far from Kingdom understanding that they are seemingly incapable of understanding that Christianity costs anything.

The second strain is "the belief that pain and suffering are not to be expected or even a part of being His disciple." This is not just denying pain and suffering. It is the conviction that pain and suffering should not be. Period.

Of course no one wants pain or suffering. No one, I hope, deliberately creates pain or suffering except those who are intent on hurting others. The truth is that pain and suffering teach us lessons we could never learn any other way. That is no longer accepted by a growing mass of human beings. NAM (New Age Movement) is reinforcing this strain in the media and various sectors of the modern church. It is a new meaning of the word "soft." It is more than that. It is an incapability of perseverance, patience, and long-suffering.

However pain is endemic to life. It is "always the means to our end or the end to our means."[20] We use pain to grow into the image of Christ, or we allow pain to paralyze us, freeze us in time, and kill our growth. This is why Christians must be conscious of these current strains of paganism affecting too many.

Third is "the belief that there are no moral absolutes." John Naisbit in *Megatrends* is correct in saying we no longer live in a culture/society that understands moral absolutes let alone believe them. It is interesting that he would say this. He borders on being a new age supporter. He may be more than this. But he is still correct in his assessment in this matter that is found in education, economics, the judicial system, the media, the church, etc. This is the mindset: a thing is morally right because I choose to believe it is right, but what is right for me is not binding on anyone else. Surely the problem with this is clear. Ramifications from this amoral mindset that is rampant in our culture/society is deep and frightening as it erodes our culture/society.

Reflecting back on the preceding epochal trends will easily reveal correlations between them and the strains of paganism stated to this point.

The fourth strain is "the erosion of personal responsibility." In another time and place there was a people most of whom believed that they were responsible for their actions. They seldom if ever talked or whined about their rights. This historical time is a dim memory.

Kids do not do well in school because they are lazy and irresponsible, but parents blame the teachers or the system. Or this. Aids is the fault of the environment, the President, or the government but not the fault of people acting like barbarians having abnormal sexual relations so abnormal that bleeding results. How stupid can a cultural mind-set be in a culture/society which is supposed to be so advanced?

There is a cure to this, and it is free of charge. Stop behaving worse than animals and stop sleeping around with the low-life of the earth. Keep sex pure, holy, wholesome, and joyful in the marriage bed only and always.

This foregoing kind of wimpy mindset is played out by politicians in too many areas to list here.

Fifth is "the denial of consequences." If this was not so true it would be such a waste of time to mention it. In so many areas of life there are many people who are actually bewildered when other people's lives are disrupted by their behavior. They refuse to believe that what they do today not only immediately affects those and us around them, but the effects could go on for generations. This is so weird, but it is alive and well and dumb.

One example of this is divorce. Some people who go through this trauma have a most difficult time comprehending why their children do not understand, why they can't adjust, why they can't get on with normal living and not be bothered by this growing problem. Nor do the divorced understand why their friends and other family members are angry, threatened, hesitant, confused, hurt, distrustful or otherwise affected.

Some pastors cannot understand why their divorce affects

their congregations. Why should the congregation want them to step down? Is divorce the unpardonable sin? Not at all, but congregations are affected in strange ways when this happens.

Mike Yaconelli, from whom so much of the forgoing about paganistic strains is siphoned, and I am grateful for his bold wisdom, has been divorced for ten or more years. He said that he has bled during all of those years as a Christian over the consequences it laid on other people's lives.

These trends and "strains of paganism" are all about worldview yet the church at large is doing little with this in education.

Therefore to reverse these post-Enlightenment trends and strains of paganism calls for effective Christians, who are informed thinkers. I call it a sanctified worldliness which means living fully and freely as God's servants and stewards in wonder and delight at this world that He has given to them to attend. If the church is to be led into the 21st century in any kind of effective penetrating power, Christians as never before have the responsibility and obligation as citizens of His Kingdom to understand intellectually, emotionally, and spiritually what has happened to create our crises abounding as a result of the foregoing epochal trends.

This is not some other-worldly disregard for our present sphere. It is the celebration of the here and now in Christ demonstrating that Christians know the source of their challenges facing them. The Christian is summoned to tackle with special energy the problems destroying life and culture/society. It is a call for God's people to Coram Deo - live all of life in the presence of God. It is living life in a sense of acute God-awareness. Right now the church needs this almost as much as the world. It is the big idea of the Christian life. It is the big idea that can revolutionize the church and the world. It is all about world-view understanding and a healthy church singing the Lord's song in an alien land. But what about the health of the church as a whole? Most churchmen really do not want to consider this. But we must.

Unhealthy Evangelical Church

As a churchman carrying on a lover's quarrel with the church, I will not lead anyone to believe that all is well in the evangelical Church family in this nation. I have to include the Christian Church-Churches of Christ heritage in this concern. I have no doubt as to the possibilities that authentic Christianity offers a civilization falling by chunks. But we have to get our own house in order, and do it rapidly.

In May, 1989, The National Association of Evangelicals and Trinity Evangelical Divinity School, a top-ranking seminary, co-sponsored a consultation on "Evangelical Affirmations" in an effort to ferret out those weaknesses and cracks forming in the evangelical foundation. Some of these cracks are no doubt partially the result of allowing something less than the theistic/Christian world-view leak into the camp. In the opening pages of the publication of the papers that were read and the responses given at this consultation, these words were clearly stated for impact. The situation has not changed.

> Evangelical Christianity is engaged in a broad conflict on many fronts. Internally, it is struggling over moral improprieties, doctrinal lapses, and problems of self-identity. Externally, it is carrying on a lingering battle with liberal Christianity and seeking to plug the leaks in its doctrinal structure that still come from the source. Moreover, new pressures are rising from the occult and from various syncretistic movements combining elements of paganism, Islam, Buddhism or other historic religions with Christianity. In Western Europe and North America and increasingly in other parts of the world as well, modern secularism has become a major foe of evangelical Christianity.

> Each of these religious movements presents its own conception of reality, and all differ from evangelical faith in doctrines that lie at the core of biblical Christianity.

> Modern secularism sees the world without God; or if it formally acknowledges the existence of some ill-defined "god," it squeezes God and all religion to the periphery of life. Either

way, a theoretical atheism or a practical, functioning atheism views the universe as controlled merely by natural or human forces. Logically, the exclusion of God from the universe rules out the very possibility of miracle in any biblical sense and yields a world-view without incarnation, resurrection, and judgement. Unfortunately it is possible to give lip allegiance to theistic or even Christian beliefs while choosing to live practically as though God does not exist.

By contrast, historic Christianity has always affirmed that God lives and acts in this world. Evangelical faith insists on the reality of divine action in creation, providence, revelation and redemption. History is not a mindless process, but the unfolding of events through which the triune God works out his purpose in the universe. The God and Father of our Lord Jesus Christ, and the God of the Bible is the sovereign Lord who controls the destiny of the nations and guides the intimate details of personal life. The hairs of our head are numbered, and God sees every sparrow that falls.

. . . . Recently, however, some have declared that several evangelical doctrines are theologically innovative and do not represent the central traditions of the Christian church. . . . We are shamed by our inconsistencies in living out the ethical values we profess, and we recognize the need to confess our sins before God.

In the last decade of the twentieth century, a number of these troubling issues have come into sharper focus. We realize that our own house is not entirely in order. Many of our worst problems we have brought on ourselves. Not only on the outside, but even within our own ranks, some confusion exists as to exactly who are evangelicals.[21]

Until Christians struggle with world-views and see how much they are effected by those that are opposed to the theistic/Christian world-view, a new song from the Lord for most of the Western world that is an alien land foreign to and alienated from God and grace will not be clearly sung and stated. I cannot help but believe there is a famine, not of food, but of spiritual truth that can be remedied, and millions will rejoice once again with life. Ponder the following before moving into other segments of this Part of the book.

On a trip to Moscow in the spring of 1990 Charles Colson shared the work of his Prison Fellowship Ministry with Soviet leaders. Vadim Victorovitch Bakatin, minister of Internal Affairs and one of the most powerful men in that changing nation, called the meeting to order. Colson spoke tracing the cause of crimes and individuals making wrong moral choices. Bakatin, the fourth-ranking Soviet leader, listened intently as Colson said without tongue in cheek that "an endless spiral of lawlessness is inevitable in an atheistic society with no transcendent values," that is, values through a personal relationship with God in Christ.

As Colson continued his presentation, this Soviet leader leaned forward asking Colson to explain the prison ministry work in detail. Colson did so without hiding that all they do with prisoners and families is to find the source of truth and strength in Christianity. "That's the answer," Bakatin declared. "That's what we need here. What you're doing, we will approve in the Soviet Union. Whatever you need to get into our prisons, you have my permission." Colson could hardly believe what he was hearing. But this Soviet power-leader with a twinkle in his eye smiled as the men in the meeting parted, and said, "And God be with you."[22] This can be an encouragement for the church to mature and get with it. Spiritual growth and maturity creating a healthy church can come when we understand and assimilate the following. In the following we can see why we as a secularized nation must attempt and do to keep God out of the public domain when Russians want Him back.

World-Views In Constant Collision-Synopses

This is an invitation to other worlds. Authentic biblical Christianity (the theistic/Christian world-view) which once furnished the assumptions, presuppositions, standards, and the ideals for intellectual, political, economic, and artistic life in the West has been swept aside by the masses. The effort to continue this sweep is not complete. While it was the dominant influence in the Western world, including our nation, there was consensus from Christians and masses of non-Christians alike as to God-ordained absolutes, right and wrong, good and evil, values, ethics, and hopes that enhanced life and culture.

There were goal-posts and boundaries to life which gave man freedom and purpose and direction. Our society was not ravaged by such epidemics as aids and the mass murdering of babies by abortion plus other deep-seated social ills.

Now this previous consensus is overshadowed by a secular culture/society filled with world-views not on a collision course but in actual collision with one another. AS they collide in the battle for the mind of modern man and the dominant influence and control of culture/society, man and society become more confused and fragmented in every parameter of personal and social life. Part Five elaborates upon and illustrates the fragmentation in some of society's spheres and disciplines.

In the morass of so many problems resultant from world-view battling in our secularized culture/society, this has to be said: Christianity helped give rise to the secular overshadowing by the work and working of the Os Guinness "gravedigger thesis." The thesis is: "Christianity contributed to the rise of the modern world; the modern world, in turn, has undermined Christianity; Christianity has become its own gravedigger."[23] How did this happen? That was a partial reason for the afore-mentioned Evangelical Affirmations Consultation in May, 1989.

The morass of life and social ills is the natural result of casting aside the demonstrated, proven, time-tested theistic/Christian world-view as the dominant influence in the Western culture/society. Once again, I state my presupposition and con-victed belief. When various world-views are studied it is realized over and over that the theistic/Christian world-view is the only one which answers coherently, consistently, meaning-fully, and lastingly the basic questions that man has asked for centuries about life and living. These questions were stated and defined in Part One.

In the midst of various world-views in collision, because the Christian world-view is no longer the predominant influence, Dr. Richard C. Halverson, Chaplain to the United States Senate, gives a "profile of our contemporary culture."

> In the wisdom of Proverbs, it is stated: "Righteousness exalteth a nation, but sin is a reproach to any people." (Proverbs 14:34)
>
> We are fast becoming a no-fault society: no fault insurance - no fault divorce - no fault choice . . . in effect, a "no fault democracy" . . . which is a contradiction in terms! Implicit in democracy is order - individual as well as corporate discipline. Democracy without order is anarchy - and anarchy breeds chaos and tyranny!
>
> We demand freedom without restraint - rights without responsibility - choice without consequences pleasure without pain. In our narcissistic, hedonistic, masochistic, valueless preoccupation, we are becoming a people dominated by lust, avarice and greed. We demand the right to sin but deny the right to train in righteousness . . . demand the right to oppose religion but deny the right to propagate religion.
>
> In the name of "pluralism" we demand a distinctiveness, monotonous, meaningless syncretism in which morality is ridiculed, and a-morality is celebrated. And with sublime naivete we wonder at the futility of efforts to eliminate crime, drug abuse, alcohol abuse, child abuse, wife abuse, suicide, war (hot or cold) and the absence of peace (within or without).
>
> We promote consumerism, acquisition, accumulation and prosperity - while we "tip the hat" to poverty, hunger, homelessness, disability, and human need all around us.
>
> Is it any wonder we are losing our influence, our leadership in the world? ". . . sin is a reproach to any people." (Proverbs 14:34)[24]

This profile compounds the difficulty of attempting to live by Christian values in an age of uncertainty created by world-views in collision; an age that is busy discarding biblical values for life and society.

The Revealing And Rewarding Technical Dimension

In order to see world-views in collision, I must include material that develops a synopsis of various world views by running each through a grid of several related categories: God; cosmos; man-created, fallen, redeemed; ethics; death; and history. This is the correct and proper way to reveal and demonstrate which world-view of several world-views gives, has demonstrated, and still demonstrates the following: that set of presuppositions or assumptions that is wholistic, consistent, coherent, foundational with freedom-giving boundaries plus lasting purpose, direction, hope and history for life and culture/society. The world-views and resultant value systems causing different lifestyles for which I will give a brief synopsis are: Theism, Deism, Naturalism, Nihilism, Existentialism, Eastern Pantheistic Monism, Secular Humanism, and The New Age.

This is the clearest and most correct way to see what happens when the theistic/Christian world view is bypassed or refused by modern man. No one has to take the word of anyone else. Even a synopsis study of world-views supports, reinforces, and demonstrates my position of insisting that the theistic/Christian world-view accepted and lived out is the only way to bring the collision of world-views to a halt for the possible healing of life and culture/society. A detailed study would only enhance this brief approach.

The handwriting on the wall becomes crystal clear as to why modern man and life is so fragmented, frustrated, confused, puzzled, and problem-filled with a growing morass of personal and social ills. A more technical study that I hope this book will encourage people to do reveals that once the theistic/Christian world view is rejected for any one of the other world-views, the attempt to live life and function in society is like taking away a piece of a puzzle or leaving out part of a building or driving an auto on three wheels.

One can see a graphic breakdown of life and culture/society as soon as the theistic/Christian world-view is rejected. Each of the other world views attempt to build a foundation for man and culture/society by discounting or completely removing some dimension or several dimensions of the theistic/Christian worldview. Every ensuing world-view was and is an attempt to remedy the problems which surface in the other world-views. For example, the major reason the new age is so influential now is that secular humanism failed. What will modern man turn to when the new age fails? Which it will.

We have nearly two thousand years to demonstrate the truthful validity and the positive, pragmatic, functional results of the authentic theistic/Christian world-view when lived out in the categorical grid forestated. Furthermore there are many solid apologetic reasons in some excellent books to support the theistic/Christian world-view.

The best and most readable books on Apologetics for the novice is *Reason Enough* by Clark Pinnock, and *Why Do We Believe* by the late Paul Little. The apologetic reasons Pinnock gives called "circles of evidence" should be logically studied and explored here, but space is our problem. But they can be stated.

These five circles from Pinnock—"pragmatic," "experiential," "cosmic," "historical," and "corporate"—if studied in depth cannot be ignored and bypassed by even the most rebellious and cantankerous kind of person who is out to stop the theistic/Christian world-view. Any person of integrity just cannot ignore the apologetic strength of this evidence.

Having written about the challenge and reward of technical studies, I believe it essential to do some of that now. To see the theistic/Christian world-view channeled through the aforementioned categorical grid revealing its wholistic picture of life and then to briefly show what the other world-views attempt to do in their fragmented effort will be quite helpful.

The Theistic/Christian World-View Examined Through The Grid

We start with a brief effort of making sense of your world from a biblical world-view, the theistic/Christian world-view viewpoint, to be able to see the contrast with alien world-views.

The prime proposition in theism is with the nature of God. This is the *first* category in our grid through which all world-views need to be channeled for study. Drawing from James Sire's classic book *The Universe Next Door,* my major resource (quoted material) for the overview of the theistic/Christian world-view, we commence with God by breaking down a long proposition into parts.

The first thing to be said about God from the theistic/Christian world-view is that "God is infinite, personal, transcendent and immanent, omniscient, sovereign and good." To say that God is infinite is to say "that He is beyond scope and measure as far as we are concerned." All else in the universe is secondary to God. No other being can challenge Him in His nature. He has no twin. He is the "be-all and end-all of existence."

God is personal in that "He is not mere force or energy or some existent substance." God is He; He has personality with two required characteristics: "(1) self-reflection and (2) self-determination. . . God is personal in that He knows Himself to be." He thinks and He acts. "One implication of the personality of God is that He is like us." Of course, in this dimension of the category of God, He is also triune, that is, in the one essence of the Godhead "we have to distinguish three persons who are neither three gods on the one side, nor three parts or modes of god on the other, but coequally and coeternally God." To know God means "knowing more than that He exists. It means knowing Him as we know a brother . . . or our own father."

God is also transcendent and immanent. To be transcendent God is beyond us and our world. He is "otherly." But to be immanent means that God is also with us. He is present. This is not a contradiction. "God is immanent, here, elsewhere, in a sense completely in line with his transcendence," because "God is not matter as you and I." He is Spirit.

God is omniscient. God is all-knowing. He is the beginning and the end. "He is He Who knows." Psalm 139 expresses this beautifully.

God is sovereign which "is really a further ramification of God's infiniteness." This expresses God's concern to rule not as some tyrant but to pay attention to all the actions of His universe, because He cares like a real father cares. "It expresses the fact that nothing is beyond God's ultimate interest, control, and authority."

God is good, so good! This is a "prime statement about God's character. From it flow all others. . . . As being is the essence of his nature, goodness is the essence of his character."

God's goodness is expressed in His holiness and in His love. His holiness emphasizes His absolute righteousness which "brooks no shadow of evil." His goodness is expressed as love. The ultimate of God's love for the human race was the sacrifice of Himself on the cross. Modern man may scoff at this, but what will he do with two thousand years of changed lives simply because of the crucifixion and resurrection of Jesus Christ?

What is so meaningful about this, that the church has not really explained to the world, is that in Christ where one does experience and realize God's goodness, man is not a puppet on a string. God's goodness gives man freedom of choice and he has to live with the consequences. But if man makes the choice that a Father God wants him to make, then: "God's goodness means then, first, that there is an absolute standard of righteousness (it is found in God's character) and, second, that there is hope for humanity (because God is love and will not abandon his creation). These twin observations will become especially significant as we trace the results of rejecting the theistic world view."

The *second* part of the grid for looking at the theistic/Christian world-view is that "God created the cosmos ex nihilo to operate with a uniformity of natural causes in an open system." This means that God is "He Who is" and He is "the source of all else." He did not make the cosmos out of Himself. He "spoke it into existence. It came into being by His word." It was not some preexistent something.

What is meant by the cosmos being "a uniformity of natural causes in an open system" is that the universe is orderly. "God does not present us with confusion but with clarity." The system is "open" meaning it is not programmed. "God is constantly involved in the unfolding pattern of the ongoing operation of the universe. And so are we as human beings." This will become more significant when we look at the fifth grid. But for now it must be understood that "the course of the world's operation is open to reordering by either" God or/and man in this context: The universe was dramatically reordered by the Fall of Adam and Eve from God's grace by their disobedience. But God made a choice to reorder the universe via man's obedience in redemption through Christ.

> The world's operation is also reordered by our continued activity after the Fall. Each action of each of us, each decision to pursue one course rather than another, changes or rather "produces" the future. By dumping pollutants into fresh streams, we kill fish and alter the way we can feed ourselves in years to come. By "cleaning up" our streams, we again alter our future and so forth. If the universe were not orderly, our decisions would have no effect. If the course of events were determined (if the universe was closed), our decisions would have no significance. So theism declares that the universe is orderly but not determined (closed). The implications of this become clearer as we discuss humanity's place in the cosmos.

The *third* part of the grid is that "human beings are created in the image of God and thus possess personality, self-transcendence, intelligence, morality, gregariousness, and creativity." The key phrase is the "image of God" as stated in Genesis 1:26-27; 5:3 and 9:6. In short this means that we are like God in that His image is in our creation.

"We are personal because God is personal," and "we know ourselves to be" because we are self-conscious. This is not the mentality of "I need to find myself." We can know ourselves only because God makes it possible. We make decisions because we possess self-determination. "We are capable of acting on our own" volition and according to our own character. We are not locked in wherein we can only react to our environment. We participate in part in a transcendence over our environment. That is a way of saying that the cosmic system as God has created it is open to reordering.

We have personality, because God is personality, and if man attempts to break away from that closeness the results are as Pascal wrote: "There is a Godshaped vacuum in the heart of every man." Augustine wrote, "Our hearts are restless till they rest in thee." How then does God fulfill our ultimate longing?

He does so in many ways:

> by being the perfect fit for our very nature, by satisfying our longing for interpersonal relationship, by being in his omniscience the end to our search for knowledge, by being in his infinite being the refuge from all fear, by being in his holiness the righteous ground for our quest for justice, by being in his infinite love the cause of our hope for salvation, by being in his infinite creativity both the source of our creative imagination and the ultimate beauty we seek to reflect as we ourselves create.

This conception of human nature is summarized by saying that like God we have "personality, self-transcendence, and intelligence" all of which is the capacity for knowledge and reason. We have morality which is the capacity for seeing and understanding good and evil. Our gregariousness or "social capacity" is "our characteristic and fundamental desire and need for human companionship" such as community represented by the male and female aspect of life. Our God-given creativity is "the ability to imagine new things or to endow old things with human purpose and significance."

A bottom line is that in theism human beings are dignified, because we are a reflection of the "Ultimately Dignified." This does not make us God, but it gives us great humility and gratitude for what God has done for and in us. Christians are sort of mid-point people. We are above the rest of creation for God has given us dominion over it, but we are still below God for we are not autonomous. We are not on our own. This is, therefore, the ideal balanced human status.

It was in failure to remain in that balance that our troubles arose, and the story of how that happened is very much a part of Christian theism. But before we see what tipped the balanced state of humanity, we need to understand a further implication of being created in the image of God.

The *fourth* part of the grid is that "human beings can know both the world around them and God himself because God has built into them the capacity to do so and because he takes an active role in communicating with them." Thus "the foundation of human knowledge is the character of God as creator." God has taken the initiative in making this knowledge possible in what is called revelation in two ways: general and special revelation.

In general revelation God speaks or reveals Himself through "the created order of the universe." God's existence and nature as Creator and powerful sustainer of the universe is in God's prime "handiwork" that is His universe. There is order and beauty, but when we look at humans we see something more. But general revelation can go only so far. As Aquinas said, "we can know that God exists through general revelation, but we could never know that God is Triune except for special revelation."

Special revelation is "God's self-disclosure of Himself in extra-natural ways." One way of special revelation was the spectacular form of the burning bush when He defined Himself to Moses as "I am who I am." He was the same God who had acted before on behalf of the Hebrew people. In this identification to Moses God identified Himself as more than the God of power and might. Here He identified Himself as a personal God. (Exodus 3:13-14)

Later God revealed Himself in the Ten Commandments, through the prophets, and finally as the Hebrew epistle in the New Testament reinforces what we know from the Gospels, God revealed Himself in even more special revelation in His own Son. This was God's final self-disclosure. "Jesus has made God known to us in very fleshly terms."

The main point for us is that theism declares that God can and has clearly communicated with us. Because of this we can know much about who God is and what he desires for us. That is true for people at all times and all places, but it is especially true before the Fall, to which we now turn.

The *fifth* part of the grid is that "human beings were created good, but through the Fall the image of God became defaced, though not so ruined as not to be capable of restoration. Through the work of Christ, God redeemed humanity and began the process of restoring people to goodness, though any given person may choose to reject that redemption."

Human history can be studied under four terms: creation, fall, redemption, and glorification. Beyond the essential human characteristics already considered, we add "that human beings and all the rest of creation were created good." But we did not stay as we were created. That is the tragedy of the universe and the world. Adam and Eve, who were historical characters, had the choice of remaining or not remaining in the perfect close relationship by obedience to God. They chose to disobey and "violated the personal relationship they had with" God who is the Creator and Father of all. The result all down through the centuries of history has been subsequent generations of personal, social, and natural turmoil. The image of God in man was "defaced in all its aspects. In personality we lost our capacity to know ourselves accurately and to determine our own course of action freely in response to our intelligence."

Our "self-transcendence was impaired by the alienation we experienced in relation to God." As Adam and Eve turned away, God let them go. As "humankind slipped" from that close fellowship and relationship with God, they lost their ability to stand over against the universe, understand it, judge it accurately and therefore make truly "free" decisions. Humanity became a servant to nature instead of a free servant to God. Humankind's "status as God's vice regent over nature was reversed."

"Human intelligence became impaired." No longer could man reason without constantly falling into error. Morally, man "became less able to discern good and evil." Socially, man "began to exploit other people." Creatively, man's "imagination became separated from reality; imagination became illusion, and artists who created gods in their own image led humanity further and further from its origin." The fullest expression of humankind turning away from God and the results of such are clearly defined in Romans chapters 1-2. It reads like today's newspaper of social evils and ills when man goes sour by turning away from God's grace.

The picture of the Fall can be put in four captions depicting the essence of fallen humanity. Man was alienated from God; from himself causing the question asked more and more, "who am I;" from others; and from the cosmic world.

But because God cares He made the way for humanity to be redeemable from east of Eden and come home. He has already done this. The question is, why does man reject it? For the same reason Adam and Eve rebelled: they wanted to be equal to God, and they lost the wonderful freedom and beauty of life which is possible in a relationship to God as Father. Now in Christ even in this fallen world, that relationship is possible.

The story of the Creation and the Fall is told in three chapters of Genesis. The story of redemption takes the rest of the Scriptures.

> The Bible records God's love for us in searching us out, finding us in our lost, alienated condition and redeeming us by the sacrifice of his own Son, Jesus Christ, the Second Person of the Trinity. God, in unmerited favor and great grace, has granted us the possibility of a new life, a life involving substantial healing of our alienation and restoration to fellowship with God.

Here is the beauty of this redemption that is possible in theism in the matter of the universe being "open" in the "uniformity of natural causes in an open system." It means that "redeemed humanity is humanity on the way to the restoration of the defaced image of God." There is substantial healing which takes place in every aspect of human life-personality, self-transcendence, intelligence, morality, social capacity, and creativity.

"Glorified humanity is humanity totally healed, and at peace with God, and individuals at peace with others and themselves. But this happens only on the other side of death and the bodily resurrection." But in this world redeemed humanity in the meantime finds significance and meaning to life, because "they are essentially godlike and though fallen can be restored to original dignity." Reams of paper would be filled with the powerful and possible results this fact can have for our modern world that is staggering like a drunk with no place to call home.

The *sixth* dimension of the grid is that "for each person death is either the gate to eternal life with God and His people or the gate to eternal separation from the only thing that will ultimately fulfill human aspirations." This dimension must be kept in the context of the fifth dimension, but it is singled out here because attitudes about death are a part of every world-view. It is a very personal issue. Does it make any difference about life's significance and purpose now if death is the end of it all with nothing better beyond? Does life have nothing better to offer than what a very crude and gross bumper sticker states: "Life Is A Bitch and Then One Dies." Do I continue after the resurrection of all by Christ's power in a transformed existence in an everlasting relationship to God because of what Christ has done for me, or do I take the other choice: Hell, a word seldom heard in most modern Churches? What is my choice? Christian theism gives us this choice.

Existence forever separated from God is the essence of Hell! G. K. Chesterton remarked that Hell is a monument to human freedom, and we might add, "human dignity." Hell is God's tribute to the freedom He gave each of us to choose whom we would serve. "It is a recognition that our decisions have a significance that extends far down into the reaches of foreverness."

The *seventh* dimension of our grid is about ethics. In theism ethics are transcendent and objective, and they are based on God's character as good, holy, and loving. This is the implication of the first dimension of the grid. Theism teaches that not only is there a moral universe, but there is an "absolute standard by which all moral judgements are measured." This is an objective truth and fact rejected by much of modern culture/society and by some of the contemporary church. The results of this are not difficult to discover.

God Himself is the standard, and Christians and Jews hold to the conviction that God has revealed His standard in laws and principles in the Ten Commandments. For Christians the Sermon on the Mount, and Paul's ethical teachings are parts of this standard. "There is thus a standard of right and wrong, and people who want to know it can know it."

However, the fullest embodiment of the good, the ethic and ethics of God, is in Jesus Christ. He is the complete man. He is humanity as God would have it be. So ethics, while very much a human domain, is ultimately the business of God. "We are not the measure of morality. God is."

The *final* dimension of our grid for theism or for any world view is the issue of history. In theism "history is linear, a meaningful sequence of events leading to the fulfillment of God's purpose for humanity." This means that people's actions, as chaotic and confusing as they are, are still "a part of a meaningful sequence that has a beginning, a middle, and an end."

In the theistic/Christian world-view, history is not reversible, it is not repeatable (Like causes may produce like results); it is not cyclic, it is not meaningless. History is teleological, going somewhere, directed toward a chosen end. "The God who knows the end from the beginning is aware and sovereign of all human action."

> In short, the most important aspect of the theistic concept of history is that history has meaning because God—the Logos (meaning itself)—is behind all events, not only "upholding the universe by his word of power" (Heb. 1:3), but, "in everything . . . <working> for good with those who love him, who are called according to his purpose" (Rom. 8:28). Behind the apparent chaos of events stands the loving God sufficient for all.

It is certainly clear that the theistic/Christian world-view is primarily dependent upon its concept of God, for theism holds that everything stems from Him. Nothing is prior to God. "He is He Who Is. Thus theism has a basis for metaphysics" (the essence of being or meaning), "a basis for ethics" (God is the worthy one), and "a basis for epistemology" (how do I know I know). Theism is a complete world-view with the greatness of God as the central tenet for it.

Even now in the midst of so much chaotic confusion in the Western world about life and its meaning, when so much convulsion is going on in society as we watch it constantly deteriorate spiritually and morally plus other ways, the world is as Manley Hopkins once wrote, "charged with the grandeur of God." Therefore "fully cognizant Christian theists do not just believe and proclaim their view as true. Their first act is toward God—a response of love, obedience and praise to the Lord of the Universe—their maker, sustainer, and, through Jesus Christ, redeemer and friend."[25]

Theism is about a world-view and a God who made and sustains the world and who is infinite. It is the Christian world-view. To say that is to say that everything is about God. This means we must see Christianity not simply as a personal relationship with Jesus, not simply as a faith system or a belief, not simply as a religion, but rather the truth about all of life. The God-given duty of Christians is to all of creation, striving to make it reflect the wonderful character of God. The late Francis Schaeffer eloquently preached it: we must examine every aspect of life under the Lordship of Christ.

Abraham Kuyper, Dutch theologian, philosopher, educator, founder of a Christian university, newspaper publisher, eventually prime minister, and considered the most influential man of his generation argued that if Christians are going to stand against the philosophies of secularism and other world-views, they must articulate their philosophy about every aspect of life and society as fully as the secularists. His world-view, a distinct theistic/Christian world-view, looks to Jesus Christ as both Redeemer and Creator of all. The world, the cosmic world and man is to be reconciled to the Lordship of Jesus.

Only this will remove the narrow view most Americans have of the Christian faith that sees it as something that relates only to a personal relationship with Jesus. They do not understand that the theistic/Christian world-view Faith is to relate to all of life. Christians who do not have this distinctly Christian philosophy about life—a view of the entire world informed by biblical truth—will easily be suckered into living by the world's standards during the week and attempting to live by Christ's on Sunday or Wednesday evening. Surveys reveal that only one out of three Christians believe that Christianity should have any effect on how they live. That is a clear clue to the cause of the spiritual, moral and social crises of our culture/society. The salt remains in the salt-shaker through the week.

This is why that even if church pews are full on Sundays, secular values still dominate our culture/society. America's half-hearted Christian faith leaves plenty of room for an anti-Christian value system during the week. With such halfhearted faith and poor understanding of the theistic/Christian world-view, Christians can't recognize false ethics in the marketplace and how they can counter them. Or they don't understand justice and how to achieve it in government. There can only be an impact by Christians when Christians become able to discern our secular society with the eye of God's gardener.

Other World-Views Examined Through The Grid

The proper way to do this is to follow the same but more brief technical procedure used in the presentation of the complete, consistent, and coherent theistic/Christian world-view. Although that is not the overall purpose of this book, as an introduction to world-view studies with illustrative materials to encourage others to do the technical study, it must be done. Excellent in-depth study material is available for those who really want to take on the world. The church must and can do that.

The same kind of technical study used for theism demonstrates how the other major world-views: Deism, Naturalism, Nihilism, Existentialism, Eastern Pantheistic Monism, Secular

Humanism, and New Age reveal many different perspectives on the various grid dimensions leaving nothing but fractured and fragmented world-views by which man cannot live fully, holy, or hopefully. They also reveal the genesis of what develops in a culture/society when they are the dominant influence. When studied in this manner they reveal nothing but chaotic results for life and culture/society.

To illustrate how these other world-views delete or change what the theistic/Christian world-view believes and follows, I will take each of the other alien world-views and state what major change or changes they make in the various dimensions of the grid. It takes only a minimum of thinking and imagination to realize the results of each of the other world-views. Enlightenment ideas are clearly evident in them.

Deism: A world made by God but now on its own. God created the cosmos but is no longer involved in the ongoing operation of the universe. The cosmos/universe is closed to God and man. It is like a clock-work world. Nature is run only by natural laws. Man must try to read God's will from the book of nature by reason alone rather than the Bible by faith and reason. He loses some hope and freedom. Ethics follows the dictates of natural religion. What is, is right. Death for the deist is the same as theism, but history is linear and predetermined. This world-view has cracks in it.

Naturalism: A world without God. God does not exist. This world-view could carry the label of atheism. Matter is all there is, and it has always been. It is eternal. The cosmos is totally closed. Man has very little freedom. Man is a complex machine. His only cause for uniqueness is reason. Ethics in naturalism is based on there is no "ought." All values are man-made with some underlying attempts to follow theistic ethics, but they cannot consistently. Death is the extinction of the individual, and history is linear with no goal or purpose unless evolution can bring up something. The cracks in this world-view are larger and leaves man in more of a fragmented state than deism.

Before continuing in the remaining world-views, please note

and ponder how that as soon as one breaks away from the theistic/Christian world-view, there is something like falling dominos happening in that each world-view progresses further from the complete world-view of theism to a more fractured view of the various dimensions of the grid. This leaves more and more unanswered questions and puzzling issues. Everyone of these unanswered questions or issues have destructive effects on man and culture/society.

Nihilism: The result of the failure of naturalism. There is no God. Man cannot be certain of any reality or of anything. The cosmos is totally closed; life is alien and absurd. Man does not belong, and he finds no significance for living. Thus man is filled with despair in an irrational and impersonal universe. In nihilism there are no values made by God in relation to ethics. Man does his own thing. The main course of action is anarchy. Death is the extinction of the individual. History is totally meaningless.

Nihilism is the pessimistic reaction to the results of modernity rooted in the Enlightenment. There is quite a roster of familiar names who reacted in pessimism. Nietzsche and Dostoesvky were two. Jean Paul Sarte saw the hopelessness in this modernity and flings at it the attempt to create meaning out of absurdity. Camus was in the same camp. Ernest Hemingway in *The Old Man and The Sea*, expresses his nihilism in a sad story of an old fisherman whose prize catch is eaten by sharks before he can bring it to shore. The skeleton of the fish is a symbol of emptiness and despair. Samuel Beckett reveals his despair in *Waiting For Godot*. Others are Franz Kafka, Kurt Vonnegut Jr., and Ingmar Bergman. These are all popular names in the world of literature who play an immense role in the developing of life-values in their followers. Their values are far removed from the theistic/Christian world-view.

A most lucid and honest expression of the despair created by the modernity of nihilism was given years ago in *The Atlantic Monthly,* September, 1948 by a Britisher teaching at Princeton. I borrow it from a paper written by Doug Dickey. It was titled, "Man Against Darkness."

The universe, created and governed by a fatherly God, was a friendly habitation for man. We could be sure that, however great the evil in the world, good, in the end, would triumph and the forces of evil would be routed. With the disappearance of God from the sky, all this has changed. Since the world is not ruled by a spiritual being, but rather by blind forces, there cannot be any ideals, moral or otherwise, in the universe outside us. Our ideals, therefore, must proceed only from our own minds; they are our own inventions. Thus the world which surrounds us is nothing but an immense spiritual emptiness. It is a dead universe. We do not live in a universe which is on the side of our values. It is completely indifferent to them.[26]

When the first group of adults studied world-views with me in a class setting some of the parents discovered a frightening reality. They realized that some of their children, baptized believers in the high-school age bracket, were more nihilist than Christian.

Existentialism: This world-view is an attempt to remedy nihilism. Of course it does not. There is no God. Matter is eternal. The cosmos as something has order is the absurd world. Man finds meaning only in his own subjective world, but that evades him. This is an attempt to find some significance for man that was totally lost in nihilism. Man becomes self-authenticating and makes his own choices. In ethics man's total freedom is the source of his joy and anxiety. Death is the final absurdity and in history only the now counts. Like some other world-views, this one has variations found in two basic forms: theistic existentialism and atheistic existentialism. Both will probably be with us for a long time.

Eastern Pantheistic Monism: A world that is God. God is the cosmos and the essence of reality is the mind. The cosmos is god. Man is to seek unity with all of reality of the present known world by merging with the impersonal whole of the universe. In ethics man must work out his own karma or fate until he reaches nirvana which is unity with All. Death ends at the incarnation of

Atman which does not affect man's essential nature. History is cyclical; time is unreal.

Secular Humanism: Man is the center and measure of everything. The Humanist Manifesto II is must reading to see the fallacy and destructiveness of this world-view that is a spin-off of naturalism. Although secular humanism as a world-view is a failure according to our criterion for validity, every major institution in America, including too much of the modern church, is heavily dominated by this system. It is so absurd that such a supposedly advanced and intelligent society does not seem to grasp the destructive nature of this world-view. It cannot meet the criterion for a workable and valid world-view, so modern man is attempting to put life and culture/society together with the New Age Movement world-view. Since God is out in this world-view, death is the final absurdity and history is only now. There is no purpose in death and in history.

Secular humanism is humanism in its atheistic form. Dr. James S. Strauss of Lincoln Christian Seminary declares that this form of humanism is "the greatest single challenge to the Christian world and life view in the twentieth century." To unpack this world-view and see its massive destructive nature one would have to study it in the context of its origins, idols, counterfeit salvation, and how it is in radical conflict with the mandate of Christ to evangelize the world.

Aleksandr Solzhenitszn declared in his famous commencement address at Harvard University in 1978 that this secular humanism has sent modern Western civilization on the dangerous road to worship man and his material need. The late Dr. Francis Schaeffer affirms the same truth in his book, *A Christian Manifesto*.

The New Age Movement: There is no God. Prime reality is within the individual consciousness, making man and God one and equals. Man is perceived by his higher state of consciousness. There is no right or wrong in relation to ethics. There is no such thing as guilt. There are no absolutes. But there are, because they live by their own. The essential self lives on after death. History is unimportant. But this world-view is not new. It is Eastern religions being replayed as Western man turns eastward. This same turning inward for truth is being seen more and more in some "charismania" groups plus other healer and subjective truth movements.

Not one of these world-views gives answers to the basic questions of life in a wholistic and satisfying way that is based on true, ultimate Truth that is consistent and coherent. No one can realize what the end and compound results of these world-views are until they are studied in a detailed effort.

What the world needs now as a world-view is clear: a covenantal relationship with God. What is meant by the word "covenantal?"

> The philosophical, ethical, and cultural foundation for world-views - whether Christian or humanistic (secular humanism which along with the New Age Movement is our greatest culture/society threat) - is covenantal. The Bible defends the idea of covenant as the personal, binding, and structural relationship between the various component parts of any given society. It is the means by which we approach, deal with, and know one another - and God. It is the pattern of all our relationships. It is the divine-to-human and human-to-human social structure.

> Thus, covenantalism is woven into the fabric of man's very being. It is an inescapable reality. It gives shape to all thinking and all our doing - whether we actually know it or not. Our worldview is, therefore, necessarily covenantal in nature.

> The Biblical covenant has at least five basic component parts. It begins with the establishment of God's nature and character: He is sovereign. Next, it proclaims God's authority: He has established order and structure. Third, the covenant outlines God's stipulations: He has given His people responsibilities. Fourth, it establishes God's judicial see: He will one day sit in judgement. And finally, the covenant details God's very great and precious promises: He has laid up an inheritance for the faithful.

This outline of the covenant, though by no means absolute, can be seen, in at least an oblique fashion, in God's dealings with Adam (see Genesis 1:26-31; 2:16-25), Noah (see Genesis 9:1-17), Abraham (see Genesis 12:1-3; 15:1-21), Moses (see Exodus 11:1-22), and the disciples of Christ (1 Corinthians 11:23-34). It is also evident in some way, shape, form, or another in the Ten commandments (two tables of five statutes), the structure of the Pentateuch (five books), the book of Deuteronomy (five parts), the book of Psalms (five sections), the book of Revelation (five stages), and many other passages of Scripture in both the Old and New Testaments. (Structuring of the Bible as Grant does is a problem for many, but do not let this deter from Grant's 'other helpful thoughts)

As a result, the Christian worldview - derived as it is from the teaching of Scripture - revolves around and is defined in terms of Biblical covenant: the Sovereignty of God, the structure of His order, the pattern of His ethics, the reality of His judgement, and the hope of His promise.

Because all worldviews are covenantal at their root, it is not surprising that the humanistic (secular humanistic) worldview can also be capsulized and summarized in five primary and primordial presuppositions: secularism, egalitarianism, rationalism, anti-traditionalism, and optimism. These are the five "values, beliefs, and sentiments" that Heritage Foundation scholar, William Donohue, says are constitutive of modern humanism. And they are, he says, the values, beliefs, and sentiments "through which the ACLU (American Civil Liberty Union) sees the world as well. Side by side, the two covenants - the Christian and the humanistic - as well as their corresponding worldviews, make for a very interesting contrast.[27]

Therefore I state again that the major presupposition of this book still stands. The only world-view that will give man and culture/society a certain, proven, cohesive, consistent, and congruent value system for life and living in this culture/society is the theistic/Christian world-view; a world-view based upon truth and ultimate Truth whose name is Jesus Christ. The evidence for this is if modern man has the decency or smarts to realize it and then will commit life to it! Does the church need to understand this in their Christian education efforts? Absolutely! We will continue to see why.

The Lord's song will have to be sung and dispensed in the context of our culture/society that is an alien land foreign to and alienated from the theistic/Christian world-view.

An Alien Land

Hunter and Johnson believes that the Christian congregation is to be "a living sign of Christ in the world."[28] This possibility for the church is filled with high hope and at the same time inescapable tension. Though the church is gathered in the world in the name of Christ for the sake of the world, the church is persistently tempted to escape into various forms of piety that have the added attraction of allowing it to be comfortable and uncritically accommodated to the controlling values of contemporary culture: an alien land in reference to Christ and Christianity. How can the church love the world without trusting it, respond to the world without being conformed to it, be involved in the world, our alien land, without being overcome by it? World-view studies are imperative to help us handle all of this.

This is why this Part of the book must be considered with the utmost seriousness and understanding. Our culture/society is very much an alien land foreign to and alienated from the Christian world-view and in desperate need of an old song that is always new, relevant, life-changing, life-remaking, culture-changing and contemporary. The song is the Lord's Song, Christ's message and Christianity's offer of hope for life and society. It is the possible transforming vision of a culture/society influenced and controlled by the complete world-view that is possible only in the context of the theistic/Christian world-view. That is the mission of the church to our culture/society in the light of Scripture and the authentic Christian tradition.

To sing the Lord's Song in an alien land (Ps. 137:4) is to affirm the possibility of a joyful, graceful, and vigorous life for people and culture/society. It is a life that is a sign of Christ in the places where we live. Such life, wherever it is born and sustained, is the gift of God. But it is a gift with a task. Some, but too few, are trying to do it within the context of the topic of this book.

In this work to be done is the growing and complex tension between the values of the authentic church and the society in which our culture and sub-cultures are being constantly formed and reformed into value systems diametrically opposed to the theistic/Christian world-view. They are value systems opposed to that for which Christianity stands. Our culture/society is an alien land. It is alienated from God's transforming presence and power for a number of reasons.

One massive reason that our culture/society is an alien land is that we have an ineffective church in the midst of so-called church growth. This will disturb some. But it is still true, sadly true. Along with this reason there is the collision of world-views already considered that are battling for the mind of modern man, and because of the ineffectiveness of the church as a whole, other world-views are overshadowing the theistic/Christian world view as the dominant, healthy, workable one world-view for people and culture/society. That is distressful for a church-man who knows that the theistic/Christian world-view has proven itself for nearly two thousand years, but the church has fallen down in its God-ordained task and has allowed this alien land to become one of the most, if not the most, resistant nation on earth to the Gospel of Good News.

Furthermore much of the church has been made ineffective by an improper picture presented by liberal theology on one side and the fundamentalistic critical right of conservative theology on the other. The kind of God which some in both of these camps present and represent would not be the God of the Bible that I would want to believe in and follow. The theology of both the liberal thinker and the radical fundamentalist thinker commences with "experience" rather than with God and that is quite problematic. Both camps become very god-like. Man's experience is not the god that will save and reconcile.

171

Also our culture/society has no binding address like the Christ in Colossians 1:15-17. This is in relation to the loss of the cosmic Christ as the center of all reality in the world. This has been helped along because too much of the modern Church has moved into a form of pietism that separates itself from the real world by a form of Platonism. In the loss of the cosmic Christ the church has bypassed Colossians 1:17 and 2 Corinthians 10:5. The alien land has lost the cosmic Christ as the center of the universe and the true Truth of all truths, therefore the lament from on-the-cutting-edge Christians is like the lament of the Hebrews in Psalm 137.

Bruce Lockerbie believes that by losing this Christ as "the secret at the center," we are a culture/society of "cracked cisterns" in "an unshackled universe."[29] Our alien land has, therefore, nothing which pulls Christians and non-Christians together into a consensus of what is good and evil, and we as a culture/society are trying to handle the game of life with the goal posts down. The writer of the Old Testament book, *Ecclesiastes* would tell us today that we have something like flies in the perfume bottle: "As dead flies give perfume a bad smell, so a little folly outweighs wisdom and honor" (Eccles. 10:1). It was Toynbee, the great historian, who wrote that "this Western civilization that is now unifying (trying to) the World . . . is a post-Christian or ex-Christian civilization." The larger picture of an alien land by Lockerbie follows:

> With the retreat of Christianity, its cultural mandate also declines into chaos. Another view of culture has taken its place, an attitude derived from the secular vision of human existence. Without absolutes, without aesthetic principles, without criteria for taste, without moral direction, contemporary culture careens in trackless shambles. The dance has been abandoned, the riot has begun, with little or no concern for its consequences, as the Stage Manager says, "in our living and in our dying."
>
> Something foul now contaminates the sweet aroma of life, like flies in the perfume bottle. Something cheap reduces every human aspiration to its lowest common denominator of

greed and lust. To us whose heritage has been traditional Western culture, buttressed by the Christian vision of life, the crisis seems particularly acute. Again, the village in "Our Town" serves as a model: To a question regarding "culture or love of beauty in Grover's Corners," the newspaper editor replies: "Well, ma'am, there ain't much—not in the sense you mean. . . . Robinson Crusoe and the Bible; and Handel's "Largo," we all know that; and Whistler's "Mother"—those are just about as far as we go."

Today one wonders if the average English-speaking town can make even so modest a claim. In North America, at least, we've become a continent of philistines, engorged by trivia, yet as culturally malnourished as children fed only on lollipops. For music, we have cacophony or Muzak; for art, graffiti and painting by numbers; for sculpture, dashboard icons and lawn statues; for literature, the novels of Jacqueline Susann; for drama, soap operas and quiz games.

Our means of discourse has been minimized to depend largely upon grunts and that all-purpose substitute for thought, only know." Our tastes are determined by pollsters and ratings. This week's Top Forty are next week's Golden Oldies. Whereas ancient Greece knew the difference in aesthetics and moral tone between tragedy and comedy, we seem to have lost that power to discriminate. The result, in our theaters and in our public life, is a juxtaposition of the ridiculous with the contemptible, the outrageous with the unspeakable.[30]

The foregoing descriptive picture of our alien land could go on for pages and pages revealing in so many ways our mediocre culture/society. The question continues to haunt us: how do we sing the Lord's Song in this kind of context. In the context of our overarching topic of world-view rhetoric and concern, there are certain facts we must know that reveals much about the creation of or the reality of our land as an alien land.

Alien Land Facts

Fact One: Hunter and Johnson are sensitive and helpful in this section, and the first fact is: our culture/society is a nation and "world without Christendom."[31]

What is Christendom? From my perspective and understanding, Christendom cannot be equated with biblical authentic Christianity. In fact, Christendom stifles the need of the church's missionary identity in North America, the largest mission field in the world, a mission field that includes most of the membership of the American church. It stifles the missionary identity of the church, because Christendom is a form of Christianity controlled by culture more than by Christ.

It is a form of Christianity that can no longer critique our culture/society, because it's too much like culture/society. The Christendom heritage has been conditioned to tell the Christian story as a success story. It is Constantinian Christianity that wants to work in a world that is safe. Of course this has contributed to allowing the church to be repositioned to the slippery slope outside the center of society. The Christendom that hangs around has an urge for success and pushes for a certain amount of accommodation to culture and becomes domesticated. It becomes unthreatening to values opposed to biblical Christianity.

> Incarnation becomes domestication when the ultimate principles governing the interaction of the church with its culture are set by the culture. When the church's incarnation of the gospel is made subject to the terms of the environment, established according to its principles, validated by its evaluations, and made subservient to its ends, its incarnation has been domesticated.[32]

A "world without Christendom" as defined is no loss. "The end of Christendom," as I have defined it, "might be the beginning of the church."[33] Authentic Christianity can grow from the stump of the church if the church will cut away from being domesticated by society.

With Christendom gone, our Western urban society has nothing like a one-world-view based on the centrality of Christ, Christianity, church, and the power of related institutions to interpret and regulate, in a strong influential manner, a guiding and directing mode in virtually ever social parameter and arena of life and society. With Christendom gone other world-views battle for control.

174

Nevertheless in saying the foregoing, we do not mourn the passing of Christendom which commenced with Constantinian Christianity. (To understand the significance of this, Constantine should be studied) That brought and contained its own variety of problems for the Christian life and faith. It left what is in some ways a dark legacy. When Christianity was made legal it lost its power and real purpose as a world-view from which every aspect of life could move and live in a healthy, wholistic, and life-transforming way by the choice of risk and to some the cost of life. Much of today's church is more Constantinian than Christ-dominated. The one world-view that did reign properly for a while is the Christianity which commenced with the incarnation of Christ leading to the transformation of people wherein they were the living signs of Christ in the world.

But the truth of the matter is that the Christian congregation is gathered in a world where it cannot make assumptions about the Christian view of reality, and it is an illusion to speak of a Christian society. Our culture/society has never been Christian, and it is further away from this than ever in the history of this nation. It is even worse in the wider scope of the world. I have been told that there are fewer churches for every ten thousand people than ever before in history.

Fact Two: Accompanying the passing of Christendom was the coming and "rise of pluralism."[34] Our culture/society is an alien foreign land in that the faith we hold is held in the context of many faiths, both, religious and secular. The God we worship is recognized by fewer and fewer in the pantheon of gods in our contemporary society. "The radical monotheism of the Judeo-Christian tradition must find its way once again in the midst of a persistent practical polytheism that marks the modern mentality and experience."[35]

While many have grown up in a world where Christian thought forms and values were normative, there are now so many ways by which many are trying to interpret reality and attempting to understand one's own identity. I think they all, with the exception of the theistic/Christian world-view, will fail, because the evidence is in that they have already failed.

In the midst of this pluralistic setting Christians can no longer expect the Christian faith to be learned by osmosis as if it ever could. Many evidently thought that was possible, and that is part of the church's problem in the attempt to communicate the one tested and workable theistic/Christian world-view. Millions who claim to be Christian are trying to live out and share a second-hand faith. They have been trapped by their own choosing in what John Stott calls "the misery and menace of mindless Christianity."

Christians must remember and come to grips with the truth that in Jesus' company there is no place for a faith that is forced or mindless, but at the same time we best remember that in a pluralistic culture/society there is the danger of a "forgotten faith."

Fact Three: The church is also gathered in a "secularized" world. That is a culture/society which has pretty much discounted the presence of Christianity as even an alternative, let alone being the possible one proven alternative and value system or world-view for this era of life in history. Man, not God, has become the center and the measure of all of life. It is not working, nor will it ever.

On the other hand, "we can only rejoice in the gains of secularity over ignorance and superstition."[36] We can rejoice in the fact that the church, at least part of it, is taking responsibility for the cares and concerns of this world; a moving beyond and away from Platonic rhetoric and convictions to biblical language about the reconciliation of man to the total purposes of God.

This is so essential, because the Christian is no more separated from the world than God is separated from everyday life. "History is the arena of the Christian congregation's involvement."[37] The community of faith, the church, which attempts to withdraw from history or deny it looks for justification for such an attitude to a source other than the God of all history and His Word.

On the other hand the church must recognize that it lives in a world where life is being reduced systematically to only the horizontal plane. In a "religion of secularism" any talk of God is

176

categorized as meaningless and we have experienced in this alien land the loss of transcendence by replacing it with a world of immediacy.

> The tragedy in the secular transition is that the declaration of human autonomy has not led to the humanization of life. The Christian congregation is gathered in a world that continues to struggle with the question of how to keep human life human. Yet where God is viewed by many as an anachronism of another age, there is a blatant refusal to acknowledge the connection between the loss of transcendence and the process of dehumanization.[38]

Fact Four: As the people of Israel, from whom the concept of singing the Lord's Song in an alien land comes, had been uprooted from their homeland and scattered along the rivers of Babylon, so is our world "marked by rootlessness."[39] I think this is clearly known by any aware person living in our culture/society.

The personal life of so many can no longer be told as a complete picture but only as a series of short chapters or stories. Continuity is lost in so much personal identity. There is no overarching theme for life. This has not only affected individuals, but it has in many cases caused great loss of community or what is called the significant group.

Loneliness and alienation are a large part of our age of crowded masses. Can life be nourished at the deepest human level without roots? Can love grow without real connections that go deeper than human emotions? "With no deep reservoir of a shared past to enrich life, countless people,"[40] in and out of the church, "clutch for sustenance in whatever experience will give assurance that they are not alone," that they do matter regardless of how superficial and shallow, evil or transient that experience may be.

These are some of the facts of our world evoked by the imagery of a "foreign" or "alien" land. It is here the church is called upon to sing the Lord's Song—to celebrate life—to care about the world and social issues, to minister to valid needs, and to share the faith, to demonstrate by word and deed the only world-view that will bring a culture/society and its people into a oneness.

But to most, including many who claim to be Christian, God is a foreigner strangely quiet. In this alien land millions are exiles and sojourners without a map and often meet one another as strangers. In the context of the church, "our faith language is alien. Our story is in danger of being forgotten. Our Christian identity is being usurped by other more pressing, secular claims. Our theology, long forgotten in most congregations, is losing its power to interpret and make sense out of life."[41] The dilemma for the church as it was for the Hebrew ancestors is either resistance, capitulation, or confrontation.

Fact Five: In our alien land we are approaching another crisis, if not already there, that few have considered. It is the fertile mind of Jacques Ellul that surfaced this situation in his book *What I Believe*. This crisis entails the transition, not from one form of society and power to another, but to a new environment. For approximately the last five thousand years we have lived in an environment of society in which politics play the major role. The present change of environment is more fundamental than anything that the human race has experienced during those five thousand years.

What we are realizing and experiencing now is the technological environment. For the last two centuries industrialization has been preparing the way for it, but it is only in the last thirty-plus years that technology has begun to impose itself everywhere, to change everything, to take over all social activities and forms, and to become a true environment.

This new environment has the following features. It enables us to live (we moderns cannot live now without it); it sets us in danger the dangers so great that they threaten to bring about the disappearance of the whole human race by power, devastation of natural resources, etc.); it is immediate to us (it is not in the future); and it mediates all else (the system encompasses all things, totally, inevitably, and invincibly).

This has frightening implications. For one thing we have no point of reference by which to pass judgement on the system. Can we refer to Jesus of Nazareth who was a model only for a traditional, political society and not a technological society? No. Because then they had nothing in common with this new system. The technological system excludes what is prior to it making the prior completely unimportant and obsolete. Thus it becomes a new form of slavery with no external references, least of all the life and conduct of Christians. This system also rules out any other scale of values other than what it develops. If this system continues on the thesis of a dead God, then there is no outcome for this world. No other life is possible.

What then do Christians do with this crisis in our alien land? They have to understand the various world-views controlling this new slavery and be ready to demonstrate by word and deed that even technology must be undergirded by a world-view which gives hope for now and forever; a world-view which offers an ethical value system that gives man dignity and not slavery; a world-view that allows technology to be a blessing to modern man. That is available and workable. By being involved in world-view thinking in the context of this new immediate crisis is to be able to show the world of technology that their environment is artificial, only a human creation, and without a Word from outside, man will only destroy himself and perhaps the world with him. The proper translation of Proverbs 29:18 is correct. "Where there is no revelation (a Word from outside), the people cast off restraint (go berserk). . . ."

It is a matter of Christians being able to exegete this system and the Word and bring the Transcendent, the Owner of the farm, the Planner of the game of life into it in a positive, creative, and meaningful manner. Only this will assist those worshiping technology to realize that there is a questionable future from technology without a complete world-view such as theism to monitor and direct it.

It is not too much to say that the Christian congregation is gathered in a world that is a battleground where the fallen powers seek to dominate and enslave human life while Christ seeks to free it.

Therefore we live in the tension of peril and promise; the concluding picture of the larger picture of the major problem resulting in crises.

Raging Battle Between Peril And Promise

The Peril: This involves our shaky culture/society as to its spiritual shallowness and moral depravity in its slide further and further from the historic faith of the theistic/Christian world-view. It is also about the reality of the peril the church itself is facing.

We are hearing more and more remarks about the church such as, "What's wrong with the salt?" Contemporary faith has been labeled as "decaffeinated Christianity." Some Roman Catholics are describing the faith in the Roman Catholic church as "cafeteria Christianity" wherein adherents pick and choose only what pleases them. There is this indictment: "In spite of the prevalence of evangelicals, American society seems as unaffected by Christian values as the National Football League is by Sunday church services."

Os Guinness writes: "The gospel is being modified to become a consumer product; its proclamation is becoming a matter of packaging, and its reception a question of personal preference; preparation through prayer and study is giving way to market research, and a new type of minister is emerging, half showman and half salesman."[42]

Deans of thinking within the modern church are warning us that the American culture and resultant society is rapidly going in a downward drift toward neo-pagan values that are inevitably harmful and destructive for the good of humans and all of culture/society. We have noted what Dr. Carl F. H. Henry has written about the *Twilight of A Great Civilization*. We have noted what Charles Colson says about our peril in his *Against The Night*. Therefore Christians have to decide, and if they really decide on Christ's behalf then the theistic/Christian world-view must be sung for the Lord like never before in this alien land.

There are two basic factors among many contributing factors to our sliding into peril. The first factor is the tension between biblical Christianity and cultural Christians. In the journal *World Vision* Tom Sine wrote an article using some quotes from a previous issue in which Tony Campolo wrote an article that generated hostility from Christians. This small journal is about the hungry and starving people of the world to which many Christians respond in a wonderful way. The journal's publisher said that never had that journal received so many hostile and angry letters for one single article. Campolo had written: "Nothing is more controversial than to be a follower of Jesus Christ. Nothing is more dangerous than to live out the will of God in today's world. It changes your whole monetary lifestyle. Am I suggesting that if you follow Jesus, you won't be able to go out and buy a BMW? You got it!" Campolo was only saying that if a Christian really follows Christ that money will be used to help feed the poor and hungry and you will get by with a lesser automobile.

Why were people upset and angry? I believe the key reason was that they missed the central issue, "that is, to what extent has our secular culture shaped Christian faith in the United States."[43] Too many Christians are really unwilling to deal with the cultural captivity of the American church. Until they do they cannot be really free and available to advance the Kingdom of God, the theistic/Christian world-view, the Lord's Song in this land.

The question is: How much are Christians trying to live the American Dream with a little Jesus overlay? Christians talk about the Lordship of Christ, but how true is that of most Christian lives in this land? How different are the lives of the majority of Christians today from their secular counterparts? If the majority are just like them, to what do they have to call them as a cure for the peril?

Whether Christians like it or not, a bottom line is: Christianity captured by the culture has been reduced to a crutch to help us through the minefield of the upwardly mobile life.

Books, broadcasts, and sermons encourage us to understand what God can do for us or "me"—to help us get ahead in our jobs, color us beautiful, and find us parking places down town. Campolo also stated in the article: "God created us in his image, but we (Christians and Americans) have decided to return the favor and create a God who is in our image."[44]

In our peril there has to be recovered the fact that biblical Christianity is not a self-interested Christianity. Christianity's author, Jesus Christ, made that clear in His first sermon (Luke 4:16ff) that caused the crowd to respond by running Him out of town. Biblical Christianity does not mean living the American Dream with a little Jesus overlay. It means committing our whole lives—not just our time, but our money—to God's purposes.

Just think about what the first disciples did to follow Him, and look what they contributed to the world and to us.

A second factor contributing to both culture/society and the church sliding into our peril has to do with the understanding of God as He is in the Book. Think about the wrestling match between Jacob and God. As we consider the history of Christian spirituality and biblical events like this between Jacob and God, essential truths surface about human experience. One truth surfacing in this event is the unpredictability of God's answer to prayer and who God really is.

Jacob prayed for help against his brother. God sent an attacker who left him crippled. That often happens and in this case we must not be too hasty in saying that this harshness was only because of Jacob's shady behavior. Job also had his prayers answered with a devastating ordeal despite his righteousness. The Apostle Paul bore the lostness of thousands on his heart in selfless love and was given a thorn in the flesh. This is the story of many saints over the years. The God of the Bible is not like rice-pudding: warm, soft, and mushy. Nor is He an indulgent divine grandparent who chuckles soothingly and pats you on the head and slips money into your pocket to do as you please. Not at all!

God is the Sovereign Lord of all reality! His is the dominion over all that can ever be. He is on no one's leash. He establishes governments and overthrows them. He builds, and He tears down. There are times when God answers prayers with a parting of the seas, with an almost miraculous easing of the way. But there are other times when He comes to us in toughness and hard, hard challenges. Why? Because God is more concerned with what we become than with what we want.

We ask for help—He wants for us wholeness. We ask for prosperity—He wants for us maturity. We ask for success and fame—He wants for us the peace of integrity. We ask for pleasure—He wants for us joy. We want what we want—He wants for us what we need to become fit for eternal life. Therefore it is a dangerous thing to ask for God. Because when He shows Himself to you it will always be in a way destined to shape your life to Him. For some of us, perhaps most of us Christians the shaping can only be done with a tough experience.[45]

But our culture/society does not want that kind of God. That is not culturally acceptable in this day of mush Christianity, yet what a time of peril we have surrounding us while much of the church attempts to make a difference with cheap grace and a manufactured God. With that the peril will stay with us. It will grow even more dangerous and destructive.

The Promise: The promise is the only possible remedy to the peril. The promise is a way of understanding life and a value system for living and life and all social parameters in our culture/society; that which builds up and unites all aspects of life and strengthens humans in a way that is purposeful, productive, hope-filled, and joyful touching all parameters of the social life. It is labeled Christianity. This the theistic/Christian world-view.

But the promise calls for a people, a coram deo people, which means living in an acute awareness of the presence of God, a people intellectually, emotionally, and spiritually engaged in this promise who are stretching toward the sunrise in the fight and struggle to keep the peril from fully arriving. They are the warriors with a mission in and to the world; the Lord's singers singing His Song in an alien land.

These singing warriors are disciples of Christ, Christians who study, who use their minds to overcome the misery and menace of mindless Christianity to become aware of the fact that America's greatest battle is for the mind of modern man in the context of world-views and pagan trends on a collision course with Godliness. As we rush pell-mell into the year 2000 we are involved in a race to which world-view or views will be in control.

In this hour when our culture/society is increasingly dominated by secular, godless, pagan values, it is imperative, it is our last real hope, that Christians understand the large picture of what is happening in this battle and collision course which is affecting the church as well as our land.

I believe that one of the greatest tragedies in the history of the Lord's church is the refusal of most Christians to use their minds in this battle and be willing to study, to know, to be able to confront all of the world-views in this pluralistic society battling against everything Christians hold to be true and dear to life and land.

We have already in Part One considered the what and why of world-view studies. Apart from the leadership of the church leading Christians to take the challenge of world-view studies seriously there is little possibility not only of real communication but even of true conversion to Jesus Christ of Nazareth, King of Kings, and Lord of Lords. Christians must know that without obeying the teaching of 1 Peter 3:15 they will never be a real part of an authentic Christian pilgrimage for Christ's sake.

The non-Christian world-views in this alien land has pushed the church against the wall. Christianity by and large in the Western world is merely coasting on the residue of past strengths. My spiritual mentor, Dr. D. Elton Trueblood, warned of this in 1944 in one of his many books, *The Predicament of Modern Man*. In that book was his phrase and warning that American was becoming a "cut-flower civilization," because then this land was moving away from the historic roots of the Judeo-Christian faith. If evangelicals and other Christian believers would have heeded his prophetic and true words in all its contextual applications, our nation/land would not be in the perils it is today. Christianity would not be decaffeinated; Christianity would still be salty as Jesus mandated.

Most readers can remember when Bobby McFerrin received the 1989 Grammy Award with his song, "Don't Worry, Be Happy." That cannot be the song of the church, because the song is mindless and the church has much to face. The church cannot sleep like Rip Van Winkle through the revolutions happening all around us.

The church no longer can allow David McKenna's indictment be true. He writes that Christians "have the ability to awaken late, rush pell-mell in the wrong direction, and arrive at our destination just after the meeting is adjourned."[46],This can no longer be true. This can no longer be allowed to continue! The church's task is too audacious and large to continue this way.

The church is not only commissioned to reconcile lost individuals but also bring a saving and transforming power of God to society and culture as a whole. Personal evangelism for the ministry of reconciliation of every person to Christ is vital, but John Whitehead issues a warning in the tendency for the church to "win souls and lose the battle for society."[47] Howard Snyder in *Wineskins* also writes that "evangelism . . . will not divide people into soul and body, caring for the one and condemning those who care for the other."[48]

It is all about world-view. This culture/society will have difficulty surviving many more years unless the church becomes active in the shaping and the reshaping of our culture/society. My friend and past Professor, Dr. James D. Strauss made a plea similar to this twenty-two years ago but few listened. The church had better listen now if we intend to leave any kind of legacy for which we can be proud to future generations.

Handles for The Battle

These truths must be kept in mind and put into action. Religion without conviction is shallow and worldly. Religion without compassion is rigid and inhumane. Conviction without compassion is spineless. In God's created order, the virtues of compassion and conviction are meant to link arms and stand together, both coming from the biblical combining of mind and heart.

Furthermore there are certain other dimensions that must be brought together by the singers of the Lord's Song to be able to be the salt and light of the land. They are like graduation requirements in five words for what it takes to be a salty singer.

Word one is conviction. Word two is courage. Conviction by itself is not sufficient. Word three is creativity which gets the conviction and courage out of the salt shaker into the market-place. Word four is competence. This rises above the mediocre and superficial. Word five is community which supports and corrects our discipleship in singing the Lord's Song. These requirements are much like what King David required of men who would serve him. In 1 *Chronicles* 12:23-38 David's warriors had to have courage, conviction, and competence, because that was an age of valor.

I would like to see another age of valor and victory resultant from the theistic/Christian world-view and the singing of the Lord's Song. To see this, we as an alien land will have to heed the words of Aleksandr I. Solzhenitsyn given in his Harvard Commencement Address in 1978. "If the world has not approached its end, it has reached a major watershed in history. . . . It will demand from us a spiritual blaze; . . . No one on earth has any other way left but — upward."

Governor Richard D. Lamm of the State of Colorado wrote *Mega-Traumas: America At The Year 2000*. It is a shrewd projection of mid-1980s trends as they seem likely to continue through the decade of the '90's into a new millennium. It is far from being science fiction.

In the book Lamm has certain government officials making speeches early in the year 2000. The content of the speeches is built around the results of the continued trends of the mid 1980s. The one speech that I draw from was a hypothetical speech made by the Secretary of the Treasury to the U. S. Chamber of

Commerce on April 15, 2000. One paragraph stands out, because it contains not only probable truths about certain mistakes but also contains the cycle that civilizations seem to have gone through in history.

> The United States made the mistake all great empires of history have made. We assumed it would last forever. We took our prosperity for granted, believing that God was on our side and would protect us from harm. We should have listened to the important words of a wise man who said, "Of the world's known civilizations, the majority have died. Not from the enemy activity, but from the decay from within, and the progression has always been the same: from bondage to spiritual faith, from spiritual faith to great courage, from great courage to liberty, from liberty to abundance, from abundance to apathy, from apathy to dependence from dependence, once again, into bondage."[49]

Where is the United States in the cycle? What world-view has the possibility to change the cycle for this nation? Will the church awaken in time? Does the Lord's people have the real sense of what legacies we as Americans are leaving our children and grandchildren? Do Christians have the ability, potential, and determination to begin acting now by thinking globally and really acting locally?

Ideas have consequences, therefore Part Five illustrates what results in the church and in some social parameters when the theistic/Christian world-view is not the dominant influential world-view.

Part Five: Particular Reflections From Crises

Ideas Do Have Consequences

Ideas do have consequences. They control life and societies for good or for bad. They do it through world-views.

To reflect upon and illustrate the results of alien world-views being the dominant influence in significant major social institutions or parameters of culture/society is a humbling and disturbing experience. When the theistic/Christian world-view is pulled out or rejected as the central dominating source of influence and power, or as the "central control box," unifying factor, and value system for all of life and culture/society, and alien world-views are the dominant influence, the results are critical.

The absence of the theistic/Christian world-view as the unifying factor in influence and power in culture/society reflects the needed and intended impact of Paul's words in Colossians 1:17: "He (Jesus) is before all things, and in him all things hold together." That is, Jesus Christ orders all things for a purpose.

But the removal of the theistic/Christian world-view's influence as a "central control box" or unifying factor has allowed culture wars to reposition the church onto the slippery slope in a position of social dislocation. This dislocation of the church has been present for a long time, and the church has refused to recognize the fact.

Only three of many major social institutions and parameters will be targeted revealing the absence of the theistic/Christian world-view. They are public education, the judicial system, journalism and the media. For the purpose of this book, I combine journalism and media as one unit. I will target only these three major social institutions for reflection, because it appears to me that these institutions and the world-view or views controlling them have the most power and greatest massive effect on our society. They are significant fields of conflict. Their world-view or eclectic of world-views become dominant in other lives, and we must be aware of and understand them.

There are other significant categories of life and society that could be targeted, but I will consider only these briefly: the family, medicine, a world in tyranny, and ethics/morals. These will suffice to give particular illustrative pictures that are the results from the crises in Part Four.

The echoing absence of the unifying factor of Christ (Col. 1:17) and the working power of the theistic/Christian world-view in the foregoing stated social institutions and other categories call for Paul's words in Colossians 1:17 that have already been stated. I do not think the Church as a whole is really aware of the importance of that biblical text and its meaning. It covers more than life's spiritual dimension.

The following material will not only reinforce what I have shared up to this point, but it will also raise Christian consciousness about the crises and results in our culture/society. The material will, I hope, encourage readers to bite the bullet and get involved in world-view thinking with the intention and hope of infiltrating and penetrating our culture/society with a song from the Lord (Psalm 137:4-5) that is true, always newer, and more productive than other world-views. This may appear to some a bold and brazen conviction, but I believe that there is no other world-view that works! It is America's last and only hope for real meaning to life and the healing of a fractured culture/society.

In this seductive society, the church riding the slippery slope must become subversive as salt and light in a correct and orderly manner to infiltrate, intensely and deeply, social parameters dominated by alien world-views that are fragmenting and frustrating life and culture/society. This subversive action is part of being God's spies in our modern Babylon, pagan society.

Prior to considering the reflections about social parameters, I must look again what Christians are—the church—the bride of

Christ. I must also reveal something called societal specialization and the resultant fragmentation of various spheres of society. This all relates to world-view concerns and the reflections to follow.

Why the church again? Because our own house has to be in order before we can really take on the world. Most of the church in America, including my heritage, is close to being impotent and ineffective in the social implications of the gospel of Christ. Millions are religious, but that is a far cry from being Christians in the marketplace.

The Church: Influence Waning Rapidly

The question has been raised: "How Does America Hear The Gospel?" (See chart in Appendix) Not very well is the answer, because the church at large does not understand world-view issues and trends. At the same time the influence of the church is rapidly waning. This fact has a direct relation to the illustrative material revealing the loss of the theistic/Christian world-view in various social institutions of our culture/society. The subversion of Christianity has been quite successful as Constantinian faith has helped "success put Christianity on a slippery slope" as Jacques Ellul so brilliantly writes.

> How has it come about that the development of Christianity and the church has given birth to a society, a civilization, a culture that are completely opposite to what we read in the Bible, to what is indisputably the text of the law, the prophets, Jesus and Paul? . . . There is not just deviation but radical and essential contradiction, or real subversion.[1]

Facing this problem is telling the truth about Christian culpability in a groaning creation. It is not what most in evangelicalism including my religious heritage wants to face. Far too many Christians are determined to avoid thinking about cultural-dominion responsibility, thus allowing alien world-views, particularly secular humanism and new age philosophy, determine our cultural/societal future. The church does not seem to understand that secular humanism (man is the center and measure of all life) full-blown leads to totalitarianism. It is like the phrase, "Everybody wants to go to heaven, but nobody wants to die."

We must be reminded that the outspokenness of the prophets of Israel concerning what was wrong with their world and their religious group is also part of the vocation of Christians to bear witness to the truth about the Gospel, the waning influence of the church, and the sickness of culture/society as we are able to perceive it by world-view analysis and trends awareness. Not to voice what we see happening in our midst is to serve the one whom Jesus called "the father of lies" (John 8:44). It is also as Dietrich Bonhoeffer said in a memorable essay on this subject, "Even a deliberate silence may constitute a lie . [2]

Truth is not comforting in matters as this, but it will be clear as we progress why I must consider the waning influence of the church.

> Indeed, if our paradigm for truth is the One who made the apparently audacious but ultimately humble claim that truth had been incarnated in his life (John 14;6), then we must suppose that the abode of truth is never far away from Golgatha and that those who point to it will not likely flourish. Not only governments, ancient and modern, but average citizens as well seem to have preferred comfort to truth from time immemorial. But what kind of comfort is it that is purchased at the expense of truth, functioning as an oily surface of civility over a sea of falsehood? "We go astray," writes Dorothee Solle, "if we separate consolation and truth and allow religion to console but forbid it to partake in truth. If the Church confines herself to consoling . . . and no longer regards herself as capable of truth, then she will be offering but shallow comfort, limited to the individual person and deferred to the beyond. . . . The Spirit of God will console only by illuminating truth, not by abandoning it.[3]

This is part of the prophetic tradition of truth-telling in the church. Therefore those who want to get to the bottom of issues in biblical terms must come to grips with their own weaknesses and perhaps feel the sting of divine judgement in the process.

Judgement begins at the household of God (1 Peter 4:17). Whether we like it or not, Christianity contributed in laying the foundation for the crises of our groaning creation. Involved was Guinness's "grave-digger thesis" that has already been introduced. But it is worthy of repetition. "Christianity contributed to the rise of the modern world; the modern world, in turn, has undermined Christianity; Christianity has become its own gravedigger."[4] This can be seen clearly in the following material.

It is a critical situation! Far too much of the modern church is rendered virtually impotent by compromise and sins in its hunger for success and size at the expense of not "making disciples". Today it is often difficult to distinguish between the church and the secular world. As Christians try to ape "secular sexology" by seeing sex not as the gift of God but only for personal fulfillment, it seems that some of the Christian community is often buying into secular ideas at the top of the idea's influence, and selling out Christian ideas just when they have no place to go but up. For instance, some secular psychologists rediscover such ideas as character, virtue, chastity, celibacy, and even virginity. These become hot topics in the marketplace just as the same ideas and values seem to partially fade out of Christian use. Are modern Christians in the marketplace afraid to be clearly marked by these values?

Richard J. Mouw, in his candid book *The God Who Commands*, is deeply concerned about the growing mindset in Christians who question the necessity of obeying the divine commands of God. Some who claim to be Christian are calling this "infantile" obedience which means that developed adults come to an equal status with God wherein His authority is no longer for adults. It is no wonder and no small concern that:

> The secular world is almost wholly unimpressed by the church today. There is widespread departure from Christian moral standards. So long as the church tolerates sin in itself and does not judge itself . . . and fails to manifest visibly the power of Jesus Christ to save from sin, it will never attract a world to Christ.[5]

That quote is not cause for comfort at all, but I have to agree with its accuracy. The world really is not impressed with the church unless you have something like a dog and pony show each Lord's Day morning. Virtually no inroads are being made into our pagan society. Society is becoming more and more secularized and pagan, stripping away the sacred in the midst of so-called church growth, much of which is evidently bypassing Kingdom building in people's lives. We are forced to admit that our culture/society of alien world-views is affecting the life-style and behavior of Christians more than we are changing culture/society. The church can hardly schedule any valid activity beyond Sunday morning that does not interfere with school activities, and so many Christian parents bow to the school before they bow to the Christ. George Gallup agreed with Stott. He wrote: "Why does Christianity appear to be on the decline in some areas of the world? One reason is that Christianity is not lived—Christians are not living in such a way as to draw others to them."[6]

How did this happen? What was the process? A lecture, "Can The West Be Converted?" by Dr. George Hunsberger, is the most succinct effort that I have ever acquired that reveals some of the process resulting in the waning influence of the church. This process has contributed to the crises reflections in this Part. Dr. Hunsberger's lecture will be significant in the next few pages. It is a masterpiece work for which I thank him and give him credit for some of my thoughts and quotes in some of the following.

The cultural context of the lecture does assist us in finding an agenda for the church now in a culture/society almost, if not, totally seduced by secularization. We must discover what it must mean for the church in our part of the Western world to be genuinely "missionary in the context of our own home culture."

Understanding this process involves culture, religion, and the gospel in the American life in the context of the implications of religion in general in American life being "repositioned". All of this is set in the context of the spreading of modernization, a most pervasive influence, that continues to drive religion more and more marginal, resulting in our culture/society becoming more and more resistant to the Gospel. Therefore the Western World is part of the most, if not the most, resistant society in the world to the Gospel.

In Part One I considered the definitions of culture which involved world-views, conceptions, perceptions, knowledge, moods, patterns of moral and aesthetic preferences, pictures of the way things are, ethos, and symbolic forms by means with which man can communicate, perpetuate, and develop their attitudes toward life.

I want to add to the previous consideration about culture by pointing out that culture is often put into one of two images. One image is that which is achieved as the highest expression of the arts, literature, philosophies of civilizations and characteristics of advance. It is like saying this about someone: "She is a person of culture."

This is what *Cultural Literacy* by E. D. Hirsch, Jr. partially considers; what every American needs to know. The other image is the collective behavior of a society formed by collective choices of a society. It is the mental maps underlying culture resulting in external behavior.

These two images can create one of two results. There can be nostalgia or frantic effort to regain any lost footholds. Both of these may cause us to miss a more urgent agenda which is to understand the way our culture/society thinks, does, and acts. Also our agenda must include how to interpret self and the Gospel within such a culture.

In the revealing process of understanding the waning influence of the church, we discover what has happened to religion in general and its influence. In the end we do have to move beyond culture and religion and attempt to "carve out a place and sense of gospel," but we must consider religion as to what has happened to its place in our part of the Western world. The church cannot live totally free of the way culture and religion in general shapes the place for the church. The fundamental question is: Is there any place really left for the church? If the answer is "yes," then how do we convince the contemporary post-post-Christian culture of this conviction? Only by world-view study and awareness in a one-on-one approach.

It is a time of critical markers. Peter F. Drucker writes of *The New Realities* meaning that perhaps as much as two decades ago (1965-1973) we entered the next century moving from "creeds, commitments, and alignments" that had shaped segments of culture/society for a century or perhaps for two centuries. Others are writing and speaking about hinge-points in our culture/society. Dr. Hunsberger stated at the 1990 Van Dyke Mission Lectures that we use to hear about "neo" this and "neo" that "in theology, politics, philosophies." Now we hear and read about "post" this and that: "post-Christian, post-Enlightenment, post-critical, even post-secular." It is the end of eras. It is beyond the end of eras. It is a post-post-world. It is the issue of wrestling and struggling about Christian belief in a post-modern and post-Christian world. As one person said to another in the movie, Flashback, "Once the 80s are over the 90s are going to make the 60s look like the 50s." All of this has caused much "dis-ease" in and out of the church.

There has been such a shift of religion in general as to its place in our part of the Western world plus its secularization, that we now have a major schism as Martin Marty calls it in culture/society wherein religion has not disappeared but has been "relocated." Christians and their institutions have been relegated to the private realm "yet permitted to a degree some monitoring, inspiring and legitimizing of the larger culture/society mostly through devotional intrusion rather than with real substance."

If we were doing an intense study of this we would detail the various stages starting perhaps as early as the 20s and 30s of the "disestablishment" of religion from the public to the private which in about the 60s flowered to a further pluralization further dividing the sacred from the secular. This resulted in stripping almost totally the sacred from the secular. This resulted in Neuhaus's "naked public square."

In the midst of this time gap from the 20s or 30s to the 60s we have the civil religion emerging in the 50s with "In God We Trust-One Nation Under God" with some meaning. Even politics were included in this, but that element of public relevance for private faith went away and eroded quickly. When the Supreme Court Justice Kennedy was installed, he reinforced this stripping away of the sacred from the secular even more by stating clearly that his faith was private and irrelevant to judicial authority. Think about that!

This has placed the church in the position of being relegated to only the private realm in regards to our corporate life and witness and our personal and corporate faith while at the same time living as a people of God among the secular, and subject to the force of the new legitimations made by the secular power block. The end result is the fractured fragmentations of life produced in a culture/society for which there is no whole overarching meaning to life as Paul's words in Colossians 1:17 states. These fractured fragmentations are running through the life of the church and its people as well. The public/private dichotomy is not just dividing the church from culture/society. It also lies within our corporate lives and within ourselves.

Therefore we arrive at some implications of the shift in religion in general in our effort to understand the Gospel in relation to the American life. If religion in general has been privatized and mostly excluded from providing the legitimation for the social order of life, it is equally true that most in the Christian church have scarcely noticed it. If they have noticed it, they shrug it off hoping it will go away. It won't! They continue to live as if the alliance of the 50s was still in force. In this conviction, "the style of its life, spread of its programs and sound of its pronouncements continues on the assumption that the church's place has not fundamentally changed. Weakened perhaps but in need of only fine-tuning and increased efforts."

Christians in this stance are lulled by reports that just as many Americans believe in God today as there were fifty years ago. That is not impressive, because the issue has always been, what are they doing about Jesus as Lord in a total lifestyle? They seem to be unaware that belief in the supernatural may be formally affirmed while there is no sense of any operative relevance of the supernatural in life. Of course they do sense something is just not right in business-as-usual church patterns of life. Something is amiss. They seem to realize that, because somehow the life of the church is experiencing not "internal combustion but internal exhaustion." A certain malaise and "disease" of restlessness is "annoying the organism at its core."

Programs proliferate, new strategies abound, some people seem to keep coming back, but there is a severe lack of focus. "The ship is rudderless and we have somehow lost our grip, the loss of the privileged position to provide ultimate legitimation for the social order is at the heart of this drift." We come to the crisis point in the life of the church of which the "symptoms of malaise, exhaustion, and strain are assigned."

A most critical need of the church is to realize the way our place in culture/society has been restructured and acknowledge that it is the new reality in which we will have to live and in which we are called to witness.

We have been accustomed to seeing the church in our culture/society as sort of hand in glove but not always real sure "which is the hand and which is the glove." We have believed that our life in the church and our participation in the American way of life are part of the same cloth. We have viewed them as companion realities. The place the church inhabited in the cultural structure of things kept it distinct from political power but included it as the provider of moral influence and conscience for the exercise of that power. But "that alliance is over. The strains in the life of the church are the results of our insistence to the contrary."

What is the answer? I shall illustrate it in this manner. Some optometrists ask a patient to look at a little circle on the wall and then ask them to tell the Doctor when the circle splits into two circles. That exercise is done several times. The point is that even before the eyes saw the circle split into two images, the dot or circle at which one's eyes are looking is splitting apart. What happens is that the eyes keep adjusting and following the dots in such a manner to see them as one. But at the time of strain the single dot would divide and become two. It was dividing before it appeared to do so, but for a time the eyes refused to see it that way. How far would the eyes go before yielding to the strain admitting there were two dots and not one.

The church in North America is in the place of that strain clinging to a vision of culture/church as one, but these have been separated. The break point is here and we need to let loose and see that they are two separated dimensions of society wherein the culture/society is affecting the church more than the church is affecting culture/society. It is, as Dr. Hunsberger spoke in a "Gospel And Our Culture Network" Consultation, "cutting the Christendom knot," because "it is precisely this Christendom hangover which thwarts the recovery of the church's missionary identity in North America."

"Then we can rediscover who we are in the new arrangement and what it is our mission has to do and say." The breaking point in which the church finds itself right now is something like the following, entitled, "Sense of Something Coming."

> I am like a flag in the center of open space. I sense ahead the wind which is coming and must live it through while the things of the world do not move.
> The doors still close softly and the chimneys are still full of silence. The windows do not rattle yet and the dust still lies down. I already know the storm and I am as troubled as the sea.
> I leap out and fall back and throw myself out and am absolutely alone in the great storm.[7]

An Irony To The Waning Influence

The irony and message is related to the continuing 90s production of numerous significant books concerned about and related to possible causes of the waning influence of the church as we race toward a new century.

There is Hunter's *Culture Wars* (1991). This is about the struggle to define America and hopefully make sense of "the battles over the family, art, education, law, and politics." William Bennett's *The De-Valuing of America* (1992) is about "the fight for our culture and our children . . . in the midst of a struggle over whose values will prevail in America."

Chandler's *Racing Toward 2001* (1992) is about "the forces shaping America's religious future." It is a powerful handbook showing the results of what happens when so many different world-views battle for the mind of modern man. He covers a wide spectrum of major social parameters. His bibliography presents continued 90s material related to his topic and my book's purpose. The bibliography is impressive and essential for the more technical study of world-views and trends awareness.

One of the most essential, more technical, publications for those who really want to take on the world is *Wild Hope* (1991) by Sine. This is "a rallying call to take charge and live creatively in a changing world." It is about the "crises facing the human community on the threshold of the 21st Century." As Jimmy Carter wrote: " . . . an important book for all people of faith."

Power Religion (1992) edited by Michael Horton, the author of *The Agony of Deceit* is a collection of essays by James M. Boice, D. A. Carson, Chuck Colson, Alister McGrath, J. I. Packer, Key Myers, R. C. Sproul, Kim Riddlebarger and others. This is the thesis of the book. In a lot of ways the contemporary evangelical church is playing "me too" with the world's idea of power. We have up-to-date psychology (the self-esteem movement), sociology (the church growth impetus), and even politics (both the Christian Right and Left) The question posed is this: Have we gone too far? The essays argue that, when the evangelical church replaces its unique message with power religion, it sacrifices both biblical fidelity and public credibility.

Consumer Church (1992) by Shelley and Shelley builds around two leading questions revealing the book's purpose. "Can Evangelicals win the world without losing their souls." And, "Are we risking false advertising if we offer people the power and benefits of Christ without the costs of following him?"

This is only a sampling of significant books concerned about the church's waning influence continuing to pour forth in the 90s.

The message? The battle of world-views fighting for the mind and heart of modern man, spewing forth values effecting man and culture/society in the midst of the waning influence of the church is heating up.

But here comes the irony of it all. As the influence of the church wanes and books of warning continue to surface, *Rediscovery The Sacred*, perspectives on religion in contemporary society by Wuthnow (1992), appears. This "rediscovery" is not considered to be a biblical revival that literally transforms people and the surrounding culture/society. It is a restlessness to "rediscover the sacred in contemporary society."

The chapter titles are full of clues as to man's emptiness on the search for more than the modern world void of the theistic/Christian world-view offers and perhaps the church is not thought to have much to offer at the present. The chapter titles—"Sacredness and Everyday Life," "The Cultural Dimension," "Religious Discourse as Public Rhetoric," "Perspectives on Religious Evolution," "The Shifting Location of Public Religion." The "rediscovering the sacred" is about "reflections on the social dimensions of this quest." This latest book by Wuthnow relates to his, *The Struggle for America's Soul* (1990). The title reveals the subject matter.

The irony of it all is that the search for "rediscovering the sacred" is going on almost as if the church is not even aware of the lack of the sacred in life and every social parameter of culture/society. This causes a question. As the church's influence wanes, and as the 90s books concerned about what has happened, what is happening, and what will continue to happen in the context of a weakened and unaware church that ignores world-view issues and trends situation spewing forth destructive mindsets and values, will the church realize the irony?

Now I can begin to reflect and illustrate results of crises in the stormy time in which the church lives and attempts to witness in a land of alien world-views.

The two following sections—Societal Specialization and Society's Spheres Fragmented—illustrate not only how significant spheres of our lives and society have become through time so fragmented, but they also give a picture of how major social institutions and parameters of culture/society operate independently of one another each with their own world-view. If certain social institutions and parameters operating independently happen to have the same world-view other than the theistic/Christian world-view, they still do not have the unifying factor, values, and purpose to give man and society a healthy direction and purpose, because there is only one world-view that can do that. That is the theistic/Christian world-view. Not only have significant spheres of life and society been fragmented as stated figures will picture, but also social institutions and parameters are all going their individual direction alone. This makes understanding all of this an integral part of the witness mandate to "make disciples."

Societal Specialization

Of all the studies done on the Church, church growth methodology, and church leadership, there have been none as helpful and significant as two books by Kennon L. Callahan. They are *Twelve Keys To An Effective Church*, and *Effective Church Leadership*. It is the latter that builds on the twelve keys from which I draw the above heading in relation to the current fracture and fragmentations in the social institutions and parameters of our culture/society. It is from this that we will begin to understand what happens to significant spheres of life and society, various social institutions and social parameters when the theistic/Christian world-view is withdrawn from the center of life and society as the dominant influence, the "central control box," or unifying factor for such.

This complex issue is about a search for hope; it is about

helping pastors lead their people to be better able to sing the Lord's songs in this alien and foreign land of our own culture/society. It is about what Callahan says concerning the pastorate today: "The day of the professional minister is over. The day of the missionary pastor has come"[8] meaning that the church resides in the midst of one of the greatest mission fields in the world: the United States and the entire North American continent including the present church membership.

> The missionary pastor helps people envision the realization of some (not all) of their deepest longings, yearnings, and hopes in the present and the immediate future. The task is not so much a matter of dragging people into the present out of a past to which they are clinging and clutching. The task is more to help them discover some sense of a stable and reliable future.[9]

"Societal specialization is the emerging trend of our time that reflects a profound search for hope."[10] It is a process in which the culture/society increases the range of options available to people for their future. To illustrate this, Callahan lists what he calls spheres of our life and culture/society. His list is family, education, vocational/economic, political, civic/community, recreational, and religious. It is the search for hope that drives this "ground swell" trend of societal specializations. The situation is this. Our culture/society is specializing in delivering more options for the future of its people.

There is a given consideration that entails the value of this acceleration of possibilities. The value is providing more options for people in all of the spheres of culture/society. "As people exercise the options that best live out their gifts and competencies, they are then able to feel a sense of fulfillment of some of their deepest yearnings, longings, and hopes. They are able to create a reasonably stable and reliable future."[11]

But are these options of possibilities a reinforcement of our radical individualism in a time when people need community as well as the privilege of working out their life in various options that will no doubt give some satisfaction? And are there some unfavorable consequences in the context of the need of a positive dominant world-view being able to hold all of these options into a meaningful whole? To answer these questions, we must consider some unfavorable consequences of society's fragmented spheres.

Society's Spheres Fragmented

One clear consequence of "societal specialization" is the compartmentalizing of culture/society into separate, yet distinct, spheres that has the subsequent alienation of each sphere from the others. This is somewhat like the circle illustration (Figure 1-The Appendix). But we will use the sphere approach here.

The various spheres of culture/society used by Callahan—family, educational, economic, political, social, recreational, and religious—become cut off from one another. We will follow these consequences through in what he calls stages (See Appendix for Figures 2-9).

Prior to our modern complex world the Stage One diagram (Figure 2) illustrates the relationship of the several spheres or parameters of society. Reflecting back to the frontier, the family unit, separated geographically perhaps by days from the other nearest family, attempted to fulfill all spheres of culture/society.

As history happened and our nation developed with increased population density, a more distinctive set of relationships surfaced in terms of societal spheres. This is Callahan's Stage Two (Figure 3). In this stage we see there is now a school doing part of the teaching that at one time had been done totally at home. The issue is not whether this is good or bad. The issue is the fragmentation of life's spheres setting in. Also emerging from Stage One are distinct political and social spheres.

As this trend continued, various other spheres became separated even further from one another. What commenced like a single entity in Stage One became more like a "solar system" in Stage Two and then a "galaxy" in Stage Three (Figure 4) and finally seven virtually "separate galaxies" in Stage Four (Figure

5). In these there is very little "communication, interaction, overlap, or interchange"[12] among them.

So what? This compartmentalizing of these spheres results in alienation and the various compartments/spheres attempt to function apart from one another. Each sphere operates as though it were the whole. Strong competition sets in, and each sphere seeks to claim the full-time loyalty, energy, and development of the whole culture/society and the whole person. This is like the fallacy of calling a university by that name today. There was once a time when universities were made up of colleges and had a major centering purpose in life such as one world-view undergirding all the studies of all of the colleges. That has all gone by the wayside, so we really do not have universities. We have colleges on the campuses with a plurality of world-views competing for students' time and energies. The battle for the minds of students continues. There is fragmentation, fractures, and alienation with no unifying factor as Paul's words clearly states in Colossians 1:17.

To illustrate the horror and possible destructive outcomes of having these seven distinct galaxies acting independently of one another a question is: what can happen if they all have a different world-view than the other spheres? Put medicine in one sphere and technology in another sphere. If either of their world-view is void of ethics, if the value of human life or a basis of truth about life and reality in either of the two fields of study and action is different, what can be the results? They both can play God and not even agree on that and decide who dies and who lives how, when, and where.

The consequences of "societal specialization" has not ended. "The further consequence of societal specialization is fragmentation and dehumanization" wherein persons within culture/society experience this consequence and although they "really seek to be whole persons, they begin to internalize the compartmentalization they see in the culture."[13] What results from all of this is The Fragmented Self (Figure 6). As a person trapped in this continues to internalize this fragmentation from compartmentalization, the more he or she senses alienation with the self and the dehumanization of self.

> The foundational search for individuality is a search to be a "whole person." The search for community is a search to belong as a whole person in a whole community. Experiencing fragmentation, however, the person feels less human. To be human is to be whole. To be compartmentalized and fragmented is to experience dehumanization.[14]

Next is the third consequence of "societal specialization." It is the isolation of the church from the rest of culture/society. "The church becomes the ghetto where God lives."[15] Ghetto does not mean in this context a "slum." It means something separate from, totally distinct and isolated. When we unpack that, it is frightening to realize how much hold this has on so much of the modern conservative church in America as members use rhetoric that betrays them: words such as the worship center being the "sanctuary." Wherein biblically the sanctuary of God is the person who is in Christ. That is just one illustration of this ghetto-type rhetoric. There is also the use of "soul-winning" which is nothing but Gnostic dualism of which the Word of God knows nothing. (I have already unpacked the misfortunate use of the term "soul-winning" in a previous Part.) Yet too much of the evangelical church structures so much around these misleading and non-biblical concepts that keep God in the stained-glass ghettos.

As the different spheres of the culture/society become separate entities, each becomes preoccupied with its own direction and future, growth and development, resources and needs while most cannot yet understand what is happening in this alien paganistic land controlled by eclectic world-views. Hence "the ghettoization (isolation, separation) of the culture moves forward."[16]

The sphere of religion is left to itself. Some are delighted with this, because it is a protection from getting involved in washing away the dirt of this world as they protect the church from the world's contamination. They have always wanted this kind of "miniculture" inside the religious sphere. This picture is found in "The Isolated Religious Sphere" (Figure 7). In this kind of isolation most all of life would be lived inside the safety and security of the church. But God did not call the church into existence for that at all. The church is to be in the center of people's lives, but not just be the center of their lives.

There is another side to this issue. Others who recognize Callahan's "ghettoization" of the church often take another approach. They clearly see the compartmentalization, fragmentation, alienation, and dehumanization. But their proposal is not to withdraw from the world into religious hideout or sphere. They wish to declare the "religious sphere" as the most important, that is, the highest of all spheres. That is noble, but one ends up with "The Hierarchical Religious Sphere" (Figure 8).

This is the problem with both of these proposals. The first denies the world, evidently forgetting that a text does not say that God so loved the church. They need to remember that the text declares, "For God so loved the world." The second proposal denies the church, for when the church is "master" it is no longer church. The church is the servant, not master. "The church is called to mission, not mastery." The church is to be in the world and not above it. The church is not called as an end in itself, but to help people discover their fulfillment in the text that has the punctuation mark to change the world (John 10:10).

Therefore a pastor's central task as a missionary pastor is to help people find the theistic/Christian world-view for the center of their life and have the church as the center for the entire culture/society tying all of life's parameters together by drawing people to the Christ and then sending them on His behalf into the marketplace. It looks like "The Wholistic Religious Sphere" (Figure 9).

This is the process of building bridges in all spheres of culture/society very similar to Figure 1. It is not easy. It will not become any easier as we plummet towards the next century.

The small amount of material presented to this point can

start raising the consciousness of Christians in the evangelical world which includes my heritage if they want that to happen. As has already been stated, so many of these Christians in the evangelical world including my heritage are so steeped in allowing the Greek, Platonic, gnostic dualism form their theology that they think Christ died to save some kind of an immaterial soul instead of being crucified for the redeeming and reconciling of the mortal whole ("nephesh"-Old Testament and "psuche"-New Testament) person. This dualism has bred an insensitivity to the terrible destructive social issues and parameters of society that leads many people, who have no understanding of Christianity, to believe that the Christian has little to do with anything that is not "spiritual".

Every Social Institution Affected By The Crises

In the context of this tough challenge for the church, God's spies attempting to prepare to sing the Lord's song in this alien land (Ps. 137:4-5), I could reflect and illustrate at much greater length than I will about what has happened to just three key and major social institutions or parameters of our culture/society. The results of life-transformation by Jesus' power in the theistic/Christian world-view is not the dominant influential value system in those social spheres.

The reason for targeting public education, the judicial system, and journalism to reflect upon is that I believe these three major institutions have impacted, and are impacting, modern man as much, if not a lot more, than any other major social institutions and spheres of our culture/society.

These three powerful institutions have arrived at their fragmented and present dangerous existence, because the theistic/Christian world-view has been rejected, ignored, or bypassed in the thinking of those who control them. They are controlled by alien world-views and as "societal specialization" have moved the entire society into fragmented and separated spheres so these social institutions are contributing to that fragmentation.

It is only when the theistic/Christian world-view becomes the stronger influence in the center of all spheres of life and society (Figure 1), can the world become more safe, sane, sensible and wholistically healthy with meaning and purposeful direction for life and culture/society.

My reflections on these three major social institutions as fields of conflict are brief but I would hope sufficient to encourage God's people to study the materials available (Bibliography) about the problems in these three major institutions. Expanded studies would reveal how I have arrived at my conclusions about these three institutions plus the other significant categories of life and culture/society in this Part.

Public Education: A Shambles

Public Education! What does this have to do with world-view, the church, and Christianity? The question will be answered commencing with the insightfulness of Hunter in *Culture Wars*.

> Education is meaningful territory not because of its formal charge to pass on the basic skills and socially relevant knowledge necessary for adolescents and young adults to eventually participate responsibility in society. Rather, education is strategic in the culture war because this is the central institution of modern life through which the larger social order is reproduced. Together, the curriculum, the textbook literature, and even the social activities of the school convey powerful symbols about the meaning of American life—the character of its past, the challenges of the present, and its future agenda. . . . Public education is especially significant territory in this regard, primarily because it reflects the will and power of the state vis-a-vis the nation's public culture.[17]

What if the State is controlled by a world-view or world-views diametrically opposed to the theistic/Christian world-view? That is the situation now! There is a governmental philosophical mindset straight out of our nation's continued growth of secularization called "statism." But "statism" can never function under God. It supplants the church, and most of the church does not know this, or if it does, silence is the church's reply to the bondage. Now the situation could be labeled as statism-one nation over God.

Prior to his death, Dr. Francis Schaeffer replied in an interview that his greatest concern for America's future was "statism." That controls public education now. Therefore "statism" in the public school system controls and owns the children of America, including the children of Christian parents. There is a direct connection between the terrible failure of this nation's public education and the secularization of this nation.

It has been almost a decade since Americans began to hear warnings about public education. It was in 1983 that the National Commission on Excellence in Education presented a "Nation At Risk."

This is old information, but I find few Christians, including Christian parents other than those with whom I work, who understand the issues and who seem to want to really get involved in the dangerous public educational situation.

One would think, that in this time of unprecedented religious activity wearing Christian labels in the midst of the rapid growth of the mega-church mindset, there would begin to be some pretty strong penetration of 'saltiness' and a rather bright 'light' of true Truth glowing out from the church and getting into all of these social parameters. We would hope that particularly in public education that is certainly doing its share of *The De-valuing of America* in "the fight for our culture and our children," there would be some Christian influence working. But that is not happening. Secularism has been winning battle after battle while the church continues to raise the walls which isolate it from the culture/society. To the victor goes the minds and hearts of tomorrow's leaders.

It is a massive world-view issue that will not be solved by only larger church bodies. Not at all. There has to be some grace-filled power coming out of the church sifting into these social needs.

It appears that most, including Christians, believe pouring more money into the educational system along with the continual building of magnificent facilities will remedy the shambles of public education. It will not. "The fundamental problem," William Bennet writes in the foregoing title, "with American education today is not lack of money; we do not underspend, we underproduce." One hundred and fifty studies reveals "no correlation between spending and educational achievement." Over the past few years a "fourfold increase in spending has brought no improvement."[18] Why would it when skills instead of building a life is taught.

The issues related to the system and power of public education is larger than the students getting a good education by modern standards. The need is to help youth develop life-building values that enhance life. That is not happening, because the struggle in American education is far greater than a battle to end functional and cultural illiteracy, even though it is estimated that we have 24 million functionally illiterate people in this nation who have been through the educational system. Now we are being told that the same system, costing millions and millions of dollars, is turning out an estimated two million or more functional illiterates yearly. Now we also have "creative spelling" wherein the students are not corrected for misspelled words. That is all serious enough. But the war is between religious, traditional values and the secular, modernist values that oppose the Judaeo-Christian values. The war is going on even in mid-America labeled "the heartland."

Secularism is unified on the conviction that "traditional values" have got to go. This is how far some will go to accomplish the burial of "traditional values." In 1970, Theodore Sizer, dean of the Harvard School of Education and his wife, Nancy, produced a book entitled *Moral Education*. They claimed that every author in their anthology insisted that there was no place left in this nation's new schools for "the old morality." They believe, actually believe, that this "old morality" is our problem and moral relativity is the only solution. The following indicates just how far some will go to destroy "traditional values." In 1973 a Harvard University professor of educational psychiatry said this to a teachers' seminar.

> Every child in America entering school at the age of five is mentally ill, because he comes to school with certain allegiances toward our founding fathers, toward our elected officials, toward his parents, toward a belief in the supernatural entity. It's up to you teachers to make all of these sick children well by creating the international children of the future.[19]

We are surrounded on all sides by the wreckage of our great intellectual and spiritual tradition. In this kind of spiritual chaos, neither freedom nor order is possible. Instead of freedom, we have the all-engulfing whirl of pleasure and power. Instead of order, we have the jungle wilderness or normlessness and self-indulgence.

The world-view issue is: there is a world-view battle going on for the minds of the youth in this nation, but most of the church just allows it to continue. One does not have to have a high I.Q. to know what world-views are winning the battle. It is not the theistic/Christian world-view. The challenge is even more serious than what follows; a portion of the document, "A Nation At Risk."

> Our nation is at risk. Our once unchallenged pre-eminence in commerce, industry, science and technological innovation is being overtaken by competitors throughout the world . . . .
> The educational foundations of our society are presently being eroded by a rising tide of mediocrity that threatens our very future as a nation and a people. What was unimaginable a generation ago has begun to occur - others are matching and surpassing our educational attainment.
> If an unfriendly foreign power had attempted to impose on America the mediocre educational performance that exists today, we might well have viewed it as an act of war. . . . We have, in effect, been committing an act of unthinking, unilateral educational disarmament.[20]

Albert Shanker, head of the American Federation of Teachers, was quoted in the Wall Street Journal, August 23, 1990: "Ninety-five percent of the kids who go to college in the United States would not be admitted anywhere else in the world." To him that is how bad public education still is after years of attempted but futile reform.

Reflecting so briefly on the shambles of public education in the context of this book's purpose is an effort intended to get people to go beyond just regurgitating what many have already heard or read. The need and purpose for Christians is to look at public education in the context of the relation or non-relation of the theistic/Christian world-view to public education. Christians must also understand the results and how they come about when this singular and distinct world-view is not allowed or even considered as an alternative value system to study and consider in the midst of hostile alien world-views/value systems allowed and *promoted* in the system of public education.

That is a bottom-line issue: The imperative and just need of allowing the theistic/Christian world-view be considered as an alternative world-view in the midst of the secular, atheistic humanistic world-view and other non-theistic related values being perpetrated in the public system in what many public educators call "value-free" or "value-neutral" education. But neither of these in education is a possibility. Everything taught has values, yet the most committed Christian parents miss or ignore that mythological effort in their local schools. I can illustrate that locally.

Our local school Superintendent is a fine person deeply committed to public education, and has some relation to the Roman Catholic faith. How much and how deeply, that I do not know. In an interview about public education in the local system, he stated that:

> Public school systems are attempting to do what the church and family are failing to do, and so a big part of the problem of education is that educators have become responsible for teaching children moral values as well as teaching them read-

ing, writing and arithmetic skills. . . . Fifteen years ago, the church and family took care of teaching values, teaching enabling skills and teaching proper manners. A five—or six-year—old child came to school prepared to learn subjects, not additional values.

I have no significant arguments with the foregoing. I might question a small portion of his thinking, but his remedy won't work any more than anyone else's when it comes to "value-free" education. In the context of "values," Dr. Skurka said that "teaching values to children is not done from a sectarian base but rather, from a practical secular base." But that is "sectarian," and the community never seemed to grasp that. What he stated is not at all value-neutral. A secular base is a world-view, and that in itself ought to allow other world-views be taught as alternatives to see which, if there is one, world-view has the answers to the basic questions of life already considered in another Part of the book.

Dr. Skurka continued by saying, "We are not looking for controversy. We are teaching children the basic tenets and principles upon what the United States was founded, and on what essentially prepares them for good citizenship: integrity and respect and regard for others."[21] My question would be: how is this done from a purely secular base unless the theistic/Christian world-view is passed over as some of "the basic tenets and peinciples" of the founding fathers? Even this approach has "values," but what kind?

The crisis in public education can be partially pictured when an attempted value-neutrality in the system is tried. Such a concept is an impossibility. Anything that is taught, perceived, and assimilated into life has a value to it that can either enhance or be destructive of and to life. The fact is, there is no such thing as value-neutral education. Someone's values emerge. The Rutherford Institute continually battle the public education system in the system's effort to force children to buy into values that they and their parents do not believe.

It is no secret that the American Humanist Association from

1933 to the present time targets public education as their pulpit to change young lives and control the system by their values that are diametrically opposed to the Christian world-view. And federally funded "Values Clarifications" courses is the religion allowed by the government to carry out the Humanist's goals.

"Values Clarification" may be the most serious factor in the American educational crises. This philosophy from an alien world-view has been stripping away vestiges of moral absolutes which undergirded the unheard of prosperity of early America. This movement is controlled by people whose approach to morality is morality without content. That is, a person sets up their own morality. But how wrong they are, for without a moral point of reference of a world-view from a Word from outside such as the theistic/Christian world-view for a unifying factor, the entire educational system has abandoned the only working base for moral literacy.

"Values Clarification" courses open the door to all other relativistic values as equal, and lead right into the contemporary idiocy of educators believing that to teach "safe sex" will stop the malignant "Aids" epidemic. It is about world-views. Will Christians ever speak up and ask for equal time? The system will say this cannot be allowed because of the "church and state" issue, but that is also untrue. Most Christians have accepted the misrepresentation of the "church and state" issue.

"Values clarification" in secular education center on inviting impressionable children and young people to make a choice among options without any consideration of absolute truth and absolute values beyond man's self-imposed and self-determined values. Is lying acceptable? Is stealing permissible? Should premarital sex be approved? Well, "it depends." Situations differ. If young people have "clarified" their own value system and have chosen to do or not to do these things, education has been achieved.

Kenneth Gangel offers a valuable analogy of this bizarre program and a word-picture of the strange people who promote it. If this analogy does not open eyes, nothing will.

The contemporary values-clarification movement is a bit like giving teenagers a driver's license without a handbook or training, placing them in a car and telling them, "Anything you do on the freeway is okay, just as long as you understand why you're doing it. The important thing is that you have made the decisions." The destructive result of such a philosophy would create automotive lunacy on the highways. On the moral highway of life, values clarification is educational lunacy.[22]

The foregoing would be the same for any so-called "Value-Free" education principles that come only from man. All of this contains symptoms of something being seriously wrong. The issue at stake is what value systems are behind the symptoms. We have read or heard these symptoms before.

In 1940 the top offenses in public schools were: (1) talking, (2) chewing gum, (3) making noise, (4) running in the halls, (5) getting out of turn in line, (6) wearing improper clothing, (7) not putting paper in wastebaskets. In a little over forty years, things had changed: (1) rape, (2) robbery, (3) assault, (4) burglary, (5) arson, (6) bombings, (7) murder, (8) suicide, (9) absenteeism, (10) vandalism, (11) extortion, (12) drug abuse, (13) alcohol, (14) gang warfare, (15) pregnancies, (16) abortions, and (17) venereal disease became the top offenses.

When the foregoing is combined with the plummeting of test scores revealing continuing problems of public education we can understand Barbara Walters standing before a huge American flag looking sternly into the TV camera saying, "The alarm has sounded. The clock is ticking, but most of us are still asleep." Was this related to some nuclear war? Not at all. It was related to so-called value-neutral public education.

Walters continued: "Today's high-school seniors live in a world of misplaced values," masses of which have no sense of discipline, goals, and meaning for living. They are following the wrong absolutes and they care only for themselves with a cry for rights without responsibilities. In short, she continued, they are "becoming a generation of undisciplined cultural barbarians." The barbarianism is not the result of just low academic scores.

Barbarianism comes out of destructive values about life.

Why would anyone be surprised at her blunt assessment? After all, much modern education could not logically be expected to produce anything else, especially when "tolerant" and so-called "value-neutral" education purports to teach not one set of values and does in fact promote a value system and worldview of its own. This system is destructive to the moral restraints essential to the character and life of students and culture/society. Is this an accident or something carefully planned and executed by other value systems? The issue is much larger than the forementioned symptoms.

How much attention has been given by most educators to this conviction? What have many educators bought into that has pushed the theistic/Christian world-view out of the ball park of education, and how did this happen in a nation with church buildings all over and supposedly fifty to eighty million born-again Christians?

The January-February 1983 issue of *The Humanist* journal of the American Humanist Association justified an article written by a twenty-nine year old honor graduate of the University of Illinois. It was entitled, "A Religion for A New Age." He wrote:

> The Bible is not merely another book, an outmoded and archaic book, or even an extremely influential book; it has been and remains an extremely dangerous book. It and the various Christian churches which are parasitic upon it have been directly responsible for most of the wars, persecutions, and outrages which humankind has perpetuated upon itself over the past two thousand years. I am convinced that the battle for humankind's future must be waged and won in the public classroom by teachers who correctly perceive their role as the proselytizers of a new faith: a religion of humanity that recognizes and respects what theologians call divinity in every human being. These teachers must embody the same dedication as the most rabid fundamentalist preachers, for they will be ministers of another sort, utilizing classroom

instead of pulpit to convey humanist values in whatever subject they teach, regardless of the educational level. . . . The classroom must and will become an arena of conflict between the old and the new—the rotting corpse of Christianity, together with all its adjacent evils and misery, and the new faith of humanism, resplendent in its promise of a world in which the never-realized Christian ideal of 'love thy neighbor' will finally be received.[23]

This new religion is alive and well in public education. Is it value-neutral? Is this new religion accomplishing the utopian ideal set out in the article? Hardly. Then is it not time, as Ronald Nash has suggested, to begin to question the minds of families who turn the education of their children over to people with the foregoing mindset who might have felt very comfortable teaching "values-clarification" to "the guards in the Nazi death camps?"

If American parents, particularly Christian parents, do not do this, then the legacy of John Dewey will continue in all its power. He combined relativism, secularism, and atheistic humanism into a philosophy of education that totally opposes anything like the theistic/Christian world-view which promotes a living God and one's faith in God's supernatural power to transform life.

There is also this assumption that dominates public education today. It is the ideology that says there is no final knowledge about anything. Surely Christians understand this to be totally opposite of the theistic/Christian world-view. Or don't they care?

Unless all of this philosophy of Dewey and "Values Clarification" is challenged by Christians, it will continue to be the philosophical training of public educational workers and teachers in our colleges and universities. This mindset will rush like a flood into local school systems and on into the millions of youth who will continue to attempt life and living on a false educational philosophy that has already failed over and over. For the most part, these coming out of the colleges and universities are decent people, but they have bought into institutionalized socialism, secularism, and moral relativity and are passing all this on into millions of young lives even though that philosophy has not worked and will not work. It only continues to produce carnal wreckage of human lives.

I have to wonder why such a large number of those coming out of the colleges and universities with this alien, untrue, and unworkable educational philosophy and also teach it, send their own children to private schools in a percentage much higher than the general population.

In all fairness to the system, I have to lay much of the blame for problems in public education at the feet of parents including far too many so-called Christian parents. There is also the deteriorating family situations even within the church that has to be held responsible for our serious youth culture problems that leak out in American education. Masses of problems in public education are fostered right there, and when the youth are thrust into the public systems that say they are value free—which is not possible—anything goes.

All of the foregoing intellectual mindset so foreign to the Christian mindset has come out of three intellectual movements that are contributors to the cause of the crisis in education. The church has not seemed to be too bothered or concerned about this philosophical "stuff", and all the time the world is crumbling all around it because of not taking these issues seriously. These movements are threats to Russel Kirk's "permanent things": relativism, positivism and secularism (the secular humanist naturalistic mind). Relativism says that everything is relative and that there is no truth or absolute Truth. Positivism believes the only truth is that which can be measured by a mathematical formula or tested in a laboratory. Secularism believes that man is the center and measure of all truth and things. God really has nothing to do with life for the secularist. "Our public schools, "wrote the president of the Catholic League, "have become 'mission schools of Secularism.'"[24]

The massive amount of material that could be presented in

this segment on public education would definitely reveal what Dr. George Roche, Educator and President of Hillsdale College, a great liberal arts college, says about most public education: "American Schooling: The Training of Anti-Heroes." That is his indictment. It is so. A "hero" is one who lives by "Thy will be done," who believes that we are responsible to God with a life of "heroism" structured by "obedience to Moral Law despite all pain and peril." These trained "anti-heroes" will be part of the cause of the "disintegration of the West" according to Robert Maynard Hutchins, who believes:

> If the object of education is the improvement of man, then any system of education that is without values is a contradiction in terms. A system that seeks bad values is bad. A system that denies the existence of values denies the possibility of education. Relativism, scientism, skepticism and anti-intellectualism, the four horseman of the philosophical apocalypse, have produced that chaos in education which will end in the disintegration of the West.[25]

I refer again to Albert Shanker, President of the American Federation of Teachers, who said, "Education holds our society together only as long as what is taught has value and is important. You can't teach reading with comic books and rock-star magazines and expect kids to be be educated."[26]

We read with fear and concern in 1983 the report card on public education called, "A Nation At Risk," from the National Commission on Excellence in Education. What might be the report card on American education from the Secretary of Education in June 2000? Governor Richard D. Lamm forces us to consider a hypothetical report on this in his book *Mega-Traumas: American At the Year 2000.*

I think it is clear enough what the report card will be unless there is a radical turn around caused by a world-view at the center of this nation which has the ability and power to unify not only education, but the entire social structure of this society. You see, world-view studies are mandated by the Great Commission, because there is no way to take Christ into the marketplace of all social parameters unless we know what controls that particular segment of the social structure.

Lamm says in his hypothetical report card on education: "The year 2000 finds America with a second-rate educational system turning out second-rate students. The educational decline in our nation is truly the new American tragedy."[27]

Mortimer Adler, philosopher, educator, and architect of the *Great Books* series, has spent decades fighting battles in secular academic settings by the rules of logic and philosophy. In this era of history most would not expect such a renowned twentieth-century philosopher to be friendly to orthodox Christianity. But in 1984 he became a Christian and has moved beyond big ideas to faith's mysteries adding "some theological arrows to his quiver."

He was interviewed by a *Christianity Today* writer. He said much in the short interview and in a sermon the interviewer heard him preach at Grace Episcopal Church in Chicago, a small south-side parish of about 40 people of different race, class, and social-structure. What Adler shared relates very much to the need in public education.

On scientists he said:

> Scientists have exceeded their bounds. They are theologically naive. But that doesn't seem to stop them from talking about beginnings and endings. The beginning wasn't a Big Bang and the end won't be a Final Freeze. But don't try telling a scientist that. . . . Scientists barge in where angels fear to tread.

On the mood of the country: "Anti-intellectual." On academics: "Hopeless." Why? For all of his life,

> Adler has written, taught, and lectured on a central, classical truth: There is one, absolute unity of truth, and the philosopher's job is to discover and define it so the good life can be known to all. Now, when Adler sees scientists, scholars, and even the man-on-the-street claim that truth is merely relative,

that all individuals shop for it themselves and create their own recipe, with a pinch of culture, a dash of ethnicity, and a smidgen of serendipity, Adler sees red. Perhaps it is just this foundational presupposition—the conviction that a single truth exists—that has attracted orthodox Christians to him.

It does not take a whole lot of imagination of the tremendous change that could come into public education if that "classical truth" was taught as a world-view and then have public school teachers mandated to teach many world-views, letting the students decide which one has stood the tests of time and history and answers basic questions to life and living. This could be done if we just had some school boards and administrators who had a little courage to be honest and equal to all. I understand that is what liberal (not theological or political liberalism) classical education is all about.

Even the church, including much of my heritage, needs to really come to grips with truth and get off the idea that all truth is positive when much truth is negative. To teach that the Christian faith is always positive is to create a monster in the church that operates only on how one feels about issues and life, and they think that is biblical. Most Christians evidently have not read the Psalms of lament lately.

I share more broadsides from Adler; quivers revealing his grasp of the world-view of Christianity desperately needed in education at all levels. From his sermon: "We (Christians) have a logical consistent faith. In fact, I believe Christianity is the only logical, consistent faith in the world. But there are elements to it that can only be described as mystery."

Adler shoots off other quivers. One is the sovereignty of God: "In the beginning, the scientists forgot about God. Now when they realize he must be there, they're trying to remake him in their own image." Another quiver is the truth of Christianity: "A property of true religion is to be evangelical. When I hear the term evangelical, . . . I think about the mission. Christianity is the only world religion that is evangelical in the sense of sharing good news with others. Islam converts by force; Buddhism, without the benefits of a theology; Hinduism doesn't even try."

Adler won't talk about his conversion, but he does say: "My chief reason for choosing Christianity was because the mysteries are incomprehensible. What's the point of revelation if we could figure it out ourselves? If it were wholly comprehensible then it would be just another philosophy."

With these and other insights Adler faces the future with hope: "I'm pessimistic about the future in the short run. We won't get over relativism in 10 or even 20 years. But in the long run, by the middle of the next century, I'm convinced we can get philosophy and education back on track."[28]

I state at this point that I am pro-public education. This position may become more difficult to retain in the future. It is becoming more difficult for many parents. Private religious education is an "increasingly viable alternative to public education" and much pressure is increasing for these advocates to "support their indirect funding through a policy of government vouchers and/or tuition tax credits."[29]

Nevertheless I am an encourager to those Christians who are teaching and administering in this social institution of our culture/society. I encourage them to see this as their vocation and ministry and not just their avocation of earning a living.

They are in the ministry if Jesus is the Lord of their life. Whether they realize it or not the State has given them a mission field. In 1990 Charlotte Wheat wrote a fantastic and thought-provoking article for the *Christian Standard* entitled: "Would You Go To This Mission Field?" It was one of the better and more important articles for the year.

> Talk about a harvest. Talk about a field that is ready. I know of a mission field that is unbelievable. The need is desperate. Perhaps you have not heard of it or are not aware of its existence, because many calls for missionaries have been neglected and shunned. This field is only for those who are tough, courageous, and filled with the power of Christ. The obstacles are numerous. . . . There are tremendous advantages to this mission field. . . . You will be paid to work on this mis-

sion field by the government officials. . . . A great advantage for this mission field is that you can go home every night. . . . This mission field is not for the squeamish, faint-hearted, weak-kneed pansies. Whether you serve in public or private schools, you will need the wisdom of Solomon, the love of Jesus, and the patience of Job. You could go. Even more important, would you go? See you in the field.[30]

I like her last sentence! All Christians need her kind of attitude and mindset and then get involved insisting that the local schools be honest and present all world-views about life to the students and let the one that stands above all other world-views be its own defense. But there is almost no world-view studies being done in the local congregations, therefore even the most committed disciple of Christ could not talk and promote, intelligently and with reason, to public education Administrators or School Boards without coming off with only knee-jerk reactions.

This must be remembered. In this confrontation with public education it is the system that is being confronted and not the excellent teachers who care. Parents must assist good teachers by demanding that the system be honest with our children and remind them daily that public education is not neutral in what it teaches. This could open the door to the system presenting all major world-views and the results in life when each world-view is followed. Is that too much to hope for or to confront the system about? The system is not neutral and Christians need to say so.

In the confrontation, Christians will meet a most powerful lobby in Washington, D.C.: the NEA (National Educational Association). It is a *Trojan Horse* that is by and large diametrically opposed to the Judaeo-Christian world-view. The NEA uses its money and power on behalf of goals that reflect its secular and far-left political ideology. Some of the largest education interests increasingly align themselves with the political philosophy of the left by taking up with the NEA believing that educational problems, like most other social issues, will be solved in Washington, D.C.

The NEA has been called an "educational Mafia," by W. A.

John Johnson, Editor of the *Daily News Digest*. It "captured the high ground of American public education in the late 1800s. But the real and often hidden agenda is different. This group:

> has deliberately steered the public schools, its teachers and children down a disaster road to socialism, secular humanism, radicalism, planned failure in reading and writing, suffocation of Christianity, the trashing of basic values and the establishment of one of the most powerful and dangerous unions...[31]

Because of the guiding effects of the NEA philosophy, "many of our schools lost their focus, their confidence, and a clear sense of mission,"[32] writes William Bennett. Just think, if the theistic/Christian world-view could be taught as an alternative world-view along with all kinds of world-views in some kind of a social-studies course, "focus," "confidence" and "a clear sense of mission" about life and culture/society would be discovered by students. This could be done without preaching or proclamation. The theistic/Christian world-view does not have to be defended. It stands on its own merit as my illustrated study of world-views through a grid of questions reveals. Does the public system of education know that? Absolutely! But that system does not want truth. That system has been telling youth for several generations now that there is no truth.

Here is one analysis of the NEA materials. "It includes the delegitimizing of all authority save the state, the degradation of traditional morality, and the encouragement of citizens in general and children in particular to despise the rules and customs that make their society a functional democracy."[33]

In a confrontation that "horse" will kick and fight Christianity, the theistic/Christian world-view, to the finish. Their goal is to control the licensing and certification of teachers and to influence the election of politicians who will support their secular-humanistic philosophies with more and more federal funding.

But John Silber, brilliant and out-spoken President of Boston University, insists that money is not the answer. What the theistic/Christians world-view stands for is the answer from Silber's perspective. "If we are to recapture . . . wisdom" of solid homes, trained and properly educated children in virtues, ethics, responsibilities, etc., then "we must go back to the copybooks and primers of the eighteenth and nineteenth century"[34] insists this President of that prestigious University. He does not mean literally their textbooks but the subject matter in them about "reality" which is God. For Silber it is a return to Kipling's 1919 poem titled: "The Gods of the Copybook Headings."

Surely God's people are stronger in a proper way than any "horse" like the NEA. I guess not. But perhaps this question from Robert Coles, Harvard psychiatrist, gives Christians encouragement: "Are students really better off with the theories of psychologists than with the hard thoughts of Jeremiah and Jesus?"[35] That kind of thinking coming out of Harvard has to give the Christian some hope and desire, doesn't it, to infiltrate the system controlled by the kicking "horse?"

William J. Bennett, past Secretary of Education under President Reagan, insists in a collection of essays and speeches that there are "The Three C's" of public education that must be added to the three R's. They are "content, character, and choice."

"Content" has to do with knowing the difference from good education between ambition and greed. Content is about history, reading, writing, literature and other significant academics. This is a world-view issue.

When he completes his thoughts on "character" it is clear that he is talking and writing about a moral literacy that can only be provided by the theistic/Christian world-view. He ties in "character" with "Religious Belief and The Constitutional Order." He comes down hard on the Supreme Court as a major culprit causing this breakdown of "character" in the public education system.

"Choice" is a tension-filled issue today, but the desire for this is growing as good parents realize that what is, by and large, being taught in public education is not "value-free,"[36] and the values being taught are contributing to the development of the "barbarians" mentioned by Barbara Walters.

All of this is a world-view issue about what happens when the theistic/Christian world-view is not the dominant influence in this major social institution and parameter. Which world-view is in desperate need in public education? What world-view is needed to be presented as an alternative world-view in the midst of hostile alien world-views?

Albert Shankler says: "We are not talking about cheerleading. We are talking about thinking, about understanding our ideals, about knowing our past - the unfortunate and the evil as well as the good. That is not indoctrination. That is education in the best sense of the word."[37] What world-view has, over the years, given us ideals that have stood the storms of life of which most youth in public education have never heard? I am not at all sure that most youth in the conservative church really know about these proven ideals. Unless Christians are prepared to dialogue about this with the non-neutral educational system the issue of "A Nation At Risk" will continue and increase in danger.

Public Education—A Shambles! The future of public education in America is at a crisis! Christianity's retreat from education has left a legacy that included the creation of a public school monopolized system controlled by secularist, a resultant moral chaos, and generations of functionally illiterate people. Christians must care about public education! They have been free with their criticism as I have, and it has failed in many ways. Public education has been viewed by advocates of Christian schools as a system beyond redemption. That is not true. Christians should be deeply concerned about public schools. Even if "choice" becomes a better option for those who can afford it, the vast majority of America's children will be educated in our present system. Therefore the opportunities and large frightening challenges have never been greater for Christians to support, encourage, and influence public-school administrators and educators. This can be done only by knowing the Christian world-view and the alien world-views in the public school system and then being able to dialogue, suggest, and illustrate which world-view can salvage young life not by force, but by dialogue with the present system. There can be an alternative approach to public education by teaching many world-views and let each person decide. Christianity can stand the testing in this kind of approach. The other world-views cannot.

What follows asks the key question and also reveals the mixed and confused signals of public education at the present.

> Who's Values? Don Boys, former Indiana legislator, director of Common Sense for Today, writes: "Can you believe it? The same public schools that produced 'a nation at risk' through indulgence, incompetence and ineptness have volunteered to fight the AIDS virus! Let's see; they can't teach the kids to read, compute, and find Miami on a map, but they can teach AIDS education . . . of course, the missionaries of AIDS education will tell us that the teaching will be value-neutral. But fools know that no education is neutral. Perverts are telling kids it's wrong to be homophobic but not wrong to be homosexual. . . 'Ah, you Christians want Bible values taught to little children,' say the fanatics of the American Civil Liberties Union and People for the American Way. Right, Pilgrim: We want all children taught kindness, honesty, love, purity, faithfulness, sexual restraint, compassion, sincerity, gentleness and principled living. . . One thing is sure: Someone's values will be taught. And if I'm paying the bill, I don't want my values denied, denigrated or denounced. AIDS educators will teach school children the depraved, depressing, dangerous, and deadly "joys" of sodomy (in fact, it's already being done.) All such preachers of perversion and permissiveness should be fired and an attempt made to restore the shame, humiliation and social ostracism that follows all sexual immorality (However, I'm not demanding a scarlet letter)." USA TODAY 9/10/90)[38]

Public Education—A Shambles! All of this is about worldviews and the imperative need of Christians to know world-views—their's and other's—and enter into the fray of the fragmented system with a Word of Truth and hope. It is time for Christians to not be defeated, but keep a sense of hope and even some humor, and begin to show some "pluckiness" to our calling.

From a spokesman for the National Association of Christian Educators come these insightful words.

> . . . there is a great war waged in America—but not on the battlefield of conventional weapons. This battle is for the heart and mind and the soul of every man, woman, and especially child in America . . . . The combatants are "secular humanism" and "Christianity." Atheism, in the cloak of an acceptable "humanitarian" religious philosophy, has been subtly introduced into the traditional Christian American Culture through the public school system. The battle is for the minds of our youth.[39]

Dr. John Steven, former President of Johns Hopkin University surely raised the eyebrows in academia with these words.

> The biggest failing in higher education today is that we fall short in exposing students to values. We don't really provide a value framework to young people who more and more are searching for it.
>
> Without a value system, it is going to be very difficult to maintain high standards in the society—the failure to rally around a set of values means that universities are turning out potentially highly skilled barbarians: people who are very expert in the laboratory, or at the computer, or in surgery, or in the law court, but have no real understanding of their society.[40]

These values from "higher education" filter down and out into public education for younger children. The battle over the nation's future will continue to take place in the classroom, from kindergarten through graduate school, and conservatives have yet to mount an effective takeover of a major university. It is a serious world-view issue. The Milligan College logo is still correct and essential. "Christian Education, The Hope of The World." This "hope" must counter political correctness, multiculturalism, and generism in public education in order to get education on the road back to sanity.

Judicial System—In Danger

This brief (a judicial term) concerning the dangerous condition and crisis of the judicial system of America is built around two questions plus a certain conviction. This also relates to the significance of the theistic/Christian world-view serving as the unifying factor for judicial law as it must in other social institutions and parameters of life if they are to survive for the welfare of the human race. The brief unfolds as follows.

Part One: There are two initial questions: "How Does Law Call Moral Shots Today?" and "What World-View Influences and Strongly Controls Present Law Or The Judicial System?" The short answer to both is: The world-view that appears to carry the most weight in controlling the judicial system and present law today is secular humanism which has pushed God to the marginal edge of life and institutions. Therefore this makes man the center and measure of all life and society. Man becomes the law-maker and law-giver, therefore from that perspective the Law calls the moral shots. God is out of the picture.

How this happened is very important, yet difficult to unfold in such a brief manner. The unfolding is not what I would prefer to do in the present brief. But I believe only by the big picture being briefly unfolded can the person in the pew, who has the responsibility as a Christian to bring Christ back into the marketplace of the judicial system the same as He must be brought into every social structure and parameter of our culture/society, be able to do so.

The unfolding of the stated answers to the initial questions commences with the conviction that God is pro-life. In the context of this conviction I use the issue of abortion as a watershed factor to lead us into understanding what Dr. James Strauss calls "the tale of two nations": Germany and the United States in a time span of approximately forty years. This issue is related to a phrase used by Dr. Carl F. H. Henry: a "nation in decision . . . at a fateful crossroads. [41]

The abortion issue must never be forgotten or ignored. The issue of abortion is a denial of God as Creator and Giver of life. Yet worldwide some resources insist that at least 55 million unborn children are killed murdered every year. That is 150,685 ever day 6,278 every hour and 105 every minute. Those are the reported cases in 1990. 1.5 million of those abortions each year happens in a nation that has an inscription about God on its coins. Legalized abortion did not suddenly come center stage in the American drama of life. It is another symptom of a much greater evil in our country—the rejection of God as the Creator and Giver of all life. The issue of abortion is not new as George Grant brilliantly writes in *Third Time Around.*

It has been a silent revolution that is still happening. It is a war between incompatible world-views. One world-view places God at the center of the cosmic universe with man as His special creation to serve Him. In this value system human life is sacred, because it is created in the image of God. Other world-views move from this and put man at the center of life and the cosmic universe. Man alone becomes the measure of life's meaning and values.

Here then is the "tale of two nations". Forty plus years ago Americans were morally incensed about what Hitler did to six million, more or less, Jews and others. But what Americans were morally incensed about then—taking human lives—is now considered morally right by the masses, because it—abortion—is legal according to the Supreme Court of this nation. How can this be? What changed not only in the law but in people's attitudes about life? Therefore, we enter into the second and largest part of the brief.

Part Two: The two preceding initial questions, ("How Does The Law Call Moral Shots Today?" and "What World-View Influences and Strongly Controls Present Law Or The Judicial System?") to which short answers have been given, thrust us into another major question: "What Has Transpired To Allow The Law To Call Moral Shots?" allowing man to become the law-giver in America?

The short answer to the questions above as to what has transpired is that a powerful non-theistic world-view and other alien world-views have taken over replacing the theistic/Christian world-view. We are a nation wherein many are practicing a strange kind of law in lawless times.

Therefore abortion became a water-shed issue which can

lead, if it has not already, to other serious issues relating to the devaluing of human life. America has become a pagan society. The notion that we are really God's favorite people, and we just need to clean up our act is a terrible illusion. Our larger problem is not just the Supreme Court and not just improper sex education in the public schools. The problem is that we live in a pagan society that's covered with a veneer of manufactured niceness. The veneer is cracking.

The present world-view of secular humanism as the dominate world-view in the judicial system also poses threats to religious freedom in the context of the recent resurrection of the Tort Law that can make a conversion experience a crime. A "tort" defined "as a private or civil wrong or injury independent of contract" involves many areas of attack against Christianity. This one illustrative area will suffice to disturb. There is "tort" liability for "brainwashing, coercive persuasion, or mind control." J. Shelby Sharp, attorney, assists our understanding of "tort" in this manner.

> Second Corinthians 10:5 teaches that "every thought" is to be taken "captive to the obedience of Christ." Repentance which is essential to eternal salvation is by a change of mind and heart. When an unbeliever recognizes his or her true condition, emotional distress is usually experienced followed by a change of behavior as a result of the presence of the Holy Spirit coming to dwell in the new believer. This whole process satisfies all of the elements of the tort of brainwashing, coercive persuasion or mind control.

Mr. Sharpe, an expert on "tort" law, also warns that "while civil government has primarily concentrated on trying to keep Christianity out of the public areas of our nation, the "tort" suit is aimed within the four walls of the church to obtain money judgement for conduct considered detrimental to our society. This goes to the very heart of Christian ministry."[42] There is going to be a rapidly changing liability of the church unless "tort" is checked by integrity of the judicial system. Thousands of churches may be experience the "deep-pocket" result of

231

"tort." This experience fills the pockets of unethical and greedy attorney's pockets.

The issue of money leads to a parallel between lawyers today and priests before the Reformation. The power of priests to extract money from their flock was a major source of resentment years ago, and the power that lawyers have to extract money from clients creates similar sore spots.

A partial result of "tort" laws is that American society is trapped in litigation and the god of greed in the judicial system is very much alive. The growing number of attorneys is revealing the power of greed. It is estimated that the total number of attorneys in Japan is smaller than the number graduating from American law schools each year. The projection for America is to have one million attorneys by the year 2000—one attorney for every 250 plus people.

I return to abortion as the water-shed issue to illustrate the result in the shift of thinking and values as Law fails to relate to the Christian faith as a world-view for all of life in societal structure and parameters.

To assist in answering the major basic question at the beginning of this Part of the brief ("What Has Transpired To Allow The Law To Call Moral Shots?"), William A. Stanmeyer, Professor of Law with a prestigious track-record in teaching and involvement wrote: "Our Supreme Court, along with the lower federal courts, has been a major cause of the divorce between law and national policy on one hand, and perennial natural truths and biblical principles on the other."[43]

He believes that the roots of the process of deChristianization are deep with much of it happening only since World War II. Consider how rapidly that has taken place. Social issues in this process that have changed radically since that war involves family in society, what laws should give the family protection, the place of religion (Judaeo-Christian) as a wellspring of policy, and questions of public morality versus private choice in such controverted matters as abortion and pornography. Stanmeyer gives this charge: "Christians had better understand how the system of judicial review has contributed to these charges."[44] Dr. Lynn Buzzard wrote in *Holy Disobedience* that "the law itself is in crisis as to its nature, character, and source."[45]

A major source of the contemporary judicial crisis is that present values and beliefs of much of the judicial system are clashing with something that most lay people have never been made aware of, yet, we have taken it for granted without realizing it. It is this. "From ancient Greek philosophy through western Christendom the conviction has been that law and religion were intertwined and that law, to be valid must express the will of God."[46]

Law that was not in accord with God's will was not considered law. William Blackstone was the source and influence of much of the educational curriculum for attorneys of past years, and his curriculum held to the foregoing convictions. He also said: "The law of nature . . . dictated by God himself . . . is binding in all countries at all times; no human laws are of any validity if contrary to this."[47] That is a far cry from today, for law is based on other convictions. Therefore we have a conflict of values and a crisis in law. In view of the preceding parts of this book, I believe anyone can see where this conflict leads in church/state relations, ethics, morality, life values, etc. The clash of the conflict appears to grow louder.

In this context Dr. Buzzard maintains that: "Law is too important to be left to lawyers." In *With Liberty and Justice* he elaborates on this and the crisis in contemporary law. He is intense about the situation.

This crisis in law emerges from the collapse of our central Judaeo-Christian beliefs and the moral commitments to them in our Western civilization. From this crisis comes attitudes and world-view convictions whereby God has little, if anything, to do with life. Therefore such statements as were made by Supreme Court Justice Burger comes forth quite easy. "We are the Supreme Court," he said, "and we can do anything we want."[48] Perhaps you need to read that again. Man as power is then in the judge's seat, and God as the source of right and justice is ignored. God is out! This is why Harold Berman, attorney, suggests that the Western legal tradition is in a very deep crisis.

> The Western legal tradition, like Western civilization as a whole, is undergoing in the twentieth century a crisis greater than it has ever known before. What is the crisis? It is clearly not that we do not have legal institutions or laws. It is something more basic. Law has lost its authority, its roots.[49]

All of this is the result of the shift in historical thinking, a shift that rejected the theistic/Christian world-view as the source of all law. I show this shift with one illustration of what happened from the eighteenth century up to the present.

William Blackstone, an English law professor and renowned eighteenth-century jurist, played the leading role in forming a Christian presuppositional base for early American law. He embodied the tenets of Judaeo-Christian theism in his *Commentaries on The Laws of England*. They were so popular that more copies were sold in America than in all England. In the first century of American independence they constituted all there was of the law. God was the source of all law for Blackstone and those who followed him. But starting in the late 1700s a student of Blackstone began to challenge him and by 1870 the Dean of Harvard Law School brought in Darwinian thought to legal education that contributed to the revolution of destruction to the judicial system. The fact that Blackstone is not studied in law schools today, according to resources, most likely stems from his belief that all law commences with God.

This creates, perhaps, the biggest problem we have in relation to law. The problem is that there is no consensus or set of common values that informs the law anymore. In the formative period of American law, to which Blackstone contributed much, the Judaeo-Christian tradition and value system shaped and informed the law. Now, that is not the case.

This shift brought in sociological law that presupposes no

absolutes outside of man exist upon which law or laws can be based. Law is seen as evolutionary in character and is based upon arbitrary man-made absolutes. Law becomes that which is politically controlled, the danger about which Robert H. Bork wrote after his rejection by the Washington power-brokers in becoming a judge in the Supreme Court.

Sociological law was carried forth more into our historical era where man is devalued more and more. Oliver Wendell Holmes (1902-1932) reflects man devalued by saying:

> I see no reason for attributing to man a significance different in kind from that which belongs to a baboon or a grain of sand. I believe that our personality is a cosmic ganglion, just as when certain rays meet and cross there is a white light at the meeting point, but the rays go on after the meeting as they did before, so when certain other streams of history cross at the meeting point, the cosmic ganglion can frame a syllogism or wag its tail.[50]

Surely any concerned Christian can begin to see why we in America are living in confused times and are also living on borrowed spiritual capital as to values about life and its purpose. The logical conclusion of man's significance being no greater than a "baboon or grain of sand" found its expression in the Supreme Court's decision in Roe vs. Wade which upheld the right to abortion on demand. The unborn child as a non-person has little significance to the Supreme Court. Will that change by the end of this century?

Having rejected the Judaeo-Christian heritage, the courts have replaced law with politics. The only absolute that remains in the system of sociological law is the insistence that there is no absolute other than man or his system. The Christian base has been pushed aside because of its insistence on God-ordained absolutes. This perspective is that law no longer reflects truth, nor does it necessarily conform to higher law. Instead, law is a social process, and law is a reflection of what is going on in society. It is in process, evolutionary. It is positivism.

Positivism is the belief that law is no more than the will of a Sovereign (Man or God?), and "rights" no more than a concession by the Sovereign (Man or God?), or federal government. Positivism is made for reasons of convenience, but with no basis of belief in the natural order or the will of God. It becomes the foundational world-view for utilitarian laws that are based on the greatest good of the greatest number, calculated largely in terms of pleasure or pain irregardless of whether something is right or wrong by a higher law such as the basis for truth from God. Positivism was the world-view for the Supreme Court Roe v. Wade in 1973.

Therefore we have a world-view centering on man and a pragmatism that controls modern law, devalues man, and replaces God. This issues such watershed crises in human life as the abortion mentality. The Supreme Court is "A Law unto Themselves," and a question is, "Is Religion Whatever The Supreme Court Says?" since man is calling the moral shots? That appears to be the case.

Consider this question in view of what we have just confronted. What if some man-made court system law starts making laws about overpopulation based upon a utilitarian ethic and the calculus of convenience? Who plays God in that? Man! That is the crassness of the utilitarianism concept with abortion, mercy-killing, and euthanasia being promoted along the way. Therefore Stanmeyer has an urgent warning:

> Here is the secular humanist vision of Almighty Man, eating the forbidden fruit of egotistical rejection of any Rulemaking outside himself; man building his tower to the heavens with a base spreading antiseptically from sea to shining sea; man pursuing personal convenience and economic advantage; doctors and mothers "free" to follow the spirit of the World, regardless of the teachings of scripture, history, philosophy or even modern science.[51]

He also believes that:

> The next decade (1990s) will be a watershed for Christians. The nation can commit only so many abortions. It can tolerate

only so much divorce, sexual permissiveness, and pornography. The secularization of the schools and the erosion of family life can go only so far. At some point, the nation will either recoil from what it has done, or seek to go all the way—to erase from its laws and finally from its collective memory any vestiges of the Christian perspective.[52]

Dr. Lynn Buzzard, attorney, sees too many parallels between what has happened and is happening in the judicial system with what happened in Germany forty plus years ago. What is morally wrong from the Christian perspective is legally allowed by man's law. The German people, most of whom claimed to be Christian, allowed "truth" from God's absolute truth to shift to relativistic absolute truth in whatever man or men who were in control.

The Judicial System is in danger! William Bentley Ball, attorney, said in "Religious Liberty in 1984: Perils and Promises."

> The devastating testimony of Aleksandr Solzhenitsyn, C. S. Lewis, Francis Schaeffer, and so many others tells us that our society is not only dangerously ill, but actually dangerous. And our peril is not merely what Christian lawyers find in those lumps and lesions in our jurisprudence. What's wrong is a deeper and worse cancer—society's rejection of God.[53]

That is the bottom-line issue in the crisis of the judicial system in America. Those in the system may believe God privately, but they will not allow that to influence their decisions, because another world-view is in control of this nation and much of the judicial system.

Can this be changed? Of course, but it's up to Christians to do so. It is possible that the faces of the Supreme Court are changing to allow this to happen. Only time will tell. But this does not mean that Christians can relax. There is much to do in the way of bringing back the influence of the church in these matters. It can be done!

Christians must think more carefully about politics and government and jurisprudence which is a philosophy of law. Most of the Evangelical movement in this country has never even vaguely considered this. Most of the movement is too busy building institutions called "church" that are filled with non-converted people. There are too many Christians who think that all we need to do is stop a few Supreme Court decisions, get *Penthouse* out of convenience stores, and we'll be back to good ol' Christian America.

The issue is so much larger than that. When a nation loses its fundamental sense of values, it does not get "less" law, it gets "more" law. When you lose big law, you do not get "no" law, you get "more' law. When you do not have any fundamental values from outside man to give guidance and upon which to build all of life and society from a larger-than-man consensus, then someone has to make the rules. But you can't write enough rules because people keep thinking up new situations.

The only remedy is the theistic/Christian world-view returned to this pagan and alien land, because we cannot write enough rules and laws to keep a society from self-destructing. Only the dominating influence from the theistic/Christian world-view can reverse the crisis of our present judicial system.

How much longer will the church allow culture/society reposition it by judicial power out of the center of culture/society onto the slippery slope? Hunter, in *Culture Wars*, maintains:

> The depth of the current cultural conflict in conjunction with the tremendous ambiguity that characterizes church and state law can only mean that there will be more and more litigation—for such litigation will force the courts to clarify its position. In all likelihood, that act of "clarification" will result in the advancement of the interests of one side of the new cultural divide and the diminishment of the interests of the other.[54]

Some reasons that contributed to the systematic removal of Christianity from expression in public life wherein litigation is out of hand are as follows. First, the rise and power of secularism (man is in-God is out) has brought about an increase in hostility towards Christianity and God's supernatural power. Second, the courts are a place for those intolerant of Christianity or anything religious that looks like Christianity (some hate God with a passion) to attempt indirectly what they cannot do and are too cowardly to do openly and directly: attack the belief in the Creator God to whom we are all accountable. Third, the out-of-control litigious nature of our culture/society has prompted people to file lawsuits against anyone for the most trivial, silly, and greed-controlled matters.

Journalism/Media— The Prodigal Press

This is not an exercise in media bashing. But as in the reflections on public education and the judicial system, I present what happens to the press/journalism/media when the influence of the theistic/Christian world-view is pulled out. Journalism/media becomes what Marvin Olasky labels the *Prodigal Press*, an excellent expose to help reveal the present challenges and needs in journalism/media. I am indebted to him for his efforts.

The visible results as to values and mindsets that pour forth from the media appear to be for many Americans and Christians a major cause of the world-views and value systems that are destructive to our culture/society. This social institution is believed to be "responsible for the dissolution of fundamental American values."[55] But have Christians considered the possibility that the media is just reflecting these destructive values, and perhaps the church along with the media/press is also part of the major decadent problem in America? I have to believe that it is.

Olasky gives this picture of "departure" into the decline of American journalism and what he calls the "prodigal" press.

American journalism is one of Christianity's prodigal sons. Until the mid-nineteenth century American journalism was Christian. But ...journalists influenced by anti-Christian humanism and pantheism abandoned their Christian heritage and ended up wallowing among the pigs. The situation is not completely analogous because the Biblical prodigal son soon was starving, while prodigal reporters of the present are well-fed. But in spirit, the living death is parallel.

The flight of the prodigal press has been hard on American Christians because journalism has departed in spirit but not in physical presence. The prodigal frequently files reports full of hatred for Christianity. Many Christians have responded angrily. Just as church-bashing is a favorite sport among some reporters, so media-bashing is the pastime of many Christians. . . . (However) there are ways for Christians to reclaim American journalism.[56]

What happened to journalism, and why have Christians failed to know about the shift into the prodigal state? Studies by Paul Vitz of New York University and other sources have revealed that the majority of textbooks in the American school system go to great lengths to omit and avoid reference to the part religion (Christianity) played in early American history. Likewise standard journalism history texts provide the same distortion. A most used textbook deals with the 1800-1833 era of American journalism without ever mentioning the "Christian world-view that characterized many major American newspapers and magazines." Presswatchers noted: "Of all the reading of the people three-fourths is religious," and "of all the issues of the press three-fourth are theological, ethical and devotional. " During that era (1830) the New York *Christian Advocate* had the largest circulation in the country and the Boston *Recorder* had the second largest circulation in that city.

Other textbooks do not mention that New York City had fifty-two magazines and newspapers that called themselves Christian, and that from 1825 to 1845 over one hundred cities and towns had Christian newspapers. The facts are irrefutable: "In the early nineteenth century, American journalism often was Christian journalism."[57]

Newspapers then covered everything from neighborhood problems to foreign affairs. Christian papers never restricted themselves to just Church activities. The circulation success of the Boston *Recorder* came from gaining "the attention of the public" but also "stirred up the minds of Christians to duty." What is realized now through discovering the truth is that "Christian newspapers through the mid-nineteenth century attempted to provide a Biblical worldview on all aspects of life." For instance:

> One Ohio newspaper declared in 1858 that the Christian newspaper should be a provider of not "merely religious intelligence, but a newspaper, complete in every department of general news, yet upon a religious, instead of a political or literary basis." Another, the *Northwestern Christian Advocate,* proclaimed in 1860, "Let theology, law, medicine, politics, literature, art, science, commerce, trade, architecture, agriculture—in line, all questions which concern and secure the welfare of the people—be freely discussed and treated, and this, too, for God, for Jesus Christ, and the advancement of the Redeemer's kingdom among men.

Many early journalist did not fail to show an awareness of how the Word of God uses bad news to show man the wages of sin in order to prepare people for understanding the necessity of the Good News. "The journalists knew that general statements about man's corruption were far less gripping than coverage with specific detail of the results of sin and misery."[58]

As a transition into the "Sunset for Christian Journalism" and the reasons for it, there is some revealing information about the great Christian newspaper: *The New York Times.* Harvard, Yale, and other great universities founded by Christians are now by and large preaching and endorsing either an atheistic or a watered-down gospel. So the story of the great newspapers can be told in the same way. *The New York Times* is one of these.

This newspaper was founded in 1871 by Henry Raymond who was a Bible-believing Presbyterian. It became known for its accurate reporting of news and for exposing political corruption and such issues as abortion practices. It is interesting that one can find the political exposing in history books, yet the abortion stories are ignored. But this issue of abortion being reported had long-range impact revealing how significant Christian journalism could and can be.

Abortion in New York City was rampant in the 1840s-1860s even though it was officially illegal. The *Times* editorials claimed that "perpetuation of infant murder . . . is rank and smells to heaven," but little was done about it until a story with the headline, "The Evil of the Age" hit the paper as the result of persistent investigative reporting by Augustus St. Clair of which Olasky writes:

> The story began on a solemn note: "Thousands of human beings are murdered before they have seen the light of this world, and thousands upon thousands more adults are irremediably robbed in constitution, health, and happiness." St. Clair then skillfully contrasted powerlessness and power. He described the back of the abortionist's office: "Human flesh, supposed to have been the remains of infants, was found in barrels of lime and acids undergoing decomposition." He described the affluence of a typical abortionist: "The parlors are spacious, and contain all the decorations, upholstery, cabinetware, piano, book case, etc., that is found in a respectable home.

St. Clair, as an able reporter for the *Times* on the abortion issue, continued searching, researching, investigating, and reporting on the seriousness of the issue. He listed key abortionists by name. He noted their political alignments and from this abortionists began to talk to him revealing much about the kind of people who went to the abortionist. Some of the finest women in the city were brought to the abortionists by politicians. You can read between the lines here. The reporter concluded his story with a call for change. "The facts herein set forth are but a fraction of a greater mass that cannot be published with propriety. Certainly enough is here to arouse the general public sentiment to the necessity of taking some decided and affectual action."[59]

Public interest and concern was aroused, but there was still a need to further galvanize readers into action. Providentially, for the effort against abortion being put forth, St. Clair exposed a true horror story of a young woman whose death had been caused by abortion. The story headline was: "A Terrible Mystery." For several days the brutal gruesomeness of this story was played out in the *Times*. It was the final tool to arouse action in New York City, and the abortionist involved in the young lady's tragic death was convicted and sentenced to seven years in prison. That is a far cry from what happens to abortionists today simply because the Supreme Court has made the murdering of babies legal.

This was not sufficient to stop the abortion business, because only a change of mind and heart in any culture/society will accomplish that. But New Yorkers were so grieved by what had been going on, it became clear that abortion would no longer receive approval. "Abortion continued to be considered disgraceful until the 1960s, when a much-changed *New York Times* and other newspapers began pushing pro-abortion."

A reading of the *Times* and other Christian newspapers of that era revealed that editors and reporters wanted to glorify God by affecting this world. Olasky informs:

> They did not believe it inevitable that sin should dominate New York City or any other city. They were willing to be controversial. One *Times* anti-abortion editorial stated, "It is useless to talk of such matters with bated breath, or to seek to cover such terrible realities with the veil of false delicacy. . . . From a lethargy like this it is time to arouse ourselves. The evil that is tolerated is aggressive." The editorial concluded that "the good . . . must be aggressive too."[60]

Nevertheless the sunset for Christian journalism eventually happened wherein aggressive journalism by Christians ceased "soon after one of its major successes, for four particular reasons and two underlying causes." In relation to the disappearing of aggressive Christian journalism in the *New York Times*, one generation died or departed from the faith as the reason for aggressive Christian journalism ceasing. Various slogans barred such reporting like St. Clair, because anything unfit for breakfast table-talk or considered unfit to print was ignored and tolerated. "Several generations later, it was embraced."

A second reason for Christian journalism disappearing was that Christian publications began to use "happy talk" for their writings. It was like the constant effort today of seeing everything as positive and constantly ignoring what is called negative even though it is true. This kind of writing at that time gave the impression that man was not a fallen creature and this refusal to cover evil resulted in "dullness of copy, because without real villains there is little real drama." One Christian publication caught in this "happy talk" ran this news report: "There is literally nothing stirring."

The third reason for the demise of Christian journalism was the refusal to come up to the communication demands of a growing fast-paced marketplace. Whether the publications are elite or popular, careful scholarship must always be present. "Some Christian magazines . . . seemed to pride themselves on unnecessary verbiage."

The fourth reason for the disappearing of aggressive Christian journalism was that "denominational infighting was on the rise."

Underlying this were "two . . . theological trends. One was anti-Christian, one operated within Christendom; but they worked together to provoke journalistic retreat." The trend outside was obvious, because generally speaking during the last two-thirds of the nineteenth century Christian principles upon which the American society had been founded were being thrown aside by the American society. "Every area of American life was affected by this shift."[61]

By this time New England was the "cockpit" of theological liberalism and *The Boston Recorder* was hard hit by the mindset. It held its own against the Unitarianism that captured Harvard College. This newspaper attempted to get people to understand the fallacy of believing in man's natural goodness, but in the mid 1830s materialism and pantheism merged for a new and stronger attack.

In this context Christian publications had to face Rousseau, Kant, Emerson, and other purveyors of intellectual romanticism wherein they and others believed man's reason did not have to operate within God's revelation. Man could create his own truth. The Transcendental Club was established and gave birth to The New York Tribune. In all of this man is god. This was the forerunner of the present New Age movement. Was the church aware of what was transpiring in the history of thought? Evidently not. Therefore the church contributed to the problem.

Revivalism comes along separating the sacred from the secular preaching a message full of gnostic dualism with the idea that all the church was to do was to "save souls" as if the total man and the world did not matter to God. "Soul" was apparently translated from "nephesh" in the Hebrew Old Testament and from "psuche" in the New Testament into a gnostic dualism implying the soul as something immaterial and separate from the body.

> Revivalism . . . did not particularly help those Christian newspapers that were endeavoring to cover every aspect of God's creation and perhaps "stir up the mind of Christians to duty." The great revivalists' focus on evangelism tended to be specifically individualistic: world-view was not stressed. Furthermore, many Christians begin to believe that the general culture inevitably would become worse. They thought that little could be done to stay the downward drift. Christian publications should cover the church news, they thought, and ignore the rest of the world.

For most conservative Christians in America that is still the mindset. They believe the only purpose of the Good News is to "save souls" in the gnostic-dualistic sense and ignore the world in which the Good News has to be proclaimed, both, for personal reconciliation of man to God and then take that Good News as the salt and light into a decaying and decayed culture/society. Continuing on with what developed historically:

> The anti-Christian trend and separatistic Christian reaction combined to end the Christian presence in the newsroom. As

journalists who had embraced materialism and/or pantheism advanced in newspaper and magazine work, Christians who embraced separatistic revivalism retreated. Some Christian newspapers may have died after being overrun, but many evacuated the social realm without even engaging the invading forces.

The general result of the two underlying movements was that the Reformational idea of Christ as Lord of all of life was neglected. Relations of ministry and laity, and of sabbatical and general church activities, also were affected. Calvin and other leaders of the Protestant Reformation had argued that good work outside the pulpit glorified God as much as the activities of the ministry proper. But as views of inevitable cultural decay began to grip nineteenth century American Protestantism, some editors began to consider journalism inferior to preaching. The editor of one Ohio newspaper said the "work of a Christian minister" was far more important than the work of an editor.

. . . Sometimes it even seemed that a sense of "Whew! Glad I'm saved" had replaced a strong sense of God's sovereignty over all areas of human life. The theological vision of social defeatism and separatism had some immediate consequences. With many Christian journalists hiding their light under a bushel, the newspaper field was wide open for the triumph of "yellow journalism" at the end of the nineteenth century,and the expulsion of God from the front page early in the twentieth. By 1925, Christians often were voiceless, except in publications that largely preached to the choir.[62]

My heritage, very dear to me, still has not learned to clean up its rhetoric. It keeps reinforcing the separatistic idea of elevating some Christians' special ministries above others.

It was at this time, 1925, that the "monkey trial" was held in Tennessee. Major newspapers were then dominated by non-Christians and the trial of 1925 made "monkeys" out of Christians, because evidently there was no Christian journalist brilliant enough to counter the liberals and others.

To further see the results of journalism when the theistic/Christian world-view is not the dominant influence, there is a bitter pill that Christians also need to swallow. This is something Cal Thomas, a syndicated columnist who demonstrates a strong Christian commitment, wrote in an article: "The Media or The Church . . . Which Needs Redemption The Most?" In the article Thomas insists that "the ultimate problem in America is not the media. It's the church." He is a needed representative for the cause of Christ in the world of the "media," a word that he does not like. In the context of world-view issues and the illustrative results of what transpires when the theistic/Christian world-view is removed from such major influential social spheres of culture/society such as public education, the judicial system, and the media, we are bound to consider Thomas's convictions with the utmost seriousness. He keeps one from getting one-sided in this issue. We must listen to him if we want to have the renewal and revival of Christian journalism enabled to reenter into the mainstream of the journalistic world. The aforementioned article reveals the depth of truth of his mind and heart.

First, Thomas refuses the indictment: the media is responsible for "the gutting of values in America." He insists, and rightfully so, that most of the followers of Christ have not really listened to God's Word to see the press and entertainment world as part of the church's mission field. "We would rather curse the darkness than light candles." From his perspective most Christians are all wrapped up in the next life complaining about the way things are "instead of plotting strategies to change them." The only contact that many Christians have with the media world is when they write letters to people in the media and call them secular humanists or communists, which they may be. But,"is it any wonder," Thomas asks, "that members of the media perceive followers of Christ as being judgemental, hypocritical, uneducated and basically humorless?"

Thomas is not giving the media a blanket approval. He is helping us to see where the church fits in as part of the problem in the lack of Christian journalism. Thomas insists that the "press doesn't destroy values - it reflects them or at least some of them. To say that the media is responsible for our decadence allows Christians off the hook" too easily.

Thomas strongly believes the church and not just the media to be a major problem in America. It is the problem of the followers of Christ who have been conformed to this world and not transformed by the renewing of their minds. "It is a cliche now," he writes, "but there is more of the world in the church than there is the church in the world"

He actually gets letters from believers looking for justification to put their children in public schools where they learn that they come from "slime" or they are wanting an okay "to have sex before marriage as long as they use a condom." Like a pastor who is really on a roll Thomas believes that:

> Christians have lost their power because they have lost their mandate. They've lost their vision. We are more interested in the praise of men than the approval of God. We are not interested in holy living. How many preachers stand up and preach about the sins that many of the people in their own congregation commit? Not the obvious sins . . . but the ones that eclipse holy living which demands deep commitment and daily devotions and a zeal for winning people to Christ?

Thomas concedes that his profession of journalism draws people who are of the liberal political mindset, while the conservatives politically and theologically are getting their degrees, taking advantage of the free enterprise system and ignoring the world's needs. Liberals, he believes, have an integrated world-view while Christians too often divide their world-view separating loyalties to God and man when the theistic/Christian world-view is integrated for Christ to be Lord of all of life. I have to agree.

How then do Christians reach out to the media world? One person at a time remembering that they "are persons before they are members of the media." It is not giving them a tract but living and speaking a life that has integrity, honesty, and openness demonstrating that the theistic/Christian world-view is your integrated world-view and value system and you are not fearful of having your world-view scrutinized and questioned. You see, most Christians today cannot do that because most do not know what they believe and why. The largest need of the church in its educational effort is the study of apologetics and world-view understanding.

The start of getting the Christian world-view back into the mainline of the media is the result of Christians taking the commission mandates seriously and reaching media people who are outside of or are not committed to Christ. It is a matter of knowing not only the Christian's world-view but also the world-view of the media person to whom a Christian may be witnessing. Thomas says it beautifully: "God will take care of the big picture when we are faithful in small things."

> If we can turn on the lay people in the country to realize that they are not going to a spectator sport on Sunday morning, but that by worshiping God and receiving His power they are being energized to go out and do the real work of the church during the week, at their job, at home, at school, then maybe, just maybe, God will be pleased to send that revival that we now only read about in history books.[63]

Thomas has such stature, awareness, and clarity of convictions about getting the theistic/Christian world-view back into journalism/media. No one can have trouble understanding him. He shows clearly the weakness of the evangelical and restoration camp in relation to lack of understanding and having an integrated world-view for witness and work in the marketplace. The picture becomes even more clear as to what happens when the theistic/Christian world-view is not the dominant influence in this social institution of journalism/media.

> Conservatives, whether political or religious or both, have been struggling for several years to regain territory they surrendered without a fight (Olasky's departure and exile study of Christian journalism). Their retreat from the intellectual

and informational arena has created a vacuum that alternative world views have been unable to fill. The absence of a world view based on an enduring moral order has brought about the present social, economic, and political crises that now grip our land. In an information age, it is important that those who hold the key to the problems that beset us receive a hearing in the public arena.

For too long, conservatives have been content either to criticize the media or to publish and broadcast their views through their own outlets. That has had and will have little or no effect in promoting cultural change. Only a penetration of existing media structures and the proclamation of such views in the public arena will attract a large enough audience to make a difference.

I call this book *Occupied Territory* because it reflects my view that the editorial pages of the nation's newspapers are the territory, or marketplace of ideas, that must be penetrated and occupied in order to influence enough people to make a difference in our culture. I am "occupying" this territory, not in the militaristic sense, but as one who has managed to squeeze his way into a highly competitive field at a time when I believe the nation is ready to listen to the philosophy I represent.

Thomas has insightful and blunt words to help Christians move from media-bashing into what it takes to get Christian journalism back and restore the press from being a prodigal.

But even if you grant that there is bias in the media (we are all biased to some extent—what the critics are actually complaining about is a lack of fairness or balance), why are there not more conservative young people in the journalism schools and working their way up through the ranks of small-town newspapers and TV stations?

I'll tell you what I think is the answer to that question. My own experience has shown me that many conservatives do not have a well enough developed world view. They do not understand that history is a battle of ideas. They are not willing to sacrifice the MBA at Harvard for the toil and often low pay (with the exception of those in Dan Rather's category) of the journalism profession. When they have made their fortunes in business, they would rather invest in oil wells and stock than in the ideological health of our country. They hold a lot of meetings, usually to talk about the "liberal threat," but they do nothing.

Liberals understand all too well that a powerful idea is worth more than a lot of money. Money only buys things that ultimately must become obsolete, but ideas fuel revolutions that change the course of history.

After the cursing of the darkness has been completed, one is still left with darkness. But light always dispels darkness and if only a few of those conservatives who are upset by what they see on television and read in the newspapers would put their money where their ideology is, what a bright world this would be. Until then, I am afraid that many of my conservative brethren will be regarded as bunch of cry-babies.[64]

This journalism/media world-view issue is much wider and deeper than can be presented here. Toffler's *Powershift* reveals media's power in writing history from the questionable perspective of balance, truth, and integrity. Media is notorious for reporting the size of Christian gatherings in Washington, D.C. The police force of that city always accounts for more Christians present than does the media.

Studies at Columbia University in 1982 clearly revealed the negative bias of media against Christianity. Neil Postman's book, *Amusing Ourselves To Death,* should be read by every Christian. He may come down a bit too much on the side of television being more destructive than it may be, but his Forward justifies space here.

We were keeping our eye on 1984. When the year came and the prophecy didn't, thoughtful Americans sang softly in praise of themselves. The roots of liberal democracy had held. Wherever else the terror had happened, we, at least, had not been visited by Orwellian nightmares.

But we had forgotten that alongside Orwell's dark vision, there was another-slightly older, slightly less well know, equally chilling: Aldous Huxley's *Brave New World.* Contrary to common belief even among the educated, Huxley and Orwell did not prophecy the same thing. Orwell warns that we will be overcome by externally imposed oppression. But in Huxley's vision, no big Brother is required to deprive people of their autonomy, maturity and history. As he saw it, people will come to love their oppression, to adore the technologies that undo their capacities to think. What Orwell feared were those who would ban books.

What Huxley feared was that there would be no reason to ban a book, for there would be no one who wanted to read one. Orwell fears those who would deprive us of information. Huxley feared those who would give us so much that we would be reduced to passivity and egoism. Orwell feared the truth would be concealed from us. Huxley feared we would become a trivial culture, preoccupied with some equivalent of the feelies, the orgy porgy, and the centrifugal bumblepuppy. As Huxley remarked in *Brave New World Revisited*, the civil libertarians and rationalists who are ever on the alert to oppose tyranny "failed to take into account man's almost infinite appetite for distractions." In *1984*, Huxley added, people who are controlled by inflicting pain. In *Brave New World*, they are controlled by inflicting pleasure. In short, Orwell feared that what we hate will ruin us. Huxley feared that what we love will ruin us. this book is about the possibility that Huxley, not Orwell, was right.[65]

Every Christian should study Otto Scott's, "Revolutionizing The Media." It is blunt. It is jarring. It is about a tax-ruling that The Public Affairs division of the IRS in Washington, D.C. allows "the communications monster"[66] (television) to get away with in taxes. It's a world-view issue. In the context of the tax-ruling, we pay taxes to the government for the television part of journalism/media to misrepresent so much about our part of the world, the church, and Christianity as a whole.

The studies related to journalism/media as a world-view

issue seem unending, but nothing seems to ever be accomplished by them. Why?

The late Malcom Muggeridge clearly understood the emptiness of the media in journalism and television when the theistic/Christian world-view has no influence in the social institution of the media. From my acquaintance with him via his writings, my personal visits with him when he visited this country to speak, and when my wife and I had the privilege of being guests in his home where he and Kitty, his kind and gracious wife, made us unequals feel his equal, it was clear that he thought the medium of television is not a neutral thing that can be used equally for good or evil. He believed, instead, that television is innately hostile to such beneficent purposes as telling the truth and fostering high morals. He had little to say of the value of any part of the media.

Muggeridge knew of so many fabricated lies in the BBC television industry. He had done that himself at one time. It is, no doubt, done in the United States. Nevertheless television was used for good when Mr. Muggeridge appeared on William F. Buckley's "Firing Line" show. It was not more of the almost silly and phony idealized conversion stories or "docutestimonials" that usually distorts, biblically, the way the Holy Spirit normally works in the lives of real people. The power of the Muggeridge broadcast on "Firing Line," "was its simple explication of the unadorned life of faith. It communicated the gospel in the context of one person's authentic spiritual journey, not in some vain, show-business performance slickly designed to capture souls for Christ."[67]

Stating this is not an effort to refute Malcom Muggeridge's strong conviction. It's only to reveal that television, as part of journalism/media can be used for the cause of Christ when Christianity is presented in a mature, honest effort with integrity that rises above religious almost silly side-shows of which we have too many.

If the exiled journalism/media is once more influenced by Christians and they return mature and honest Christian journalism influence back into the major media streams, Christians will have the most insightful and exciting news publications and programs in the United States.

Other Significant Categories: Illustrative Crises

Four of many other significant categories reveal what happens when the theistic/Christian world-view is rejected, ignored or not lived out. Each require intense detailed study. But I will state brief explanatory reflections related to the four areas.

Family: Foundation For Society—Deteriorating

It is an understatement to say that the American family is in deep, deep trouble. It is a sad indictment to admit that much of the Christian family in this nation is almost as bad off as the American family that has no part in the church. Marriages do not last long. Over half of the weddings taking place in this nation are for couples who have lived together often for two and three years. Their weddings have little joy. It is just a legal bonding that they hope will work.

This institution is in such need that a year's sermons could be built around marriage and the family and still not touch all of the crises in the American family in need of the theistic/Christian world-view as the source of the needed unifying factor for their lives and homes.

Never has the father been under a more severe attack. Little, if anything, is being written on honoring the father. Books are numerous about fathers "loving," "caring," "spending time," "prioritizing," "training," and "playing with" their children. Did God make a mistake with the Fifth Commandment? Did He mean to say "Honor your son and your daughter?" Everyone knows of the Dan Quayle/Murphy Brown episode. The media completely misrepresented what Quayle was saying about the need of a father.

The entire parental picture, even in the Christian community, seems out of control. I am amazed at how many Christian parents allow the kids to set the agenda and value-system for the entire family. It is to the point where many Christian parents end up worshiping their children and bowing to every option the kids want. An Oriental father once said, "I am amazed at how well American parents obey their children." That would fit far too many Christian homes.

I have a series of sermons that I preach every three or four years entitled: "How To Keep Moonlight And Roses From Becoming Daylight And Dishes." Every time I bring them more up to date with constant changes without compromising Truth, the response to them is gratifying and quite revealing: Even many marriages of many years are hurting. It is about homes finding new basis for living and loving in the theistic/Christian world-view. That goes for Christian and non-Christian families and homes that are too often only houses where people congregate. It is surely revealing of something lacking in the American Christian family when the number of Christian families parading to counselors is growing rapidly. The "therapeutic revolution" from the Recovery Movements seem to be replacing the cross of Christ.

Medicine Absence of Ethics—Playing God

This is rapidly becoming one of the most urgent yet fuzzy areas of culture/society for Christians to be concerned. Most Christians will say "what does this have to do with world-view?" Think about it. National health care cost is skyrocketing. We continue to murder babies, because its legal. More and more convictions about dying with dignity and euthanasia are softening. This is a difficult dilemma for all, but in all of this, human life is being devalued more and more.

Aids is becoming more and more a threat to society and the entire world. We really have not been told the whole truth about the amount of "Aids" all around us. Drug use is out of control. Thousands of babies are born drug-addicts and alcoholics. Doctor and patient relationships are becoming strained. Because of the career of one person very close to me I happen to know that the god of greed certainly controls too many of the medical professions as they drain the poor and others with outrageous and questionable charges.

There has been documented experiences that open-heart surgery is used much more often in affluent communities than in the poor areas and the charges are much more. Some Godly physicians are sharing some of these factors. Is this about world-view? Absolutely! When the theistic/Christian world-view ethic is not the unifying factor in the medical world, chaos results as it does in every other sphere and institutions of culture/society. Most of the conservative church is doing little if anything about confronting or teaching the people about these truths.

To read the section on "Bioethics—A New God?" in Chandler's most recent writings, *Racing Toward 2001*, "the forces shaping America's religious future" is like reading something from a space trip into an unknown world! Christians had better begin to struggle with what part does the theistic/Christian world-view play in this dimension of our society.

A World In Tyranny—Why

The life of Whittaker Chambers reads like a novel. The book, *Witness,* is the account of a remarkable life. But it is more than the account of one man's life. Dean Curry believes that "*Witness* stands as a classic statement of the crisis that confronts our contemporary world—a world that is no longer tethered to a belief in God. In rejecting communism, Chambers came to the realization that tyranny is the inevitable by-product of the denial of God."[68]

Whittaker Chamber's witness to the crisis of our time has been all but forgotten in the context of God and tyranny. The sources of contemporary tyranny lies in this fact: "Of all the changes that have revolutionized the modern world, none is more important—or neglected in the study of international politics—than the decline of Christianity and the rise of secular, naturalistic worldviews."[69]

Modern man, Christians included, cannot escape the fact that every situation of life involves deciding about world-views.

But most Christians still act like that is none of their business hoping that all of these problems will disappear like a poof of wind. But modern tyranny that is the product of the crisis of faith in Christ and the theistic/Christian world-view will continue its march until man realizes his dependence upon his Creator. Tyranny is a call to evangelize and make disciples. This is the first necessary step in fighting modern tyranny. The second step is to understand that man's claim on God's creation is limited. Ultimately it is freedom in Christ that is the antidote to modern tyranny, and Christian education in the church by and large has no comprehension of this and is not even considering the study of the issue.

The modern evangelical church cannot continue with a fragmented world-view that is concerned only with the spiritual aspect of man. Of course the remedy commences there, but the whole person must be reconciled to God. To continue only the spiritual emphasis is to reject both mandates of God: the dominion mandate of Genesis 1:22-29 and the witness mandate of Matthew 28:16-20. It's all about world-view!

Ethics/Morals—Whose

This is one of the greater challenges facing our culture/society to which the church has to speak and witness. Christ is the ethic of life and from Him filters out all aspects of ethics and integrity, because the theistic/Christian world-view answers the basic questions of life coherently and consistently. As long as modern man attempts to make life work by relativism and ethics based on what man chooses, there will be chaos in all aspects of life and society.

But here is the dilemma. You can stand on most any soapbox today and speak out: "What our nation needs is ethics." Most will agree. But as Charles Colson writes: "But what no one seems to realize is that while we all want ethics, ethics are meaningless unless based on some value system. And the problem is, our society cannot agree on common objective values on which common ethical standards must be based."[70]

This dilemma can be illustrated in connection with the great educational institution of Harvard University. John Shad, former chairman of the Securities and Exchange Commission, donated $35 million to the Harvard Business School to establish an ethics chair and department.

That was in 1987 and as far as I know up to 1992, the University has come up with only a flimsy-sounding "values" course. Harvard is still sitting on the Shad grant unable to find an ethicist to head up the department. Why? Whose ethics shall they teach? It is a world-view issue clashing with other world-views. How many Christians, including pastors, could wade through many alternative world-views and demonstrate that the coherency and consistency of the theistic/Christian world-view is the only option for such a chair?

Whose ethics in the midst of the death of ethics in America will be taught? Harvard's problem parallels that of our larger society. Our nation demands and desperately needs ethics but abandons the objective moral base on which any real standard of ethics must logically rest. "Our society deplores the proliferation of scandals," such as the Wall Street, HUD real-estate sales and the Savings and Loan fiasco, "yet rejects the basis for an ethical code designed to restrain the human passions that cause those scandals."[71] Surely, Christians do understand that America really has no moral base left but man.

This quandary was expressed by Harvard President Derek Bok in *Harvard Magazine* (May/June 1988). He described Harvard's origins. After the school was expanded from a training ground for ministers to include other students, Massachusetts law mandated that "the president (and) the professors . . . shall exert their best endeavors to impress on the minds of youth committed to their care and instructions the principles of piety and justice and a sacred regard for truth." Bok speaks almost wistfully of returning to such absolutes by which to formulate ethical decisions. "But he hastens to note that faculty members react with tepid interest and outright skepticism to the idea of teaching any kind of ethics."[72]

Let Cal Thomas respond to this need of ethics.

If a consensus in our society really wants ethics on Capital Hill, on Wall Street, in the worlds of business and academia, we must be willing to base those ethics on a firm foundation. And in Western civilization that foundation has been twenty-three centuries of accumulated wisdom, natural law, and the Judeo-Christian tradition based on Biblical revelation.

Until we look again to these classic sources, Harvard will continue to waste both its $35 million and the hearts and minds of its students; Capital Hill will continue to be a play-ground for opportunities rather than a place of service for statesmen; and our culture at large, loosed from any absolute foundations of morality, will continue to drift helplessly in a moral quagmire, all the while pitifully pontificating about the lost of ethics.[73]

That has been clearly realized in the latest scams of the check-bouncing in Washington, D.C., and the slow uncovering of questionable ethics in the House Post Office.

Whose ethics? What world-view will be the source of getting the likes of Harvard and our nation out of the dilemma? Will the church speak to that with high-level Christian education so the people of God can really speak to such issues?

Is there however a glimmer of hope in the area of morals and ethics beginning to shine forth in some higher places, socially speaking? In a remarkable commencement address May 10, 1987, to graduating seniors from Duke University, Ted Koppel ABC anchor man sounded like a solid conservative preacher that the media too often likes to deride. His theme to these children of the sexual revolution: "ethics and morals."

His address was intensely serious. He deplored the superficiality of a culture "that elevates a Vanna White to stardom on television's Wheel of Fortune." In the context of the media's hedonistic messages, Koppel reflected back to his parent's time, telling the Duke graduates: "We have actually convinced ourselves that slogans will save us. 'Shoot up if you must, but use a clean needle.' 'Enjoy sex whenever and with whomever you wish, but wear a condom.'"

He then jumped into the topic with the force of a lecture from parents trying to straighten out children, which most college graduates still are. Koppel said:

> No. The answer is no. Not because it isn't cool . . . or smart . . . or because you might end up in jail or dying in an AIDS ward-but no . . . because its wrong. Because we have spent five thousand years as a race of rational human beings trying to drag ourselves out of the primeval slime by searching for truth . . . and moral absolutes.

What? Is that a misprint: "moral absolutes" from such a powerful media voice as Ted Koppel? And he continued:

> In the place of Truth (his capitalization) we have discovered facts; for moral absolutes we have substituted moral ambiguity. We now communicate with everyone . . . and say absolutely nothing. We have reconstructed the Tower of Babel and it is a television antenna. A thousand voices producing a daily parody of democracy; in which everyone's opinion is afforded equal weight; regardless of substance or merit. Indeed, it can even be argued that opinions of real weight tend to sink with barely a trace in television's ocean of banalities.

> Our society finds Truth too strong a medicine to digest undiluted. In its purist form Truth is not a polite tap on the shoulder; it is a howling reproach. What Moses brought down from Mount Sinai were not the Ten suggestions. . . they are Commandments. Are, not were.

The entire text is something to behold from a man in high places saying things like the foregoing to a society awash in ethical mishmash that says nothing. Koppel continued with elaboration of the Ten Commandments and the tension between them and our frivolous sick society. He talked about why the Hart campaign foundered in relation to a Commandment. What is so amazing is that Ted Koppel gave this address at a major American University in the late 1980s, and the graduates and others were

260

willing to listen to it. Does that tell us that most of the church is not giving a clear sound from the Word of God? Probably so! Is that not a glimmer of hope in the need and search for an ethical base in our culture/society? It is a world-view issue.

Koppel concluded with some remarkable thoughts for a person who is not viewed as part of a religious community. He said that the First Commandment was the "most controversial of the Commandments," because it "requires that we believe in the existence of a single supreme God. And then, in the Second, Third and Fourth Commandments: *prohibits* the worship of any other gods, *forbids* that his name be taken in vain, *requires* that we set aside one day in seven to rest and worship Him."

The real irony but yet a real hope was that Koppel gave this address to an audience of students many or perhaps most of whom were from public schools in which the posting of the Ten Commandments is prohibited by the Federal Courts, because they say that it is an unconstitutional act. The danger of this is that the First Amendment has received a misguided interpretation that has elevated it to a "position of greater power and worship than the First Commandment." Thus in our contemporary world the courts have decreed "thou shalt have no other gods before the state."

Then in a most poignant moment Koppel sounded like a pastor giving the conclusion of a sermon to move people to decision and commitment.

> I caution you, as one who performs daily on the flickering altar, to set your sights beyond what you can see. There is true majesty in the concept of an unseen power which can neither be measured or weighed. There is harmony and inner peace to be found in following a moral compass that points in the same direction, regardless of fashion or trend.[74]

That is a glimmer of hope in the current ethical malaise from one that our culture/society hears and sees often in the media. May his tribe increase, and may the Lord's church have the wisdom, boldness, and willingness to become world-viewish marching boldly into the marketplace to carry out the mandates and commissions of our Lord.

But in that glimmer of hope we must understand that we may yet be on the brink of a new Dark Age. We must keep before us the truth of the West's 20th-century rejection of biblical values, its wholehearted embrace of secular, anti-Christian philosophies, its worship of science, its avid consumption of decadent entertainment, its relentless pursuit of pleasure and self-fulfillment, its clamor for rights without duties. Dr. Carl F. H. Henry insists that today "Western society manifests a quantum leap of immorality and indecency unprecedented since the fall of the Roman Empire."[75]

His question is "Can The Church Save Our Culture?" Of course not! The church cannot save anything, but it can be strong enough to influence culture/society sufficiently wherein Christ has an opportunity to turn the world around by turning people to Him. But this will not happen if "to the world we (church) seem like Hogan's Army waiting for Godot."[76] It's all about world-views that must become part of the local church's educational agenda.

In the context of everything that I have written, Christians must heed the words of Dr. Marshall J. Leggett, President of Milligan College: "We Christians stand on the threshold of a new decade, a new century, and a new millennium. We must read 'the signs of the times' because the 'kingdom continues to unfold' even in our midst."[77]

We are in the new decade. Does the church as a whole really know it and know where it (the new decade) is going unless the church comes alive in high-level thinking and a willingness to risk more than ever before? The tragedy of the modern world can continue, the tragedy being that we are a world without heroes, or the church can develop the only real heroes there are: those willing to do His will.

We live in a flawed world—fallen according to Christian theology. We cannot create a faultless society. But we can create a better or worse one. Harold O. J. Brown wrote: "Our older, nominally Christian America had its faults. But is our present 'pluralistic' chaos preferable—or even viable?"[78]

His thoughts causes me once again to stimulate thinking and discussion and to possibly give a password to recovery by stating something that was stated in another part of the book. It is Millendorfer's statement: "The future will be Christian, or it will not take place."[79]

Tomorrow's Agenda Today

Ideas do have consequences! Let us never forget that the war of ideas is a real war, with real casualties. If the church continues to fail on the slippery slope with business as usual, the casualties will be enormous.

We cannot predict the politics and perils of tomorrow exactly, but the enemies of Christ and His order for life, society, and morals change little. The enemies will continue to be exploiters and the wielders of power and privilege. The enemies will take positions against the traditional and normal, against family, against distinction between man and woman, against human nature itself. This enemy stance will take positions that will treat people as mere conveniences to somebody's plan, not as "individuals of infinite worth".

This enemy is "sin," and those controlled by "sin," the "fatal conceit" in mankind. The red flags are up against Christ, His church, and His people who call themselves "Christians." I concur with Dr. George Roche, President of Hillsdale College. The words are addressed to a wider audience than the church, but they certainly speak clearly to the church right now:

> There has never been a generation in the history of America which has had such an enormous opportunity to make a clear choice and to have a hand in implementing that choice. We can play our part in shaping the world now emerging, or we can stand aside and be overrun. The other side is working against us. We have to be better. We have to lead with the right ideas.

Dr. Roche, who believes that the modern tragedy of this

society is that we are a *World Without Heroes*, heroes are those who do the will of God, also says: "We have moved a long way from the idea of the hero. We have allowed anti-heroes to befoul our morals, manners and culture. Only a willingness to face them down and say that right is right can restore the health of the Republic." That is tomorrow's agenda today!

The church has to be more vocal than ever before to remind our society that all civilization is based on shared religious (Christian) belief: a common understanding about what is right and what is wrong. Only one world-view offers that. Sound institutions, including the church, are built on this alone. It is persons of integrity who must build them, recognizing that we are children of God and responsible to God, to ourselves, and to one another to find answers not just for our "felt needs," which is a modern cry weakening the church, but we are responsible to a sense of transcendent purpose for God's glory. Someone said about man: "we are not ants in an anthill," but creations of God for the purpose of bringing glory to Him by doing His will for Christ's sake.

We are not called to save the world. That has been done for us by Christ. Our task and privilege is to tell the world the message through the church, and introduce the world to Christ and His world-view, the only world-view that can keep a world from the horrors of self-destruction by the self-centeredness of man.

I conclude with more words from Dr. Roche, one whom too few people have read or are reading. What I share from his mind and heart is what it is partially all about to sing the Lord's Song in an alien land and time, and get the church off the slippery slope.

> You and I know, and maybe the world will know one day, that when our lives are given salvation and eternal hope, every day can be exciting and joyous and fun instead of bleak and grim. When we remember the old teachings and understand them, happiness is given to us freely. Of old, the angels told us, "Rejoice and be exceedingly glad . . . ."

New-think (alien non-theistic world-views, liberal, and leftist Marxist thinking) gave us barbed wire, machine guns, slavery and life stripped of meaning ...Everybody hated it. Many died trying to escape it and many more found God in the teeth of (or because of) its slave labor camps and engines of thought control. What more do we need to know about it?

I love to laugh, and I'll bet you do too. We can laugh and we do, simply by accepting life as a gift from God who called His creation good. The words, "Thy will be done," give our lives just the right foundation. Without them, we build our houses on sand and will never find a real smile. With them we are the salt of the earth, and we do, one by one, each with his own gifts, all that is good in this world.

If we are called on to do even more than we do now, it is not a burden but a blessing.[80]

Tomorrow's Agenda Today Is Growing More Urgent As The Speed Toward An Unknown Complex Century Seems To Be Rapidly Increasing!

Epilogue
Reclaiming Culture With
The Christian World-View

The good news is that more people are paying attention to the bad news. The bad news is that Christianity has been marginalized and no longer considered as a serious and alternative option for the high ground of contemporary study and intellectual debate in life and society.

This book has been birthed as a hopeful contribution to the laos (People of God) to assist them in realizing the need of the reinstatement of the historical Christian Faith on the high ground of intellectual debate starting at the congregational level. Movements within the church, such as the Restoration Heritage, must enter into this debate or talk only to the church. It appears that is about all that is presently happening now.

The primary thesis of the book has been to reveal and illustrate the inadequacies of major world-views when contrasted to the theistic/Christian world-view that can answer life's basic questions. This world-view can serve as the only unifying and healing factor for life and our fragmented culture/society that is alienated from the historic Christian Faith.

The Christian/theistic option is by and large ignored today. It's relegated to the private world. Public education and the secular media in most all categories portray an entirely secularized society. God is illegal in our schools, and children in the new Russia have more religious freedom than Christian children have in schools in the United States.

But relegating Christianity and God to the private world is a misrepresentation, because there are multitudes who still hold firm to the historic Faith. Serious writers and commentators take little or no account of this or of the Christian dimension of life. If they do mention it, they often imply that there is little difference between one religion or another. The Christian religion has become a private religious option for the individual choice rather than a matter of objective truth that should be publicly debated and studied. The result of not seeing and believing this objective truth is resulting in a culture that is rapidly becoming more and more pagan in its presuppositions and assumptions about values in life.

It's beyond high-time that this situation be exposed. That has been a basic purpose of this book as an introductory primer and practical tool to assist the laos in this urgent need. Bishop Huge Montefiore of England has written his concern and desire for Christianity to reclaim the high ground. Here is his response to secularism: "At almost every point the Christian religion has a very high claim to truth, and an even higher claim to the high ground of intellectual debate."[1]

He is correct, but I am convinced that the church is largely to blame for this state of affairs wherein the intellectual world believes that Christ, Christianity, and His church has little to bring to the debate floor. After all, this is the 1990s, and the cultural mindset is that modern man is beyond all this Christian information and the claims of Christianity.

I realize the statement of blaming the church for our modern predicament will cause some to say that I do not love the church. That is just not true. I have had a lover's quarrel with the church for a long time, because I believe the church and its message as the last bastion of hope. But I see the gap widening between what the authentic church is to be. What I see now in a society where the great biblical principles are waning, even among many pastors whose pastoral life centers around church growth at any cost, is pastoral institutional management as CEO officers, and planned pizzazz in praise and worship that will appeal to the "baby boomers" and their consumerism plus bowing to their "please me or lose me" mindset.

On the one hand the church has been inward looking locked in a survival or success mindset. The survival mindset in the heritage that I know best is part of the result of the leadership crisis in most congregations. Most congregational affirmed leaders (elders, deacons, etc.) have little vision, very little understanding of the world situations in the area of world-views and trends, too often lack a real emotional desire to lead, and often hold back pastoral leadership that has vision, balance, and biblical integrity. The congregational leaders seem to be fearful of giving a pastor too much freedom as a decision-maker to lead. Many, many pastors are very discouraged and belittled by this mindset that treats them as just someone with a label. A major cause of this leadership crisis is that leadership studies for development does not have a high priority in most congregations of my heritage, and leadership is mostly by office than by function.

The success mindset and the success that may go with it is usually led by the pastor being something like a CEO. The truth is that today it is the CEO arrangement along with pragmatism that works, and because it is working, then the conviction is that it must be the proper and correct direction to take in church work. Unless real leadership by elders and deacons surfaces with a new mindset that is biblically grounded, then the recourse for the modern church is the CEO approach. That does not mean that I am for it, but at least it works and gets something accomplished. There is great tension over the attempted effort of the CEO arrangement in old established congregations. What is the remedy for both, the survival and the success, mindsets to stop the inward looking direction? I would suggest both mindsets need some radical overhauling and a new balance.

On the other hand church leadership, beyond what was stated in the previous paragraphs, in some of the modern church has become preoccupied with the political and social dimensions of the church at the expense of standing on the Christian claims of truth.

Therefore even though the opening sentence of this epilogue is, I believe, true, the bad news can only be remedied by the real Good News. But I fear that most Christians, including my heritage, really do not know what they believe and why in order to be able to communicate the Good News in the context of the bad news. This remedy requires not only that Christians know God's Word but also God's world and various mind-sets via world-view studies as already suggested. In this process of becoming students of the Word and the world, and exegeting both, there is a rewarding and developing dimension of the Christian life from this approach in Christian education that can now be stated.

The people reached by the church with the Good News during the rest of this century will need to go through world-view studies to realize from where they have come intellectually, spiritually, emotionally, and politically or their faith in and commitment to Jesus Christ as Lord will not be what it can and must be in this kind of world. Their new life in Christ will be enhanced immensely when they are able to see how the theistic/Christian world-view fills the blank places in the puzzle of life and society and makes both new in Christ.

They must be assisted in understanding that civil society (a term describing all the transactions within a society) has triumphed via the wrongly manufactured wall of separation of church and state, and as Thomas Molnar states, civil society "now surrounds us and defines our material and intellectual environment exactly as church and religion and state authority defined the environment centuries ago."[2] The central thrust of civil society is to rule, enforce its program, and interpret social forces and interest groups in its own best interest. In this so-called separation and the pipe-dream of civil society that makes-believe every interest group in a pluralistic society finds complete freedom of thought and action,(which they do not, because there is always some mindset or world-view that attempts to control), the question to face is: "Has the church gained freedom through its separation from the state and its acceptance of an interest-group status?"[3]

The answer is an unequivocal "no." The church, whose primary content is about faith with a morality and a mission, cannot be regarded like any other "interest group" such as gays, business people, satanists, feminists, salesmen or what-have-you. But a civil society that is controlled by secular humanism and other alien non-theistic world-views tries to constrain the church to fit itself in civil society's agenda as just another group equal to all others.

Therefore, things being as they are, "the church has only limited elbow room and even more limited choices." Liberal civil society will "forever suspect the church of not playing according to the rules of the game," which it cannot "without denying its founder and its own vocation." A "political party" as part of the civil society can run the road of concessions and compromises. A "business enterprise" can accept higher taxes and some curtailment of its area of activity. But no church can "accept in good faith the curtailment of its mission . . . and the spreading of its message. The dilemma is serious."

If the church "adapts" to the assigned status of an "interest group," it dilutes its essence while remaining always suspect "in the eyes of those who supervise the appropriate and appropriately liberal functioning of civil society." If the church "opposes" civil society and the rules of civil society's game, it is immediately accused of "breaking the social contract." So it is a choice between "losing its essence or losing its license to function." The almost obligatory consequence is that the church accepts "working at half steam." From a vigorous presence in "doctrine and morals," it is tempted to emphasize only one of its many aspects, but not a whole lot differently from other social agencies in schools, hospitals etc. These are parts of the church's possibilities, but "a caricature of the whole Christian endeavor."

> As soon as the church oversteps the narrowly defined function—by opposing abortion, biogenetic manipulation, homosexuality, moral deviation, and so on—its so-called partners, the other interest groups, denounce it in violent terms, with powerful politicians echoing these denunciations. Meanwhile, liberal civil society instructs its lawmakers and judges to bend in favor of those pressure groups whose agenda, absolute freedom and secular humanistic norms, coincides with the one it tacitly holds.

Civil society is achieving its program. It rapidly achieved half of its prison-like program, "the separation of church and state." It is now working with great success on the next half, "the separation of church from society." The total aim is to weaken strong commitments—except to liberal dogma and a secular humanism that can be defined and redefined according to need to keep them in control. The church had best get with it!

How can it be more forcefully stated? The church must regain its influence on the high ground! That is the purpose of this book as a tool to help Christians get started. The liberal content of civil society is not the result of some conspiracy or of "historical derailment." It is the product of centuries, a reaction to "the power monopoly of state and church gradually broken and replaced by the power monopoly of liberal ideology."[4] The task for regaining influence, therefore, is the penetrating of the culture/society with another kind of vocabulary; concretely, the education of a generation that rejects the terminology of secular humanism. It is a long and tough process, but worth all the best efforts of God's people.

Can the west be reached and changed by God's power through His people? Culture wars that have repositioned the church onto the slippery slope will continue. Therefore Christians must be equipped as active cultural warriors to bring a Christian effect into every social parameter and the disciplines of study in every aspect of the humanities.

The stance of Christians cannot be that of a theology of pessimism nor a theology of blind optimism. The stance must a theology of reality and confident, convicted, and expectant hope. The reality of the world must be known and the hope must be from an expectant belief that God in Christ can transfuse into every person reached for Christ's sake so that person will and can affect and effect all of culture/society.

But none of this will happen, and culture wars against Christ, Christianity, and Church will continue and win, if the bride of Christ is ravaged by an unconverted pastoral ministry of weak shepherds and hirelings who may be leaning into the subtle lure of liberalism or sold out to peace, affluence, and selfish individualism presenting the Christ, not as Lord or Lords and King of Kings, but as Christ-the-need-meter.

This book is written under the conviction that there are a

271

sufficient number of Christians who want to take on the world for Christ's sake; disciples who want to go beyond just church growth. Although we may be confident in Christ's Lordship, we do not hide the fact that the increasingly de-Christianized societies of the West present a difficult environment for Christian life and mission. Many structures of the modern Western world work to undermine Christians' ability to maintain their distinctiveness from the secularized cultures wherein they live. At the same time disciples of Christ who are intent and determined to make a difference in culture/society also observe a widespread secularization of Christian teaching and ministry. Today, in this secularizing of the Christian position, faith in God's revelation and obedience to it is being attacked both directly and indirectly outside and inside the churches. This is an assault that all Christians must resist, but they will not be able to do this without the imperative arm of world-view studies in Christian education being taken seriously.

Therefore the next step from this book is a sequel to it that involves a continuing breaking the church out of the seductive society, getting if off the slippery slope to start penetrating more effectively the same society. The sequel is keeping *The Church Off The Slippery Slope* and repositioning it back into society. It's a call to seduce society with the Lord's Song. This sequel will consider the following handles for penetration.

Tomorrow's agenda for today is developing a brighter road ahead to reclaim our future. But before the church can liberate itself to become a penetrating force it will have to face some reasons for being an ineffective church in the midst of church growth. The church will also have to have an understanding, a better understanding than most of the church has faced, of the challenge and difficulty of the church relating to society without compromising the Gospel. This involves grappling with perspectives about our situation, developing principles that will work, unloading deficiencies that distract, use reminders of past failures to keep from doing it wrong again, and there are special requirements before the world and requirements before the Lord.

Along with the foregoing major issues to face, there must come from the church a restoration of secularity, not secularism, but secularity (bringing the sacred, the transcendent into the secular, the now). There must be a redemptive fellowship that is committed, incendiary, and firmly theologically placed, a responding with proven and workable alternatives for values and life to an intellectually skeptical world already turned off from Christianity. It's being the proper kind of strangers among strangers, *The Company of Strangers* doing Christ's mission His way, crossing the river like Joshua to take the land. It is going public with one's faith as strangers in Christ to those who are strangers to Christ.

To cross the river will require an *Uncommon Decency* of "Christian civility in an uncivil world," a "convicted civility" as Richard Mouw recently published. His question is: "Can we be faithful and polite too?" My questions are: Do we really want to emerge from the chaos discovering the abundant life as the gift of God's grace, realizing that God is in the chaos waiting to be discovered afresh? Do we really want to see Christianity reestablished as the dominant, most influential world-view in our day? If we do, we must be willing, available, and prepared. But it is nothing new to say that the missing element in most Christians today is, preparation. That is partially what this book is about. Preparation.

An audacious task to be certain, but with the faith of David as he stood before Goliath, it can be done. It must be done. Once again, and for the final time, I use the words of the Austrian systems analyst, Hans Millendorfer: "The future will be Christian, or it will not take place."[5]

Christians must heed the credo of Dante which was: Have a "fear of being a timid friend to truth." The implication? Be a very bold friend to truth and see what happens! Find out what it is to live a dynamic Christ-follower's life in a post-post-Christian world.

Coram Deo: Live acutely aware of the ever present God who loves His people, the church. It is living under His authority and unto His glory.

273

Notes

Preface
1. James W. Sire, *The Universe Next Door*, 17.
2. John D. Castelein, *Christian Standard*, 5 July 1992, 5.
3 Steve Rabey, *Christianity Today*, 22 June 1992, 37.
4 Tom Sine, *Christianity Today*, 22 June 1992, 37.
5. Rabey, 38.
6. Russell Chandler, *Christianity Today*, 22 June 1992, 38.
7. Rabey, 38,40.
8. Sine, 40.
9. W. Gary Philips/William E. Brown, *Making Sense of Your World*, 17.
10. Arthur Holmes, *The Making of A Christian Mind*, 29.

Introduction
1. Hans Millendorfer, Christian Vision Book, *Man And State: Religion, Society, and The Constitution*, 93-94.
2. Ibid.
3. George Roche, *A World Without Heroes*, Cover.
4. *Time* Magazine, 8 April 1949.
5. Walter Brueggemann, *The Message of The Psalms*, 74-77.
6. Not everyone who refers to Genesis 1:26-29 as humanity's dominion mandate can be classified a dominionist or reconstructionist. One can find in Reconstructionism some of the most extensive, solidly researched, and carefully constructed Christian social thought available.
7. Charles Dickens, *A Tale of Two Cities*, 35.
8. Walker Percy, *Lost In The Cosmos*, 1.
9. Quoted in *The Stewardship of Life in The Kingdom of Death*, iii.
10 Quoted in *Christian Standard*, 6 May 1990, 6.
11 Quoted in a study monogram by Dr. James Strauss.
12. From a lecture by Dr. James Strauss.

13. George Barna, The Frog In The Kettle, 17.
14. Lesslie Newbigin, *The Gospel In A Pluralist Society*, 232-33.

Part One
1. W. Gary Phillips/William E. Brown, *Making Sense of Your World*, 17.
2. D. Elton Trueblood, *The Teacher*, 111-113.
3. Ibid.
4. Carl F. H. Henry, *The Christian Mindset In A Secular Society*, 84.
5. Ibid, 82.
6. Ibid, 93.
7-16. Craig Van Gelder, "The Gospel And Our Culture," a newsletter, January 1992, 3-4.
17. Lesslie Newbigin, "The Gospel And Our Culture," a brochure.
18. James Sire, *The Universe Next Door*, 17.
19. Ibid.
20. Charles Kraft, *Christianity In Culture*, 53.
21. Os Guinness, *The Gravedigger Thesis*, 30-47.
22. Frank E. Gaebelein, *The Christian, The Arts, And Truth*, 43.
23. Kraft, 53.
24. Ibid, 54-57.
25. Richard J. Mouw, *Distorted Truth*, 75-76.
26. Ron Boehme, *Leadership For The 21st Century*, 9-10.
27. George Grant, *Truth And Error*, 127.
28. Douglas John Hall, *The Stewardship of Life In The Kingdom of Death*, cover.
29. Harvey M. Conn, *Down To Earth—Studies In Christianity And Culture*, 154-155.
30. Ibid.
31. Ibid.
32. Terry Ferguson, *A Journal For Christian Studies*, 29.
33. Earl F. Palmer, *The Communicator's Commentary*, 29.
34. Sire, 18-19.

35. Tony Campolo, *Wake Up America*, 114-115.
36. Sire, 19.
37. James W. Sire, *Discipleship of The Mind*, 33.
38. Kenneth A. Myers, *All God's Children And Blue Suede Shoes*, 19.
39. Paul Johnson, *Intellectuals*, 1-2.
40. Francis A. Schaeffer, *The Great Evangelical Disaster*, 47.
41. Paul Johnson, quoted in *Against The Night*, by Charles Colson, 152.
42. Hall, flyleaf.
43. George Barna, *The Frog In The Kettle*, 112-122.
44. Rodney Booth, lecture by Dr. James D. Strauss.

Part Two
1. George Barna, *The Frog In The Kettle*, 23.
2. Ibid, 111-13
3. Ronald E. Osborn, *Our Message Is Jesus Christ*, Myron J. Taylor Lectures on Preaching—Westwood Christian Foundation, 1991, 1-2.
4. Doug Dickey, Personal correspondence.
5. Douglas John Hall, *The Steward*, 2-3.
6. Jurgen Moltman, *Creating A Just Future*, 1.
7. David McKenna, *Mega Truth*, 21.
8. Pascal's *Pensees*, 121.

Part Three
1. Bruce Shelley/Marshall Shelley, *Consumer Church*, Cover.
2 Tony Campolo, *Wake Up America*, 114-115.
3 Robert M. Woods, "Church Growthism: The New Heresy?", *Restoration Herald*, 5.
4. Os Guinness, *Tabletalk*, January 1992, 53.
5. Guinness, February 1992, 52.
6. Ibid.
7. Ibid.
8. Guinness, March 1992, 52.
9. Ibid.

10. Ibid, 53.
11. Ibid.
12. Ibid.
13. Hans Kung, *Tabletalk*, March 1992, 53.
14. Guinness, April 1992, 50.
15. Ibid.
16. Ibid, 51.
17. Ibid.
18. Guinness, May 1992, 51.
19 Guinness, June 1992, 51.
20 Collection of essays by Os Guinness for *Tabletalk*.
21. John F. Crosby, *First Things*, December 1991, 28.
22. James Davison Hunter, *Culture Wars*, 287.
23. Alasdair MacIntyre, *Culture Wars*, 315.
24. Tom Sine, *Wild Hope*, 68-254.
25. Howard A. Snyder, "Master Trends of The New Millennium," *A Journal For Christian Studies*, 2-13.
26. Tom Sine, "Shifting The Church Into The Future Tense," *Perspectives*, March 1992, 8.
27. Ibid, 11.

Part Four

1. Douglas John Hall, *The Steward*, 75.
2. Carl F. H. Henry, *Twilight of A Great'Civilization*, 22.
3. Ibid, 18.
4. Charles Colson, *Against The Night*, Cover.
5. Douglas Dickey, Research Paper, School of Theology at Claremont.
6. Lesslie Newbigin, *Foolishness To The Greeks: The Gospel and Western Culture*, 33.
7. Robert Benne, *Ordinary Saints*, 4.
8. Ibid.
9. Ibid, 5.
10. Jacques Ellul, *The Technological Bluff*, ix.
11. Benne, 7.
12. Ibid, 8.

13. D. Elton Trueblood, *The Predicament of Modern Man*, 59.
14. Benne, 9.
15. Ibid, 10.
16. Richard John Neuhaus, *The Naked Public Square*.
17. Benne, 10-11.
18. Charles Colson, *Wellspring*, TEDS journal.
19. Mike Yaconelli, *The Wittenburg Door*.
20. Ibid.
21. Kenneth S. Kantzer, *Evangelical Affirmations*, 27-29.
22. Charles Colson, *Jubilee*, June 1990.
23. Os Guinness, *The Gravedigger Thesis*, 15.
24. Richard C. Halverson, *Perspective*, #12.
25. James S. Sire, *The Universe Next Door*, 25-44.
26. Dickey, 12.
27. George Grant, *Trial and Error*, 118-120.
28. Victor L. Hunter/Phillips Johnson, *The Human Church in The Presence of Christ*, 19.
29. D. Bruce Lockerbie, *The Cosmic Center*, 97, 29, 123.
30. Ibid, 21-22.
31. Hunter/Johnson, 23.
32. George R. Hunsberger, "Cutting The Christendom Knot," a GOCN consultation paper, 5-6.
33. Douglas John Hall, *Has The Church a Future?*, 31-37.
34. Hunter/Johnson, 23.
35. Ibid.
36. Ibid, 24.
37. Ibid.
38. Ibid.
39. Ibid.
40. Ibid, 24-25.
41. Ibid, 25.
42. Os Guinness, source unknown.
43. Tom Sine, "Will The Real Cultural Christian Please Stand Up," *World Vision*, October/November 1989.
44. Ibid.
45. Ibid.

46. David McKenna, *Megatruth*, 26.
47. John Whitehead, *The Second American Revolution*, 41.
48. Howard Snyder, *The Problem of Wineskins*, 43.
49. Richard D. Lamm, *Mega-Traumas*, 16.

Part Five
1. Jacques Ellul, The Subversion of Christianity, 3.
2. Dietrich Bonhoeffer, *Ethics*, 332.
3. Douglas John Hall, *Imaging God*, 21-22.
4. Os Guinness, *The Gravedigger File*, 15.
5. John R. W. Stott, *Confess Your Sins: The Way of Reconciliation*, 49.
6. George Gallup, "Worldwide Trends In Religion," 17.
7. George Hunsberger, "Can The West Be Converted?," a tape.
8. Kennon L. Callahan, *Effective Church Leadership*, 4.
9. Ibid, 126.
10. Ibid.
11. Ibid, 129.
12. Ibid, 129-132.
13. Ibid.
14. Ibid, 133.
15. Ibid.
16. Ibid.
17. James Davison Hunter, *Culture Wars*, 174.
18. William J. Bennett, *The De-Valuing of America*, 55.
19. Kenneth Gangel, *Schooling Choices*, 131.
20. Quoted in *Mega-Traumas*, 119.
21. Dr. Charles Skurka, an interview, Gary Post Tribune, December 1990.
22. Kenneth Gangel, 127.
23. Walter Puckett, "Commentary," *Gary Post Tribune*, Ma 1989.
24. Hunter, 202.
25. Robert Maynard Hutchins, *A World Without Heroes*, 211.
26. Ezra Bowen, *Time*, August 1987, 56.
27 Richard D. Lamm, *Mega-Traumas*, 61.

28 Terry C. Muck, interview with Mortimer Adler.

29. Hunter, 209.

30. Charlotte Wheat, *Christian Standard*, 10.

31 W. A. John Johnson, Daily News Digest, advertisement for *NEA: Trojan Horse In American Education* by Blumenfield.

32. Bennet, 50.

33 Chester Finn, *Reader's Digest*, May 1984, 92.

34 John Silber, *Straight Shooting*, 8.

35. William J. Bennett, *Our Children and Our Country*, 83.

36. Ibid, 15-21.

37. Cal Thomas, *Uncommon Sense*, 174-175.

38. Curtis Dickenson, *Witness*, October 1990.

39. Hunter, 201.

40. "Milligan Milepost," Fall 1990.

41. Carl F. H. Henry, *The Christian Mindset In A Secular Society*, 9,16.

42. J. Shelby Sharpe, *The Coming Nuclear Attack On Christianity In America By Attorneys*, a document, 2-6.

43. William A. Stanmegry, *Clear And Present Danger*, 61.

44. Ibid.

45. Buzzard/Campbell, *Holy Disobedience*, 29.

46. Ibid.

47. Ibid.

48. Ibid.

49. Ibid.

50. John W. Whitehead, *The Second American Revolution*, 52.

51. Stanmeyer, 87.

52. Ibid, 30-31.

53. David C. Cook III, *Innovations*, Winter 1985, 24.

54. Hunter, 271.

55. Cal Thomas, "The Media or The Church . . . Which Needs Redemption Most?" *Tabletalk*, February 1990.

56. Marvin Olasky, *Prodigal Press*, xi-xii.

57. Ibid, 17-18.

58. Ibid, 19.

59. Ibid, 20.

60. Ibid, 22.
61. Ibid, 22-23.
62. Ibid, 25-26.
63. Thomas, 6-10.
64. Cal Thomas, *Occupied Territory*, 1,190-191.
65. Neil Postman, *Amusing Ourselves To Death*, vii-viii.
66. Otto Scott, "Revolutionizing The Media," *Chalcedon Report*, September 1989.
67. Quentin J. Schultz, *Redeeming Television*, 20.
68. Dean C. Curry, *A World Without Tyranny*, 112.
69. Ibid, 127.
70. Charles Colson, *The God of Stones And Spiders*, 91,
71 Ibid, 92.
72. Ibid, 91.
73. Cal Thomas, *The Death of Ethics In America*, 133-136.
74. Ibid, 136.
75. Carl F. H. Henry, *Wellspring*, TEDS Journal, 4.
76. Carl F. H. Henry, *Twilight of A Great Civilization*, 18.
77. Marshall J. Leggett, *Megaopps*, 27-28.
78. Harold O. J. Brown, A Christian Vision Book, *Man And State*, 76.
79. See Introduction.
80. George Roche, *One By One*, 203-214.

Epilogue
1. Huge Montefiore, *Reclaiming The High Ground*, 7.
2. Thomas Molner, A Christian Vision Book, *Man And State*, 76.
3. Ibid., 77.
4. Ibid., 78-80.
5. Harold O. J. Brown, A Christian Vision Book, *Man And State*, 94.

Appendix

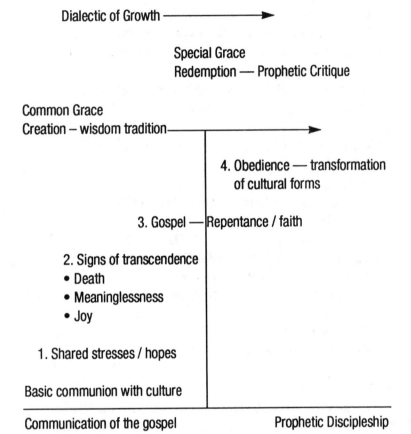

Dialectic of Growth ⟶

Special Grace
Redemption — Prophetic Critique

Common Grace
Creation – wisdom tradition ⟶

4. Obedience — transformation
   of cultural forms

3. Gospel — Repentance / faith

2. Signs of transcendence
   • Death
   • Meaninglessness
   • Joy

1. Shared stresses / hopes

Basic communion with culture

Communication of the gospel   Prophetic Discipleship

Source: *How Does America Hear the Gospel?* —William A. Dyrness

In a culture / society that is mostly alien to the gospel, disciples have to start witnessing, evangelizing, and enlisting where the people are at in understanding life, Christianity, authentic needs, and common aspects of life that Christians and non-Christians have. If Christianity was the dominant world-view of the western world, witnessing could start in most cases at step three. Now that is not the case.

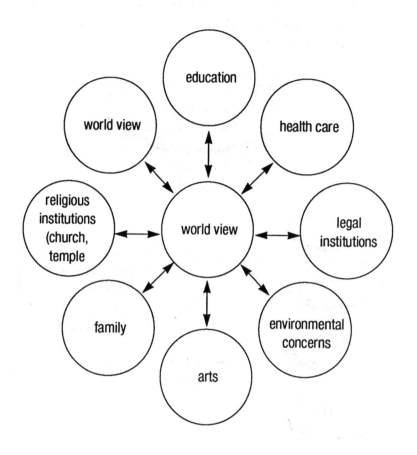

Figure 1

Source: *The Transforming Vision* —Brian J. Walsh/J. Richard Middleton

An illustrative picture of how world-view or eclectic world-views affect, interact, influence, or even control various social parameters of a culture / society. Consider the implications of what happens when any world-view opposed to the theistic / Christian world - view is the most influential or in control.

Source: *Effective Church Leadership* —Kennon L. Callahan.

The following stages of sphere relationships are very important for Christians to understand in order to assist them in world-view studies and issues.

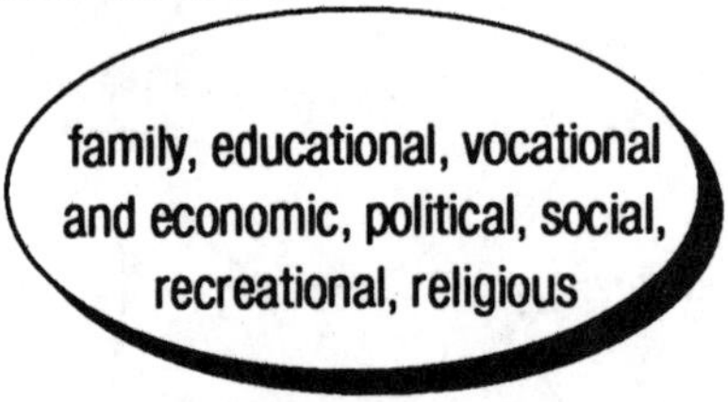

family, educational, vocational and economic, political, social, recreational, religious

Stage One
Figure 2

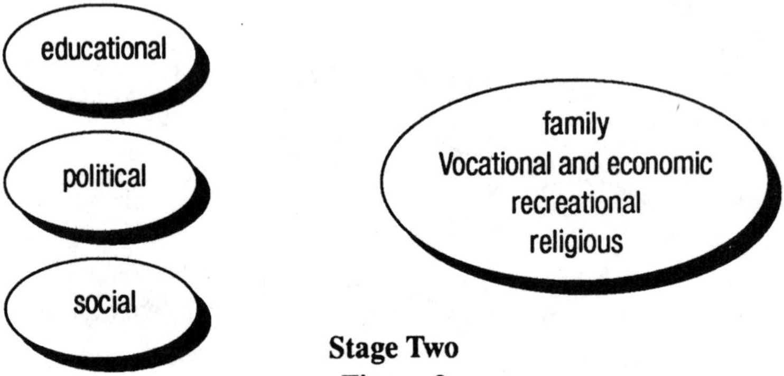

educational

political

social

family
Vocational and economic
recreational
religious

Stage Two
Figure 3

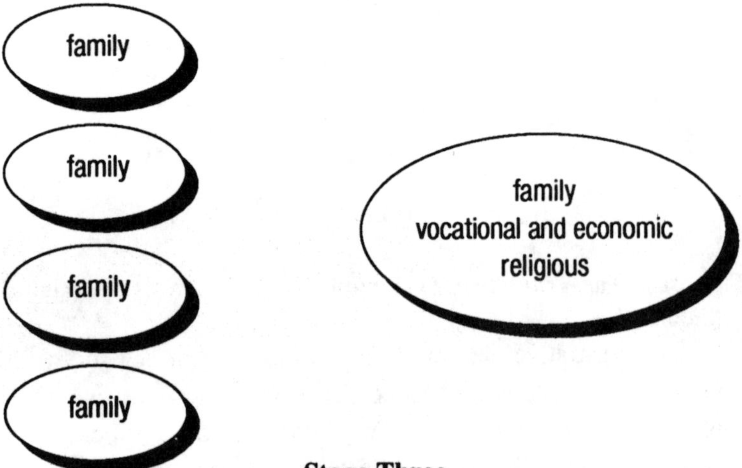

family

family

family

family
vocational and economic
religious

family

Stage Three
Figure 4
284

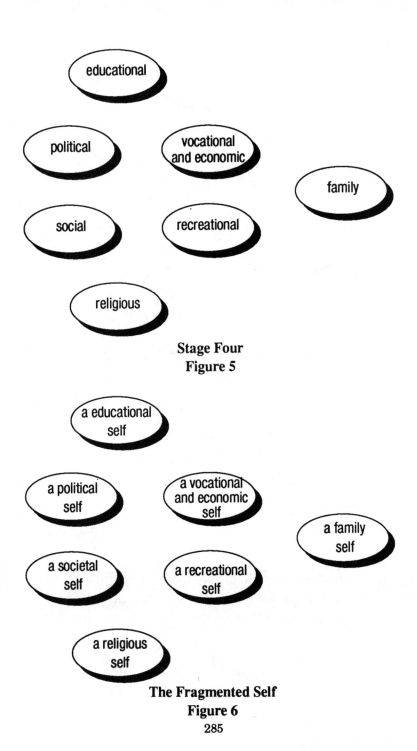

educational

political   vocational
                 and economic

                                        family

social   recreational

religious

Stage Four
Figure 5

a educational
self

a political   a vocational
self   and economic
                 self
                                        a family
                                        self

a societal   a recreational
self   self

a religious
self

The Fragmented Self
Figure 6
285

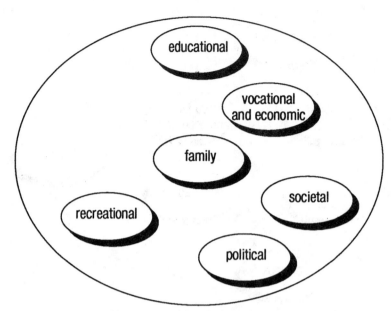

The Isolated Religious Sphere
Figure 7

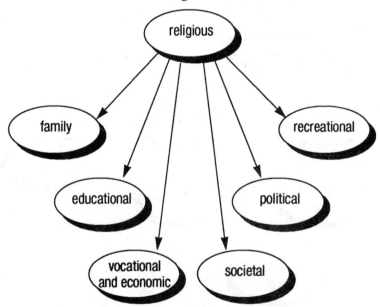

The Hierarchical Religious Sphere
Figure 8

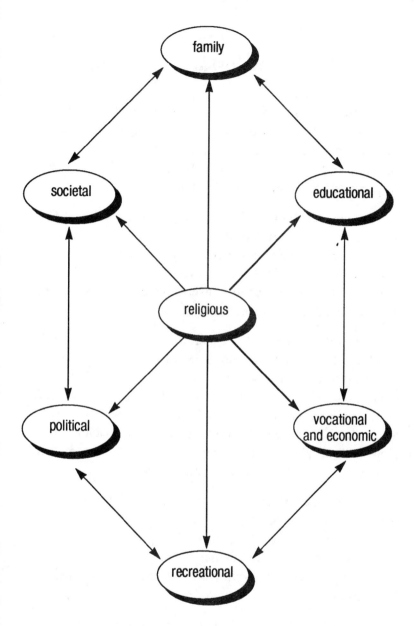

The Wholistic Religious Sphere
Figure 9

Glossary

Cosmos: God's entire universe; an ordered whole. Cosmology is the study of the entire form of the universe. In ancient Greece, Egypt, and Asia the order of the universe was thought to reflect the divine order. To participate in the cosmic order enabled one to participate in its divine source.

Cosmic world-view: This encompasses the relation of God to human beings and to the entire creation; a view of life, society, and the world that is larger than just this physical world. This sets forth cosmic thinking wherein Jesus Christ is Lord over the totality of life and the universe. Through Christ we find our place in the larger order of the cosmos.

Culture: In a broad sense culture is the patterned way in which people do things together. Expanded, culture means the total pattern of human behavior and its products embodied in thought, speech, and action. It's about the activity of man. It reveals whether man is noble or vile, and the cultural activity of man reflects his values and arises from basic convictions, religious and moral, about life. Culture is a social phenomenon. Culture may consist of various separable parts.

Culture/Society: Society is the result of culture as a social phenomenon developed from the culture or cultures operating within. Society is the whole of the culture or cultures. What world-view or world-views carries the most influence in a culture/society is the issue. Values are defined and developed by these world-views.

Humanism: This word has been abused by many right-wing, ultra-fundamentalist Christians. There are many facets to humanism, and one can quickly tell that many Christians, including Christian leaders, have not done their homework with this word. So many conservatives dump anything that is against God into "humanism." That is incorrect.

The many facets to humanism are not all bad from a Christian point of view. In its classical sense humanism is concerned with the value of general culture, rather than academic specialization and vocational education. Commitment to humanism in the classical sense is to care about the well-being and the betterment of man and does not require one to oppose or have a religious commitment. In this context Christians can work with a non-Christian humanist for both are concerned about the well-being and betterment of man. However, Christian humanism is the need of the hour in Western culture/society.

Pluralization: This is the enormous accelerating increase of choice right up to faith itself. It is a state of mind. The increase in choice has led to a decrease in commitment and continuity with any one truth statement or world-view or value system. For instance, with all the growth and demand for "fulfillment of self" in our culture/society fragmented by a plurality of world-views, one-man and one-woman faithfulness is out even in much of the church. If anyone dare say anything about that, you are liable to be labeled a "blue nose" by the powers in control, because most do not want to be offended with Truth. The church is soft on truth in a "political correct" society.

This is the process by which societies have come to have an increasing number of world-views available for their members, none of which is any more true or right than the other. There are a variety of world-views within one society, and not one world-view is in control unless it would be the spin-off of naturalism leading to secular humanism.

Pluralism: This relates to pluralization. In a pluralistic culture/society we have diversity but no ultimate unity to bring the diverse things of our experience together into a coherent whole. We have particulars but no universals. We have the relative and all kinds of absolutes, but which absolute/absolutes are worthy of unifying life and culture/society?

This is not the same as plurality which describes the many diverse views of peoples, etc. But add the suffix "ism" on the end of the word plural and you are saying there is only plurality and no unity, no one world-view, or no one true Truth. There are no correct standards by which to measure or to judge values, truths, purpose, beauty, etc. in society. This is too widely accepted in much of the modern church resulting in a very weak Christianity if it can be called that. No one truth is any more right or wrong than another. It is this that contributes to our society being very seductive.

Pragmatism: Some insist that this philosophy has its origin in the United States. It is a dominant influence in producing a lifestyle in America. The pragmatist says, "I don't have time in my life to figure out all the mysteries that are clouded in the universe about ultimate reality and ultimate purpose and all that sort of thing that has traditionally concerned religion and philosophy. I have been too busy with living. My life revolves around encountering a myriad of problems and so, I've got to find the solutions to these problems."

The pragmatist is interested only in "what works?" What brings results. Truth has nothing to do with it. The conflict between Christianity and pragmatism is the conflict of what is right and true and what is expedient. John Dewey the educator was a leading spokesman for this idea and saw education's purpose as this. Much of the American work ethic derives from this. Truth does not really matter. What works is not measured by any eternal norm or norms from someone called God.

A lot of church growth is pragmatism instead of discipling for conversion. Multitudes are added to the church by pragmatism, not by truth, but there is no subtraction of sin by conversion.

Presupposition: Some would say assumption. It is that which we suppose to be a truthful starting point for the building of what we consider truth and true Truth. Example: The basic presupposition for Christians in world-view studies is that the theistic/Christian world-view is the only valid world-view historically and in a contemporary and future way that will put man and God together and man and man together in this world. It is God's intention for life.

This presupposed world-view is based on revelation by God's self-revelation plus the Word of God. The presupposition upon which we are working is that the theistic/Christian worldview unifys and touchs every social parameter of society objectively. There is a Word from outside for man to measure every aspect of life and living. The presupposition is that no other world-view can say that totally. It is the only unifying world-view in the world.

Privatization: This is also part of society's seductiveness. Privatization is not individualism, but the result of the cleavage made between the public and private spheres of people's lives. Faith only flourishes in the private sphere of one's life. It is the ignoring or the refusing of the Biblical mandate to redeem/reconcile the whole world (cosmos) to God. It is a retreating into only the "soul saving" attitude of a Platonic gnostic-dualism approach to the Gospel as if man has some immaterial soul separate from his body. It is greek philosophy. It is not biblical.

It has, because of Christians privatizing their faith, left the public square "naked," meaning the influence of Christianity is no longer felt and realized to any real degree in the public domain of culture/society. It is a glove compartment type of Christianity that is crushed when the church really gets on with the theistic/Christian world-view.

Positivism: There is no higher law than what man makes or decides. Truth is only truth when it can be measured or tested mathematically or in a laboratory beaker. This is in the judicial system as man becomes the only lawmaker and morality is no more than legality.

Reality/reality: What is real and what is Reality? The best way to understand this is that the real is what we know and see by our senses; the world in which we live. The really real, Reality with a capital "R," is God as the ultimate reality.

What is happening in modern science in the face of the breakdown of the modern mentality in a post-modern world is causing science to take another look at what is real and beyond man. If this world is the ultimate in life, and in view of the issues modern man is facing, the question opens minds to see the possibility of the really Real, that is God. It is about world-views.

Sacred/Secular: These are not contradictory terms, but complementary for the simple reason that in this life the sacred can only be expressed in time while the secular has no meaning apart from the Transcendent.

The difference between sacred and secular is not that one is good and the other evil. Rather, the two are faces of the same coin. The sacred points to the Transcendent—the Eternal One—while the secular points to the temporary—the speculum, or world of time in which we live.

Secularism: This is secularity that has repudiated the transcendent—the God of Scripture—and therefore assumes to itself the absolute sanctions once reserved for the Creator. Secularism is a religion.

Secularity: This is a "holy worldliness." In this sense as used here, it is that which keeps the Transcendent—the God of Scripture in the unity of the sacred/secular. It challenges secularism by bringing the secular once more under Divine judgement.

To restore this secularity, the call is for the church to recover the offensive. It is to affirm the rightful Lordship of Jesus Christ over all of life as set forth in the Scriptures. It is to deny to the principalities and powers their right to absolutize the institutions of men. To restore secularity is to place the nation state once more "under God" where it belongs.

Secular Humanism: This is that which sets God aside and man is center stage. This term has come into vogue and power since the 1960s. It sets man apart from God. It is the non-classical form of humanism used today, a twentieth-century philosophy of naturalistic humanism that developed in a Christianized civilization. It is an atheistic humanism and one of the greatest threats to the survival of Christianity in a time when the church demonstrates little difference in life than the man on the street without Christ. In secular humanism "man is the measure of all things."-Protagorus.

There is one thing about which we must be honest. Secular humanists, who explicitly reject Christianity, take it for granted that every person has value and significance. They do not seem to realize, however or else they refuse to admit it, that without Christian convictions it is impossible to maintain that every human being has indefeasible value.

Secularization: A process through which Christian ideals and institutions lose their social significance and influence as a result of the power of the philosophy of secularism. There are at least two causes of this.

In a world of explosive religious diversification, religion instead of being central is just one tiny item amidst all the others. The effect has been to push it onto the sidelines. The other cause is not that "religion" is banned because of being illegal. It is ignored, because it appears irrelevant.

That is hard to accept in a culture/society filled with churches or at least church buildings. Is there anything really going on in those locations? The overall result and effect of this secularization has been a retreat into the privatized world; a form of unrelated piety; a form of monasticism by biblically oriented Christians.

It appears that over the past decades most Christians are content to remain in the private sphere that restricts Christianity. Keeping unaware of core issues, they do not have to confront that which is eating away their freedom to become salt, light, and leaven for Christ's sake.

"The Gravedigger Thesis:" This has been explained elsewhere. This has to do with Christianity digging its own grave. Involved in this is "secularization," "privatization," and "pluralization."

Society: That group of people, organism, social group developed by culture/cultures. The result of the social phenomenon of culture.

Utilitarianism: The social ethic which holds that the test of "good" is not anything intrinsic, but it is the greatest good of the greatest number calculated largely in terms of pleasure or pain.

Whether something is right or wrong by a higher standard than man's majority will is shelved and put away by positivism and utilitarianism. Positivism is the foundational world-view for this ethic.

This is the basis for deciding many laws in the judicial system. It is the secular humanist vision of Almighty Man.

Post-Christian: An era when Christian influence has waned to the point that it has almost no influence in the world beyond just the personal dimension of salvation.

Post-Modern: An era beyond the time when much believed to be the last word in truth and meaning since the seventeenth-century scientific world no longer works. It is the time of the breaking down of the modern mentality or the age of modernity which has left and is leaving too many questions unanswered.

Some call our time now the post-modern age. It is possible, according to great wisdom, that we are even beyond the post-modern mind.

Is this an open door to the church if the church knows something about what has been going on as a result of being world-viewish?

A growing number of thinkers are saying we are now in a post-post-modern age which means the world is in a more critical situation than yesterday.

Annotated Bibliography

This bibliography is not exhaustive. But it is more than sufficient for those desiring to begin studies in world-views, trends analysis, plus other supportive and related material.

The following sources are gifts that the Lord has made available through the hard labors of many individuals to help others grow in Christ and be His servants in the world.

Primary Resources For World-View Studies

Geisler, Norman L., and William Watkins. *Perspectives*. San Bernardino: Here's Life Publishers, Inc., 1984. An excellent companion to what I believe and will state to be the classic catalog study of world-views for primary understanding.

Mouw, Richard J. *Distorted Truth*. New York: Harper & Row, Publishers, 1989. A helpful work written in an illuminating manner somewhat like a social commentary to help discover what every Christian needs to know about the battle for the mind. The major issue in world-view studies is basically about that battle.

Noebel, David A. *Understanding The Times*. Manitou Springs, CO.: Summit Press, 1991. A recent discovery of the results of 30 years of world-view studies two-week camp program for high school and college youth. What a powerful contribution to the Kingdom.

Phillips, W. Gary, and Brown, William E. *Making Sense of Your World From A Biblical Viewpoint*. Chicago: Moody Press, 1991. This is a very good treatment in relation to the title. It would make an excellent text for a college class or for those who are not afraid of a more technical approach. It is too technical for the majority of the laos because it is too demanding for beginners.

Schlossberg, Marvin, and Olasky, Marvin. *Turning Point*. Westchester: Crossway Books, 1987. The first book in the Turning Point Christian Worldview Series; a Christian worldview declaration that fewer and fewer Christian understand.

Sproul, R. C. *Lifeviews*. Old Tappan: Fleming H. Revell Company, 1986. A helpful understanding of the ideas that shape society today. It is what is called a crucial questions book helping to bring one's faith into the world.

Sire, James W. *The Universe Next Door*. Downers Grove: InterVarsity Press, 1988. This catalog of world-views continues to be a most useful primary book for the new world-view student. Overall it continues to be the best introductory exposition of prominent world-views. It is a most readable presentation of alternative and alien world-views attempting and accomplishing the replacement of the Christian world-view in our culture/society. The latest edition has an expanded study of the New Age phenomenon. This one book accomplishes what would take three or four others together to accomplish.

Discipleship of The Mind. Downers Grove: InterVarsity Press, 1990. Learning to love God in the ways we think is the crux of the book. An excellent tool. This book contains "A Bibliography We Can't Live Without." It is most comprehensive of the many disciplines involved in world-view studies.

Smart, Ninian. *Worldviews*. New York: Charles Scribner's Sons, 1983. A study of world-views in the crosscultural and crossdisciplinary dimensions as they occur in religion, political science, sociology, philosophy, etc. A good tool for more advanced studies.

Walsh, Brian J., and J. Richard Middleton. *The Transforming Vision*. Downers Grove: InterVarsity Press, 1984. In a society where science, technology, economics, etc. have little regard for the Christian world-view, how do Christians continue to shape a Christian world-view developing a philosophical framework? A very good tool.

Primary Resources For Trends Studies.

Aeschliman, Gordon. *Global Trends*. Downers Grove: Intervarsity Press, 1990. Ten trends affecting Christians everywhere in the world. A disturbing but true work. Imperative reading.

Barna, George, and McKay, William Paul. *Vital Signs.* Westchester: Crossway Books, 1984. A helpful easy-to-read handbook on the emerging and present social trends in the context of the future of American Christianity. It is a good opener to the more intense trends studies and helps Christians to see if they are ready to struggle against the forces undermining their faith.

Barna, George. *The Frog In The Kettle*. Ventura: Regal Books, 1990. A tool to help awaken Christians to the world around them. Like all of Barna's books, it is not very heavy but worthy of reading and study by pastors and the laos.

User Friendly Churches. Ventura: Regal Books, 1991. A sequel to the above book. It is also helpful reading for Christians who want to know what is happening in trends and other churches. This book and the one above is fair for discussion texts in group forums.

What Americans Believe. Ventura: Regal Books, 1991. It is the same kind of tool put out by Gallup, but in some ways better, because it is more readable.

Chandler, Russell. *Racing Toward 2001*. Zondervan, 1992. A book about "the forces shaping America's religious future" that can be almost overwhelming. But for those who want to be on the cutting edge, it needs to be studied. This is a classic study.

McKenna, David. *Mega-Truth*. San Bernardino: Here's Life Publishers, Inc., 1986. An excellent tool to help interpret the changing trends of society in the light of the Mega-Truths of God. Perhaps a key book to assist in another spiritual awakening in America.

Naisbitt, John. *Megatrends*. New York: Warner Books, Inc., 1982. Although this book is relating ten new directions transforming our lives is almost ten years old, it is still current. I fear that most of the modern church has not even caught hold of what this book said almost a decade ago.

Naisbitt, John, and Aburdene, Patricia. *Megatrends 2000*. New York: William Morrow and Company, Inc., 1990. This contains ten new directions for the 1990's that must be heeded by the church. Although Naisbitt is biased as a New Age believer himself, his findings cannot be dismissed. In effect, the New Age movement is nothing but the old human potential movement with eastern religions thrown in, but it's flying its full colors while the church waits in the wings in committees and cheap grace wondering just what to do.

**Naisbitt, John and Aburdene, Patricia. *Megatrends for Women*. New York: Villard Books, 1992. The authors and title tells the context. Essential reading to be aware.

Snyder, Howard R., and Runyon, Daniel V. *Foresight*. Nashville: Thomas Nelson Publishers, 1986. This book asks the question, "why trace trends?" and offers ten major trends that will dramatically affect the future of Christians and the church. It was one of many books written in an attempt to relate to Naisbett's 1982 book. It is helpful.

Primary Resources For New Age Studies

Since the New Age philosophy is a most powerful and fast growing world-view in America, and since it is being used to try and remedy the failure of the world-view of secular humanism, which it cannot do, what follows are some select books for personal and group study of New Age world-view to equip Christians to know what they are confronting.

Amano, J. Yutaka and Geisler, Norman L. *The Infiltration of The New Age*. Wheaton: Tyndale House Publishers, Inc., 1989. A helpful book to realize that the New Age movement is something to know.

Chandler, Russell. *Understanding The New Age*. Dallas: Word Publishing, 1988. An excellent and more comprehensive work than most studies. It was written by the religion writer of the Los Angeles Times. No one book unmasks the New Age phenomenon better than Chandler. Furthermore he is not afraid to name key names in the modern church whom he believes to be promoting New Age more than the true gospel.

Ferguson, Marilyn. *The Aquarian Conspiracy*. Los Angeles: J. P. Tarcher, Inc., 1980. You can read all of the best writings on New Age, but will not fully understand it and its agenda, that seems to be making rapid progress, without doing some study in this book, the bible of the New Age Movement. The author steals Christian concepts and most Americans would think it is a Christian book. Key names in every social discipline and parameters will be recognized. They may take over public education, if they have not already, unless Christians wake up and know what is going on.

Geisler, Norman L. and Amano, J. Yutaka. *The Reincarnation Sensation*. Wheaton: Tyndale House Publishers, Inc., 1986. For its small size, it is a helpful handbook to give much information on this bizarre phenomenon. It ties in with the whole New Age/Eastern Religion craze.

Groothuis, Douglas R. *Unmasking The New Age*. Downers Grove: InterVarsity Press, 1986. This is one of a trilogy of New Age studies. All three are the best combined work available in the three areas that the author covers.

Confronting The New Age. Downers Grove: InterVarsity Press, 1988. An excellent tool on resisting the growing New Age movement.

Revealing The New Age Jesus. Downers Grove: InterVarsity Press, 1990. This is an excellent study of New Age challenges to orthodox views of Christ. Very essential for those willing to challenge New Age people.

Hoyt, Karen. *The New Age Rage*. Old Tappan: Fleming H. Revell Company, 1987. A collection of essays from key people sponsored by the Spiritual Counterfeits Project. Helpful.

Kjos, Berit. *Your Child & The New Age*. USA: Victor Books, 1990. Every parent should read this to be able to spot when their children are being moved into the New Age mindset in public education. This is wide-spread in public education, but presented in names that sound harmless. The book was written by a mother who discovered this in their local school. So she blew the whistle on what was going on.

Lutzer, Erwin W. and DeVries, John F. *Satan's Evangelistic Strategy For This New Age*. USA: Victor Books, 1989. This book covers more than just New Age thinking, but it still is helpful. A good book for group study. It is helpful for a series of sermonic studies on the topic, and very good for the beginner in these kinds of studies.

Related Informative/Supportive Resources

= Imperative reading and study.
* = Excellent reading and study.
** = Very worthwhile reading and study.

#Abraham, William J. *The Logic of Evangelism*. Eerdmans, 1991. The best book available on real evangelism that initiates people into the kingdom of God. Nothing in contemporary Church Growth material comes close.

**Allen, Diogenes. *Quest*. New York: Walker and Company, 1990. The search for meaning through Christ. Interesting. Not a shallow book.

Christian Belief In A Postmodern World. Louisville: Westminster/John Knox Press, 1989. It reveals how the breakdown of the modern mentality is happening. It opens the door to rethinking the place of Christianity in the modern world since science has not answered all the questions or ever

will. The book is about the full wealth of conviction on the part of Christians who know what they are talking about and know the world to which they are speaking.

**Bellah, Robert N. *The Good Society.* Knopf, 1991. A helpful book related to Bellah's *Habits of The Heart.* It is clear about the plights of America as we move toward the next century.

**Benne, Robert. *Ordinary Saints.* Philadelphia: Fortress Press, 1988. A good introduction to the Christian life of how ordinary people become ordinary saints because of God's grace. It has some great germinating thoughts for sermonic materials in the context of the call of God, the calling of the Christian, and the callings of the Christian. It contains some excellent understandable results of the Enlightenment on the modern world.

#Bennett, William J. *Our Children and Our Country.* New York: Simon & Schuster Inc., 1989. Edited addresses and speeches of the former Secretary of Education. Every parent and person involved in public education must read the book. It will encourage on one hand and disturb on the other. Reveals why public education by and large is still a shambles.

#Bennett, William J. *The Devaluing of America.* 1992 This is informative and disturbing, Bennett style, but truth about "the fight for our culture and our children." Christians need to be made aware of much that Bennett writes.

Berthoud, Jean-Marc. "The Gulf Crisis and The Temptation of World Government." *Chalcedon Report.* Vallecito: Chalcedon, December 1989.

#Billingsley, K. L. *The Seductive Image.* Westchester: Crossway Books, 1989. This is a Christian critique of the world of film, and one of the excellent Turning Point Christian Worldview Series. An honest appraisal.

#Blamires, Harry. *The Christian Mind.* Ann Arbor: Servant Books, 1978. Blamires, an Englishman, has been labeled a worthy successor to C. S. Lewis. That makes all of his books imperative reading. This one is about how a Christian should think. One realizes not too many are thinking.

\#   *The Secularist Heresy.* Ann Arbor: Servant Books, 1980. This is about the erosion of the Gospel in the twentieth century and has the quality of Blamire's expertise.

\#   *Where Do We Stand?* Ann Arbor: Servant Books, 1980. An examination of the Christian's position in the modern world. The author makes the book imperative reading. The forward written by the late Malcolm Muggeridge makes the book more valuable. Like all of Blamire's books, it is still contemporary.

\#   *On Christian Truth.* Ann Arbor: Servant Books, 1983. The author makes the book essential. The topic of truth and related subjects reinforces the imperative need of reading it.

\#   *Recovering The Christian Mind.* Downers Grove: InterVarsity Press, 1988. This book prepares one for meeting the challenge of secularism which will be around for a long time.

**Bloesch, Donald G. *Crumbling Foundations.* Grand Rapids: Zondervan Publishing House, 1984. Still a contemporary writing for Christians to be aware and get equipped as disciples to bring God's grace into the human folly in this age of upheaval. Those who care will be challenged. Those who do not want to know will not like it.

\#Bloom, Allan. *The Closing of The American Mind.* New York: Simon and Schuster, 1987. Surely no Christian, or parent, or public educator will bypass this bestseller by a University of Chicago professor who, even though he is not a Christian, prophetically says things Christian leaders need to know and say. Bloom's thesis is how higher education has failed democracy and impoverished the souls of today's students. Many have not taken this indictment quietly. On the other hand the book has made multitudes think again.

*Blumenfeld, Samuel. *NEA: Trogan Horse In American Education* . Boise: The Paradigm Co., 1984. Must reading for all concerned with public education.

**Boehme, Ron. *Leadership For The 21st Century.* Seattle: Frontline Communications, 1989. A helpful study in the context of changing nations through the power of serving. Highly recommended by some key individuals.

**Boice, James M., ed. *Transforming Our World.* Portland: Multnomah, 1988. A series of addresses given at the Congress on the Bible II, 1987 on a call to action.

Bonhoeffer, Dietrich. *Ethics.* ed. Eberhard Bethge. London: S.C.M. Press.

#Bork, Robert H. *The Tempting of America.* London: Collier Macmillan Publishers, 1990. This is about the political seduction of the Law. It is Robert Bork's brilliant report from the front line in an ongoing cultural war. What is at stake is constitutional government. He was turned down as a Supreme Court justice, because he is well aware of what is going on in the judicial system. Christians must read it.

**Breese, Dave. *Seven Men Who Rule The World From The Grave.* Chicago: Moody Press, 1990. A helpful book on how Charles Darwin, Karl Marx, Julius Wellhausen, John Dewey, Sigmund Freud, John Maynard Keynes and Soren Kierkegaard still influence modern man.

*Buzzard, Lynn and Campbell, Paula. *Holy Disobedience.* Ann Arbor: Servant Books, 1984. Lynn Buzzard, at the time of writing this was Executive Director of the Christian Legal Society. An excellent and informative writer about Church/State issues. This book has guidelines when Christians must resist the State. A delicate task.

*Buzzard, Lynn R. ed. *Freedom and Faith*. Westchester: Crossway Books, 1982. An excellent collection of essays on the topic.

* *With Liberty and Justice*. Wheaton: Victor Books, 1984. An excellent examination of civil law and the Christian. A companion to the foregoing book.

*Callahan, Kennon L. *Twelve Keys to an Effective Church*. New York: Harper & Row, Publishers, 1983. So much more valuable than most church growth handbook's methodologies.

Effective Church Leadership. San Francisco: Harper & Row, Publishers, 1990. Nothing in church growth handbooks match this as Callanhan builds on the twelve keys.

**Campolo, Anthony. *A Reasonable Faith*. Waco: Word Books Publisher, 1983. This is about responding to secularism. Campolo is not at his best in this field, but the book is worthy of study in a more practical manner. It is not a shallow book, but it is helpful.

* *We Have Met The Enemy and They Are Partly Right*. Waco: Word Books, 1985. This is more than just a worthy book. It makes a Christian face the truth in the enemy camps of other world-views. It keeps the Christian honest in the evaluation and study of other world-views.

Wake Up America! Grand Rapids: Zondervan, 1991. Typical, bold Campolo style, but a must reading if the church is going to answer "God's radical call while living in the real world." Mega-church people need to read it and see if they have any prophets in their pulpits.

Chalcedon Journals. Vallecito: Chalcedon.

Chancellor, John. *Peril and Promise*. New York: Harper & Row, Publishers, 1990. Some interesting helps as a commentary on America's inability to manage its affairs. It is evident that

Chancellor is truly disturbed. Without saying it, which is typical for most modern journalists, there was a world-view which once held America together. He did not say which one, but his words betrayed his unwillingness or cowardice to say it was the theistic/Christian world-view.

#A Christian Vision Book. *The Christian Vision: Man In Society.* Hillsdale: The Hillsdale College Press, 1984. A collection of essays from the college's Christian Studies Program that involves visiting key renown scholars for the special themes and studies.

#A Christian Vision Book. *The Christian Vision: Man and Morality.* Hillsdale: The Hillsdale College Press, 1986. A collection of essays from the college's Christian Studies Program that involves visiting key renown scholars for the special themes and studies.

#A Christian Vision Book. *Man And Mind: A Christian Theory of Personality.* Hillsdale: The Hillsdale College Press, 1987. A collection of essays from the college's Christian Studies Program that involves visiting key renown scholars for the special themes and studies.

#A Christian Vision Book. *Man And State: Religion, Society, and The Constitution.* Hillsdale: The Hillsdale College Press, 1988. A collection of essays from the college's Christian Studies Program that involves visiting key renown scholars for the special themes and studies.

**Clark, Gordon. *A Christian Philosophy of Education.* Jefferson: The Trinity Foundation, 1988. An important work.

**Colson, Charles. *Who Speaks For God?* Westchester: Crossway Books, 1985. A collection of Colson's "Jubilee" articles for confronting the world with real Christianity. Many, many areas covered that challenge Christianity in its weakened condition in this nation.

*   *Challenging The Church Series*. Four Books:
"Dare To Be Different, Dare To Be Christian" (What It Means to
Be a Citizen in God's Holy Nation); "Presenting Belief In An
Age Of Unbelief" (How to Evangelize Our Self-centered
Culture); "The Role Of The Church In Society" (Responding to
a Watching World); "The Struggle For Men's Hearts And
Minds" (Christ and Caesar in the 20th Century Arena).
Wheaton: Victor Books, 1986. These would make excellent
studies for small groups as well as personal study. Colson, in all
of his writings, says more as a prophet than heard in most of the
American church or even said by most modern theologians.

\#   *Kingdom In Conflict*. Grand Rapids: Zondervan
Publishing House, 1987. This book written by an insider to politics
and power speaks to the pulpit and pew. A book of great purpose
for a long time from one who has really been on both sides of the
Cross. What is written cannot be taken with a grain of salt.

\#   *Against The Night*. Ann Arbor: Servant
Publications, 1989. This is imperative reading by Christians who
are not afraid to face the fact that we are living in the new dark
ages.

\#Colson, Charles. *The Body*. Dallas: Word Publishing, 1992.
This is a book long overdo on the church being the light in the
darkness. The assessments are pointed which makes the book a
disturbing but quite true and needed production. It's Colson's
best!

        Wellspring. A monthly alumni journal.
Deerfield: Trinity Evangelical Divinity School.

**   *The God of Stones & Spiders*. Westchester:
Crossway Books, 1990. More articles from his "Jubilee"
newsletter, but written to what he calls "a church in exile." Few
stones are left unturned as to social issues and the condition of
the church as it faces the 21st century. A cry for the only world-
view we know that works.

Jubilee. A monthly newsletter. Washington: Prison Fellowship.

*Conn, Harvey M. *Down to Earth-Studies In Christianity and Culture*. Grand Rapids: William B. Eerdmans, 1980.

Cook, David C. III, ed. *Innovations*. Winter, 1985. A good article on the judicial system.

**Crabb, William and Jernigan, Jeff. *The Church In Ruins*. Colorado Spring: Navpress, 1991. Can the church sufficiently repair or rebuild its foundations for the future in order to get back in touch with the people and culture it is mandated to reach?

#Curry, Dean C. *A World Without Tyranny*. Westchester: Crossway Books, 1990. This is a must book as it considers Christian faith and international politics. It is one of the excellent Turning Point Christian Worldview Series. Only the courageous will read it and wonder what has happened to Christian influence in relation to world politics. The alert know.

*Damerall, Reginald G. *Education's Smoking Gun: How Teacher's Colleges Have Destroyed Education In America*. New York: Freundlich, 1985. The title says it all. Educators by and large would probably not appreciate it.

#Dannemeyer, Congressman Wm. *Shadow In The Land*. San Francisco: Ignatius Press, 1989. This book is a warning about the growing power of homosexuality in America. He pulls no punches and reveals many true frightening situations. Endorsed by several key people with strong minds and convictions. The gays have an agenda and it is going their way, unless.

Dickens, Charles. *A Tale of Two Cities*. Edited by George Woodcock. Middlesex: Penguin Books, Ltd., 1986. The title tells it all.

Dickinson, Curtis. *The Witness*. A monthly newsletter. Lubbock: Dickinson.

**Drucker, Peter F. *The New Realities*. New York: Harper & Row, Publishers, 1989. About the new realities in government, politics, economics, business, society, and world-views. The thesis is that the next century is already here. It is about action today, quickly, in the midst of our pluralisms for tomorrow. Heavy, but essential reading.

**Dyrness, William. *Christian Apologetics In a World Community*. Downers Grove: InterVarsity Press, 1983. A very helpful tool that is not too technical in the area of apologetics in relation to various world religions and other world-views.

** *How Does America Hear The Gospel?* Grand Rapids: William B. Eerdmans Publishing Company, 1989. A very helpful tool to help realize that without understanding the title question, the church will not evangelize to its fullness. Christians must learn about and be aware of what kind of interaction has to take place in presenting the gospel to an almost totally secularized nation and culture/society.

*Ehrenfeld, David. *The Arrogance of Humanism*. Oxford: Oxford University Press, 1981. The classic on humanism and why secular humanism fails.

Ericson, Samuel. "The Supreme Court's Changing Stance on Religious Freedom." *Christianity Today*. 19 April 1985.

#Ellul, Jacques. *The Subversion of Christianity*. Grand Rapids: William B. Eerdmans Publishing Company, 1986. This is heavy, but quite understandable by any who really want to take on the world. Christianity's success in a world still operating on Constantinian principles has been put on a "slippery slope." It is a challenging work, but still offers hope. More writers like Ellul are needed. He is not appreciated by many conservatives and those in the "just think positive" camp, because he is on target and they know it. An imperative book.

*   *What I Believe.* Grand Rapids: William B. Eerdmans Publishing Company, 1989. A summary in essay of his beliefs concerning humanity, history and the Christian faith. A good way to understand his thinking and application. Extremely helpful and needed. No truths are hid. His convictions are clear.

The Technological Bluff. Grand Rapids: William B. Eerdmans Publishing Company, 1990. To read and study this book is to be aware of the mess that technology has developed while it was doing much good. It is a penetrating work on how technology has been presented as only that which is totally good with no related and resulting issues of danger. Much of the world's problems will not be understood without such a watchdog warning

**Etzioni, Amitai. *An Immodest Agenda.* New York: McGraw-Hill Book Company, 1983. Rebuilding America before the 21st century in the midst of our political, ethical, economic, and personal options for the last decade. Can it be done?

Eyre, Stephen D. *Defeating The Dragons of The World.* Downers Grove: InterVarsity Press, 1987. A good group study book on resisting the seduction of false values from such dragons as materialism, relativism, individualism, conformism, etc.

**Farra, Harry E. "The Closing of The Christian Mind." *Eternity.* January 1988.

**Ferguson, Terry. *A Journal For Christian Studies.* Lincoln: Lincoln Christian Seminary, 1989-1990.

Gaebelein, Frank C., Lockerbie, D. Bruce, Editor. *The Christian, The Arts, and Truth.* Portland: Multnomah-Press, 1985. The thinking of Gaebelein who was considered to be a great educator on the subject of regaining the vision of greatness which most believe can only be recovered through the theistic/Christian world-view.

Gallup, George Jr., and Jim Castelli. *The People's Religion.* New York: MacMillan Publishing Company, 1989. A helpful study of American faith in the 90s. It is more than just statistics.

Gangel, Kenneth, H. Wayne House, ed. *Schooling Choices.* Portland: Multnomah, 1988.

*Geisler, Norman L. *Is Man The Measure?* Grand Rapids: Baker Book House, 1983. An excellent study on the evaluation of secular humanism building around the major thesis of this world-view which is man as the measure of everything. Enlightening in its content.

**Gill, David W. *The Opening of The Christian Mind.* Downers Grove: InterVarsity Press, 1989. This is worthwhile reading in the context of taking every thought captive for Christ. A good handbook for university Christians.

**Goldberg, George. *Reconsecrating America.* Grand Rapids: Wm. B. Eerdmans Publishing Co., 1984. An informative work with a concise summary of the Supreme Court's interpretation of the First Amendment over the years. If concerned about the federal takeover of religion, read this.

Graham, Billy. *World Aflame.* Garden City: Doubleday, 1965.

#Grant, George. *Trial And Error.* Brentwood: Wolgemuth & Hyatt, Publishers, Inc., 1989. A chronological of how the ACLU has carried out policies that are against everything Christianity stands for. A documented study of this powerful lobby that carries more weight than most Christians realize or perhaps even care about.

Grand Illusions. Brentwood: Wolgemuth & Hyatt, Publishers, Inc., 1988. This is the only thorough study that does in the legacy of Planned Parenthood. It is fully documented as to the source and present power of this mindset. It is disturbing and only the mature Christian will really want to work through it. It would mature others to do so. Grant knows his topics.

\#   *Third Time Around.* Brentwood: Wolgemuth & Hyatt, Publishers, Inc., 1991. Written in the same excellent Grant style, this is a documented study of the fact that the pro-life movement began in the first century A.D. Through the years key people have stood firm against abortion and held it back. Grant clearly reveals where the current pro-life movement has erred and where it is on target. A well researched tool.

**Guinness, Os. *The Devil's Gauntlet.* Downers Grove: InterVarsity Press, 1989. A good little handbook on "The Church and the Challenge of Society."

\#   *The Gravedigger File.* Downers Grove: Inter-Varsity Press, 1983. This book is as essential as it was when it was printed, because Guinness is a very alert and aware Christian scholar. How the modern world has had subversive power in the modern church is enlightening as well as disconcerting.

\#Guinness, Os, and Seel, John. *No God But God.* Chicago: Moody Press, 1992. This production is about breaking with the idols of our age. It is the same kind of powerful book as Colson's *The Body.* It is needed in this day of "church growthism."It is a stunning testament about American Christianity as a religion without God.

*Hall, Douglas John. *The Stewardship of LIfe in The Kingdom of Death.* Grand Rapids: William B. Eerdmans Publishing Company, 1985. A groundbreaking book on stewardship in the mission of the church being much broader than most of the church faces. A good handbook for serious study of "Thy Kingdom Come . . . On Earth."

*   *Imaging God.* Grand Rapids: Wm. B. Eerdmans Publishing Co., 1986. Perhaps heavier reading than most Christians do, but essential reading for the Christian caring about dominion as stewardship in a groaning creation. It opens a field of study that I have never received in any of three seminaries attended. That ought not to be.

*   *The Steward*. Grand Rapids: William B. Eerdmans Publishing Company, 1989. An excellent treatment of seeing the steward as a biblical symbol come of age. Again, a much wider, but true, treatment of stewardship beyond just the material giving of tithes and offerings. It would break new ground for a lot of pastors.

\#   *Thinking The Faith*. Minneapolis: Fortress Press, 1991. This is the first of three volumes on theology. The other two are coming. Having every pastor or seminary student reading this could remove most of the trivial thinking in the church today. This would begin to get the church off the slippery slope.

*Hauerwas, Stanley. *After Christendom?* Abingdon, 1991. A good, but challenging effort to make some aware that "Christendom" is history and that may be the best thing that can ever happened to the Western church, because the church will have to "make disciples."

*Henry, Carl F. H. *The Christian Mindset In A Secular Society*. Portland: Multnomah Press, 1984. Excellent in its field as the title clearly sets forth. A promoter work for evangelical renewal and national righteousness.

\#   *Christian Countermoves In A Decadent Culture*. Portland: Multnomah Press, 1986. The title is clear as to contents. Imperative for all Christians, leaders in particular.

\#   *Twilight of A Great Civilization*. Westchester: Crossway Books, 1988. As in most all of Henry's books, the title reveals the jarring contents. An excellent related tool for worldview studies as all of his books are. Is our world like Hogan's Army waiting for Godot? Read it.

*   *Toward A Recovery of Christian Belief*. Westchester: Crossway Books, 1990. The Rutherford Lectures with Henry at his best in a lucid, wise and powerful manner.

Perhaps the greatest need in the evangelical church is the recovery of being able to think Christianly.

Herberg, Will. "Modern Man In A Metaphysical Wasteland." *The InterCollegiate Review.* 5 Winter 1968-69.

**Hirsch, E. D. Jr. *Cultural Literacy.* Boston: Houghton Mifflin Company, 1987. An excellent companion book to Bloom's *The Closing of The American Mind.* It reveals how little cultural literacy is left in our nation of mediocre education, thinking, and living. Much of this sickness is being perpetuated in the classrooms of American public education. How long until we wake up?

*Hitchcock, James. *What Is Secular Humanism?* Arin Arbor: Servant Books, 1982. A shorter, but concise and thorough study of why humanism became secular and how it is changing our world. Still a very contemporary study source after eleven years. The amount of material it contains will surprise the reader which says much about the writer's expertise.

*Hoffecker, W. Andrew, Editor and Scott, Gary, Associate Editor. *Building A Christian WorldView,* Volume 1. Phillipsburg: Presbyterian and Reformed Publishing Company, 1985. Extremely helpful in tracing various philosophical creations of various world-views. The questions considered are fundamental. Beginners can handle it with some thought.

**Holmes, Arthur F. *All Truth Is God's Truth.* Grand Rapids: William B. Eerdmans Publishing Company, 1977. Very good introductory material showing the non-biblical fallacy of separating sacred from secular except for definitive purposes. Written by one of the evangelical giants.

* *Contours Of A World View.* Grand Rapids: William B. Eerdmans Publishing Company, 1983. A more advanced study, but worthy of the time spent in working through it. An introductory book to an entire series with Carl F. H. Henry as Editor-In-Chief.

**Holmes, Arthur. Editor. *The Making of A Christian Mind*. Downers Grove: InterVarsity Press, 1985. A consideration of the Christian world-view and the academic enterprise.

#Horton, Michael, Editor. *The Agony of Deceit*. Chicago: Moody Press, 1990. An eye-opener to what some TV preachers are really teaching. The book is endorsed by such people as Richard C. Halverson, Chaplain of the United States Senate.

Made In America. Grand Rapids: Baker Book House, 1991. This is one of the most jarring, but needed, books that I have read for a long time. It is a revelation of how spurious and compromising the American church is becoming. Horton raises questions that the concerned believer just cannot be ignored. I think he is right is revealing how American made evangelicalism is creating super-churches and mega-churches that has, as Campolo states in his new *Wake Up America,* have little if any social effect in the marketplace. This book by Horton relates to the results of allowing world-views alien to the theistic/Christian world-view leak into the church.

Power Religion. Chicago: Moody Press, 1992. This book asks the question: Is the evangelical church selling out to the wrong kind of power? It is a collection of essays about mission, not success, about faithful witness, about proclamation, not power, truth instead of technique, and message over method. The essays will deeply disturb many, but they must be read by "church growthism" minds. The argument of the book is that "Christ's Person and work is being obscured by ideology, subjectivism, pragmatism, legalism, carnal conservatism, and carnal innovationism." Enough stated.

*Hughes, Philip E. *Christian Ethics In Secular Society*. Grand Rapids: Baker Book House, 1983. Extremely helpful with studies on many dimensions of ethics in our kind world commencing with the study of the "conscience."

Hunsberger, George. "Can The West Be Converted?" A tape-1990 Van Dyke Lectures. Grand Rapids: Calvin Theological Seminary.

**Hunter, Victor L. and Phillip Johnson. *The Human Church in The Presence of Christ.* Mercer: Mercer University Press, 1985. Worthwhile reading helping the church to be the living sign of Christ in the world.

#Hunter, James Davison. *Evangelicalism-The Coming Generation.* Chicago: The University of Chicago Press, 1987. A jarring and disturbing book about the weaknesses and dangers imposed from the lack of certainty, discipline, and conviction in much of the younger evangelical leadership coming on the scene. It is a bit disconcerting, but imperative reading for those who care.

Culture Wars. USA: Harper Collins Publishers, 1991. An imperative book for Christian leaders that is receiving critical acclaim. It is an effort to make sense of the battles over the family, art, education, law, and politics in the struggle to define America. Any person who refuses to study this production will only shortchange their own understanding of the culture wars that have repositioned the church out of the social center of our culture/society.

#Johnson, Paul. *Modern Times.* New York: Harper & Row, 1983. A giant, but not for the slow reader. Imperative help to understand the world from the Twenties to the Eighties. Johnson is hard to match as a historian.

Intellectuals. New York: Harper & Row Publishers, 1988. A demanding but essential work for the study of the minds that have shaped the modern world. By reading this book no one can miss from where our current attitudes, mindsets, and world-view value systems come.

Jordan, James B. *Through New Eyes.* Brentwood: Wolgemuth & Hyatt, Publishers, Inc., 1989. Developing a biblical view of the world.

#Kantzer, Kenneth S. and Henry, Carl F. H. *Evangelical Affirmations.* Grand Rapids: Zondervan Publishing House, 1990.

The collection of addresses given at the Evangelical Affirmations Consultation at Trinity Evangelical Divinity School in 1989 considering the cracks in the evangelical church weakening its substance and penetration ability of culture. There are attitudes in the larger evangelical mindset that need to be known. It is a related world-view study needed by all. The Restoration Heritage could benefit from this collection of essays.

#Kilpatrick, William. *Why Johnny Can't Tell Right From Wrong*. New York: Simon & Schuster, 1992. A professor of education at Boston College writes about moral illiteracy and the case for character education. Informative, on target, disturbing and Christians should be the first to read it. Educators must read it!

*Kirk, Russell. *The Conservative Constitution*. Washington, D.C.: regnery Gateway, 1990. The author justifies the reading. Kirk clears up the wrong approach being used for the "separation of church and state."

#Kraft, Charles H. *Christianity In Culture*. Maryknoll: Orbis Books, 1981. This is the classic study of Christianity and Culture in a cross-cultural perspective. A detailed study that gives strength to any study of world-view and culture.

Christianity With Power. Ann Arbor: Servant Publications, 1989. This work considers your world-view and one's experience of the supernatural. It is helpful in world-view studies, but one will have to think through some conclusions to which Kraft arrives. He makes one think about the signs and wonders that are a growing attitude today. Make your decisions about his conclusions. I have mine, but the book has much good about it.

*Kreeft, Peter. *Making Choices*. Ann Arbor: Servant Books, 1990. Kreeft is an excellent Roman Catholic scholar teaching at Boston University. His writing is refreshing and challenging. This book is about finding black and white in a world of grays giving practical wisdom for everyday moral decisions. I recommend it as have many leading conservative evangelicals.

#Kuyper, Abraham. *Lectures on Calvinism*. Grand Rapids: Wm. B. Eerdmans Publishing Company, 1987. A series of lectures first given at Princeton University in 1898. Reading this will put a stop to blanket knee-jerk pot-shots taken at Calvinism by many who have never read much from Calvin. Much could be learned from this study by many Restorationists. It is clear that every social parameter of life belongs to God, not just some kind of gnostic dualistic "soul" talk.

*Lasch, Christopher. *The True and Only Heaven*. New York: W. W. Norton & Company, 1991. It is a plea from a noted historian who is tradition's champion. Constant progress, the cornerstone of the American belief system, is pure myth. He is calling for what he calls the "prophetic tradition" embodied in such 18th century people as Jonathan Edwards and the more recent Reinhold Niebuhr. Relates to world-view studies. Requires some thought from a very long book. But that won't bother the concerned.

Lamm, Richard D. *Mega-Traumas: America At The Year 2000*. Boston: Houghton Mifflin Company, 1985. An interesting writing on how America may be seen in various social parameters of life by the year 2000. The possibilities are present for what can be by the year 2000. There are some major crises we face in getting there from here.

Langley, McKendree and McCrory, Don. "A Conversation with Carl F. H. Henry." *Eternity*. January 1988.

**Leggett, Marshall J. *Megaopps*. Joplin: College Press, 19 90 .

Leslie, Connie and Lewis, Shawn. "The Failure of Teacher Ed " *Newsweek*. October 1, 1990.

*Lindsell, Harold. *The New Paganism*. San Francisco: Harper & Row, Publishers, 1987. An understanding of American culture and the role of the church written in Lindsell style: to the point without apology. He does not dance around the fact that America is very much controlled by paganism. Some will not like its bluntness, but its truth cannot be denied.

#Lockerbie, D. Bruce. *The Cosmic Center.* Grand Rapids: William B. Eerdmans Publishing Company, 1977. The cosmic center is Christ. It makes Colossians 1:17 come alive as a key text in the New Testament. Don't let its publication date fool you. It is more essential now than it was in 1977.

Thinking and Acting Like A Christian. Portland: Multnomah Press, 1989. One of many needed books to get Christians to use their minds again as God has ordained. It puts fickle feelings where they belong reminding us that it is only through the mind's use that we break the world's pattern. Grace and love and hope are not left out of his thinking. An excellent study and discussion tool for small groups.

*MacIntyre, Alasdair. *After Virtue.* Notre Dame: University of Notre Dame Press, 1984. An excellent critique of contemporary moral philosophy. It is not for the beginner. Helpful for one who has learned to use his/her mind in deep stuff.

Marshner, Connaught Coyne. *Blackboard Tyranny.* New Rochelle: Arlington House, 1978.

**McCullough, Donald W. *Waking From The American Dream.* Downers Grove: InterVarsity Press, 1988. A readable and helpful tool to understand the fallacy of "can-do" faith and culture as well as the illusion that all one has to do is "think positive." Endorsed by Richard Halverson, U.S Senate Chaplain and other notables.

**Moltmann, Jurgen. *Creating A Just Future.* Philadelphia: Trinity Press International, 1989. You have to face some heavy questions in this very thin handbood. How is it possible to create a world society worth living in? Is there a just future in a threatened world as fragmented as our modern world? Is there any world-view to remedy this? Can you support it if there is?

**Moore, Peter C. *Disarming the Secular Gods*. Downers Grove: InterVarsity Press, 1989. A good tool to learn how to better communicate to people and other skeptics who are trapped in the secular gods.

Montefiore, Huge. *Reclaiming The High Ground*. New York: St. Martin's Press, 1990. A Christian response to secularism. Somewhat of a disappointment as a whole, but it as some key thoughts relating to world-view.

**Mosley, Steven R. *A Tale of Three Virtues*. Sisters: Questar Publishers, Inc., 1989. His concern is cures for a colorless (not as in race but in something that has some kick to it) Christianity. It is so different from anything else, but interesting and revealing as to how "light humility," "hard honor," and "open allegiance" jumps over obstacles of boredom and the abstract. I will read it again, and perhaps again.

#Mouw, Richard J. *The God Who Commands*. Notre Dame: University of Notre Dame Press, 1990. It is about ethics and world-view. Read it and be challenged as to what is going on in the field of ethics. The issues are complex. Is it "infantile" to obey God's Word on ethics? Why is the movement growing to say that there is no room for commands of morality even though they come from God?

*   Uncommon Decency. Downers Grove: InterVarsity Press, 1992. An interesting, yet significant, treatment of having "Christian civility in an Uncivil World." Can Christians be civil, yet retain strong convictions, in a world falling apart. A source of help for engaging the world in world-view dialogue.

**Moyers, Bill. *A World of Ideas*. New York: Doubleday, 1989. This is a collection of conversations with thoughtful men and women about American life today and the ideas shaping our future. Quite helpful and informative, because Moyers has such a broad contact with decision makers irregardless of whether one agrees with him and his audience or not.

#Muck, Terry C. "Truths Intrepid Ambassador." *Christianity Today.* November 19, 1990. An interview with Mortimer Adler. Excellent!

*Muggeridge, Malcolm. *Vintage Muggeridge,* Grand Rapids: Wm. B. Eerdmans Publishing Company, 1985. A series of essays by Muggeridge on religion and society, plus a lengthy interview between he and William F. Buckley, Jr. The words, wit, and wisdom of Muggeridge will be quoted for years to come.

#Myers, Kenneth A. *All God's Children and Blue Suede Shoes.* Westchester: Crossway Books, 1989. This is another of the excellent Turning Point Worldview Series that should be in every church leaders library as well as other concerned Christian's library. The book is about Christians and popular culture. What is culture? What is pop-culture? "Ken Myer's book is a must for thoughtful evangelicals . . . I only hope there are enough of them left to read it." -Os Guinness

#Nash, Ronald H. *The Closing of The American Heart.* Probe Books: Distributed by Word Publishing, 1990. Nash's one question is: "What's Really Wrong With America's Schools?" I cannot stress enough the importance of this book on public and private education. Any parent and school teacher, Christian or not, should ask forgiveness if this book does not become a part of each life. This book is the same kind of giant as Bloom's book: *The Closing of The American Mind.* Read Nash and see if the theistic/Christian world-view can be brought back into public education as an alternative? I say it can, with work.

*Neuhaus, Richard John. *The Naked Public Square.* Grand Rapids: William B. Eerdmans Publishing Company, 1984. This is the classic treatment and study of religion and democracy in America. One cannot miss the fact that the church is the culprit that took religion (faith) out of the public square. It is an indictment, but a true one.

*Newbigin, Lesslie. *The Other Side of 1984*. Geneva: World Council of Churches, 1984. This book raises radical questions about the future of western culture and the life and witness of the church within that culture. First-time readers of Newbigin are in for a treat. This book and those that follow are, I am certain, instrumental to the creation of a movement going on in the United Kingdom called "The Gospel and Our Culture." This movement has moved into the States and is growing. This says something about the slowness of the American evangelical and biblical groups not picking up on world-view issues two decades ago.

Foolishness To The Greeks. London: SPCK, 1986. This is a companion to the foregoing book dealing with the gospel and western post-enlightenment culture as a missionary problem. Must reading for world-view people.

* *Mission in Christ's Way*. Geneva: WCC Publications, 1987. A series of studies given at the meeting of the synod of the Church of South India. Continued freshness from Newbigin.

The Gospel In A Pluralist Society. Grand Rapids: William B. Eerdmans Publishing Company, 1989. Perhaps the best book I have read in the context of the title. It is a continuation and an expansion of the first two of his books in this listing. Witnessing will not be strong unless the western pluralist society is understood.

* *Truth To Tell*. Grand Rapids: Eerdman's Publishing Company, 1991. The printed lectures given at Western Theological Seminary, Holland, Michigan. The title explains the purpose.

*Niebuhr, H. Richard. *Christ and Culture*. New York: Harper & Row, Publishers, 1951. An old classic of continued importance and help.

*Noll, Mark A. and Wells, David F., Editors. *Christian Faith & Practice in The Modern World*. Grand Rapids: William B. Eerdmans Publishing Company, 1988. A collection of essays and speeches from some top thinkers considering theology from an evangelical point of view. Helpful and enlightening.

**North, Dr. Gary. *Liberating Planet Earth*. Ft. Worth: Dominion Press, 1987. Some will write this book and the author off because of its relation to reconstructionist theology. But don't do it. One does not have to buy into that whole ball of wax in order to lift some very significant biblical truths from this movement that are solid and correct. The word "liberating" will scare some off, but in the context of the book, Christianity is the only liberating possibility for this world, and the book is not about contemporary liberation theology.

#Olasky, Marvin. *Prodigal Press*. Westchester: Crossway Books, 1988. This work on the press will anger Christians in two ways. There is revealed the anti-Christian bias of the American news media. But at the same time it was and is the church that contributed to how the bias came about and still is not helping remove it. Christians that cannot accept their responsibility in allowing this bias to happen will be angry. But the book must be read and it will stop much knee-jerk reaction against journalism. Journalism is an open field for Christians to enter if they know what they are talking about and know something about worldviews. It is another excellent production of the Turning Point Christian Worldview Series.

*Olasky, Marvin and Schlossberg, Herbert, Berthoud, Pierre, Pinnock, Clark H. *Freedom, Justice, And Hope*. Westchester: Crossway Books, 1988. Another excellent production in the Turning Point Christian Worldview Series. The title tells the content which is toward a strategy for the poor and the oppressed. A challenging book.

Owens, Virginia Stem. *And The Trees Clap Their Hands.* Grand Rapids: Wm. B. Eerdmans Publishing Co., 1983. For most, the book has little interest. For me it was the key and clue to the idea of Christians being God's spies in a modern Babylon. It has to do with perception and faith.

**Packer, J. I. and Howard, Thomas. *Christianity: The True Humanism.* Waco: Word Books Publisher, 1985. Very, very worthwhile because of the two authors and the need for Christians to understand that Christianity is the true humanism. This is not only a good treatment of the topic. It is also filled with practical teaching helps and ideas about the Christian life in this kind of world.

*Palmer, Parker J. *The Company of Strangers.* New York: Crossroad, 1985. The most lucid and encouraging combination of spiritual insight and social sensibility; a helpful and practical eye-opener to the idea that into the company strangers Christians are to enter. Going public with faith is not just fashionable or a fad. It is biblical and unless the church does that it is not the church.

**Pannenberg, Wolfhart. *Christianity In A Secularized World* New York: Crossroad , 1989 . A good small treatment of our world as the title states. Easily understood after some world-view studies have been encountered.

Pascal's *Pensees.* New York: E. P. Dutton, 1958.

*Patrick, Michael. "Casualties In The Church and Culture Growing." *Action.* Charlottesville: The Rutherford Institute, October 1990.

**Peacocke, Dennis. *Winning The Battle For The Minds of Men.* Santa Rosa: Alive & Free, 1987. Christianity once turned the world rightside up. Can it happen again? Only when Christian minds are captured in developing a new and alive generation of Christians. A lot of practical and illustrative material that ties the dominion mandate of Genesis and the witness mandate of Matthew together.

** "A Commentary On World Issues." *The Bottom Line*. Santa Rosa: Strategic Christian Services, December 1990. A perceptive monthly printing.

*Peck, Scott M. *The Different Drum: Community Making and Peace*. New York: Simon & Schuster, 1987. Some very good helps on community making.

Percy, Walker. *Lost In The Cosmos*. New York: Farrar, Straus & Giroux, 1983. An interesting writer dealing with key Christian themes in novel and none-novel approaches. He has been labeled as "the moralist of the south," and "the doctor of the soul." He immerses himself in theological thinkers and the bible and worshiped regularly until his recent death. He calls this the last self-help book. Shortly before he died, his testimony about Christianity to a reporter was in a question: "What else is there?" meaning nothing else.

**Perrotta, Kevin and Blattner, John C. *Courage In Leadership*. Ann Arbor: Servant Books, 1988. A series of addresses from an Allies for Faith and Renewal Conference calling for boldness in preaching, teaching, and pastoral care. Significant thinking from significant people.

*Posterskie, Donald C. *Reinventing Evangelism*. Downers Grove: InterVarsity Press, 1989. A refreshing book on evangelism with the same message in a changing world. It is far beyond the too typical church growth book on methodology that seems to gather adherents, but I wonder if conversions are happening?

#Postman, Neil. *Amusing Ourselves to Death*. New York: Penguin Books, 1985. Postman reveals so much for Christians to realize and understand in the area of public discourse in the age of show business. The "Forward" by itself is worth the cost of the book.

#Roche, George. *America By The Throat*. Hillsdale: The Hillsdale College Press, 1985. This is about the stranglehold of federal bureaucracy. It has been a long time since I have read material as good as everything Roche, President of Hillsdale College in Michigan writes. He is saying more and saying it better than most theologians and philosophers. The Hillsdale Story is must reading as to how this College stood firm and free and still does from any kind of federal control. The Story and Roche's writings is fresh air.

A World Without Heroes-The Modern Tragedy. Hillsdale: The Hillsdale College Press, 1987. A book the likes of which we have not seen in nearly a century is the endorsement of many people like Dr. Carl F. H. Henry, William F. Buckley, Jr. and others. The only heroes are those who do the will of God. The modern world of education and other social institutions have done little more than create anti-heroes.

One By One. Hillsdale: The Hillsdale College Press, 1990. An excellent treatment of preserving values and freedom in heartland America. It won't be done by bigger and better but only one by one. Again the endorsements from key people says it all about the value of the book.

*Sample, Tex. *U.S. Lifestyles and Mainline Churches*. Louisville: Westminster/John Knox Press, 1990. An informative cultural map sketched as we enter the 1990s. Some very helpful keys to reaching people in the 90s. Far beyond most church growth material that seems to forget that the church is an organism and not just organizational methods.

**Schaeffer, Francis A. *True Spirituality*. Wheaton: Tyndale House Publishers, 1971. Dr. Schaeffer's books will be valuable for a long time, because he was the forerunner of world-view thinking commencing in the late 60s and early 70s and continuing studies in world-view, Christianity, and culture until his death in 1984.

\#   *How Should We Then Live?* Old Tappan: Fleming H. Revell Company, 1976. This a classic foundational study for world-view studies in relating the rise of decline of western thought and culture. It will always be a necessary primary study for teachers and students.

**Schaeffer, Franky. *Sham Pearls For Real Swine.* Brentwood: Wolgemuth & Hyatt, 1990. The son of Dr. Schaeffer has mellowed since his last book, but he is still a disturbing and solid writer. This book is about getting beyond the cultural dark age in a quest for a renaissance of Christianity encountering and affirming the ordinary world as an object of God's redeeming love. There is a place and need of Christians in the arts.

\#Schlossberg, Herbert. *Idols For Destruction.* Nashville: Thomas Nelson Publishers, 1983. This ranks at the top the list of Christian faith and its confrontation with American society. The idols are: history, humanity, mammon, nature, power, religion, etc. It is lucid, disturbing, and very readable.

**Schultze, Ouentin, Jr. *American Evangelicals and The Mass Media.* Grand Rapids: Zondervan Publishing House, 1990. The title itself tells the contents. It is a helpful tool for research in the area of mass media.

*   *Televangelism and American Culture.* Grand Rapids: Baker Book House, 1991. It is a tool for information and relates to the book *Power Religion* edited by Horton. It is world-view related as it helps expose the alien world-views deeper into the church that most Christians realize, or perhaps want to know.

\#   *Dancing In The Dark.* Grand Rapids: Eerdmans Publishing Company, 1991. It is about the culture that controls most youth and younger adults. It is informative, disturbing, and imperative for study.

**Sciacca, Fran. *Generation At Risk*. Minneapolis: World Wide Publications, 1990. The question is not only why our nation has discarded spiritual values, but also how we got to this desperate situation and what can be done in the area of world-view application. Or is it too late? An informative book.

Scott, Otto. "Revolutionizing The Media." *Chalcedon Report*. Vallecito: Chalcedon, September 1989.

#Sharpe, J. Shelby. "The Coming Nuclear Attack On Christianity In America." Manuscript on The American Bar Association Seminary on Tort and Religion, 1989. The title tells the story that Christians need to be reading quickly.

"The Nuclear Attack On Christianity in America Has Begun In Earnest." Manuscript on The American Bar Seminar on Tort and Religion, 1990. This must be studied by Christians.

#Shelly, Bruce and Shelly, Marshall. *The Consumer Church*. Downer's Grove: InterVarsity Press, 1992. Two questions should lead the concerned to this book. They are: "Can the evangelicals win the world without losing their souls?" And "Are we risking false advertising if we offer people the power and benefits of Christ without the costs of following him?" This work reveals the danger of seeing the gospel as something to "market" in the contemporary marketing mania in order to attract "consumers" who will probably seldom be disciples.

#Silber, John. *Straight Shooting*. New York: Harper & Row, Publishers, 1989. What is wrong with America, and how can we fix it? This book is in the quality category of Bloom's *The Closing of The American Mind*, and Nash's *The Closing of The American Heart*. Silber is President of Boston University and has brought that university back into a thriving center of excellence. Educators would profit much from his assessment of public education. More money for the public educational shambles is not the answer. He has the real answer.

Sine, Tom. "Will The Real Cultural Christians Please Stand Up?" *World Vision*. October/November, 1989.

\#   *Wild Hope*. Word, 1991. Some more excellent writing from this author. A rally call to the church to take charge and live creatively in a changing world. You will not be able to ignore "the crises facing the human community on the threshold of the 21st century." Excellent tool.

\#Smith, Huston. *Beyond The Post-Modern Mind*. New York: Crossroad, 1982. The top of the studies on the breakdown of the modern mind to the point of being beyond the post-modern mind therefore opening doors for astute Christians to be able to dialogue with non-Christian searchers trapped in a scientific world that lacks many answers to life. Written in a very understandable style from a Christian who taught at MIT for several years. That is a clue to its value.

Snyder, Howard. *The Problem of Wineskins*. Downers Grove: InterVarsity Press, 1978.

\#   *Models of The Kingdom*. Nashville: Abingdon Press, 1991. An excellent study tool to attempt to bring some balance in some "kingdom" talk extremes.

\#Stanmeyer, William A. *Clear and Present Danger*. Ann Arbor: Servant Books, 1983. This is the excellent study by a Professor of Law at a distinguished university who understands the church and State in a post-Christian America. His warnings are clear. Extremely readable by any person who wants to learn and grow and be challenged.

*Stott, John R. W., and Coote, Robert. Down To *Earth-Studies In Christianity And Culture*. Grand Rapids: William B. Eerdmans Publishing Company, 1980. The collection of papers given at a Lausanne-sponsored Consultation on Gospel and Culture. The speakers read like a "Who's Who" in their fields. Extremely helpful on defining, understanding, and applying the manifested meanings of "culture" in the context of Christianity and the world.

**Stott, John R. W. *Confess Your Sins: The Way of Reconciliation*. Waco: Word, 1964.

*Swartz, David. *Magnificent Obsessions*. Colorado Springs: Navpress, 1990. A passionate writing about Jesus' mandate to "seek first the kingdom of God." It creates an appetite for thinking and wrestling with the imperative need of this kind of obsession.

*Swindoll, Charles R. *Sanctity of Life*. Dallas: Word Publishing, 1990. Swindoll at his typical best in dealing with the inescapable issue of abortion. It is a useful, readable, practical, non-technical book for the beginner.

*Thomas, Cal. *Occupied Territory*. Brentwood: Wolgemuth & Hyatt, 1987. Thomas is a journalist with strong Christian conviction and commitment who is able to relate and communicate to non-believing journalists without capitulating to their standards. He has the respect of the opposition who occupies the territory that Christians should be occupying. This book is a collection of his most controversial articles in which he has a jarring indictment against conservatives for not having the courage and determination to enter the journalistic world. Christians would benefit much from all of his books.

\#   *The Death of Ethics*. Waco: Word Publishers, 1988. The title tells the story that Thomas elaborates about and opens up. He writes clearly about another kind of AIDS: "Acquired Integrity Deficiency Syndrome." He has a hold on the pulse-beat of the issue in all sectors of culture/society including the church.

\#   *Uncommon Sense*. Brentwood: Wolgemuth & Hyatt, Publishers, Inc., 1990. He calls this a layman's briefing book on issues. It is an equal to the previous two books. Reviews on this book are from such people as Vice President

Quayle, Senator Robert Dole, Steve Allen, and George Will, the top Columnist in America. Also a fourteen year-old girl wrote a review thanking him for the book. It spoke to her.

* "The Media or The Church . . . Which Needs Redemption Most?" *TableTalk*. Orlando: Ligonier Ministries, February 1990. A jarring, but quite truthful assessment on the issue. The church needs help.

#Thibodaux, David. *Political Correctness*. The most readable book on the craze for "political correctness" and what this is doing to education. It is about the cloning of the American mind. Excellence by one who has shifted from the support of the topic and is now warning the results of "PC" at the university.

Tillich, Paul. "You Are Accepted." *The Shaking of The Foundations*. New York: Charles Scribner's Sons, 1948.

*Toffler, Alvin. *Powershift*. New York: Bantam Books, 1990. This is the third of Toffler's trilogy which started with: *Future Shock*, continuing with *The Third Wave*, and this book. It is about violence, knowledge, and wealth and the power roles they play at the edge of the 21st century. He has been on target with the other two books and if he is on target with this one, then we are heading into the greatest fight and shift for power that the world has ever known. Toffler insists that we live at a moment when the entire structure of power that held the world together is now disintegrating. It is five hundred pages of reading that can be frightening but informative for Christians to see if they are ready for the powershift. It is no longer business-as-usual.

#Trueblood, D. Elton. *The Predicament of Modern Man*. New York: Harper and Row, 1944. This classic is more contemporary than ever before. It is in this book that Trueblood manifested the concept of the "cut-flower generation."

The Company Of The Committed. New York: Harper & Row Publishers, 1961. This book is as fresh, if not more fresh for today, than it was the date it was published. My

work on him still stands: "Elton Trueblood: Twentieth Century Prophet of Church Renewal—Ahead of His Time." Most of the American church still has to catch on to what this title means and does to the Christian life and church as well as making an impact on culture/society. This book and the next one are still the most popular of his thirty-five plus books.

\#   *The Incendiary Fellowship.* New York: Harper & Row Publishers, 1967. This book rates the same as the preceding as to value and present need in the modern church. Nothing in these two books is too old and stale for today. Nothing. These two books should be required reading for every church leader: pastors, elders, deacons, and Christian education leaders in the local congregation.

*   *A Place To Stand.* New York: Harper & Row Publishers, 1969. This is a reasoned guide for the Christian faith. It is an apologetic that any searcher or seeker can read and understand. A good primer, but still advanced enough in theology to refresh the more mature Christian. He builds around Jesus Christ being the "center of certitude." A world-view issue.

*   *The Teacher.* New York: Harper & Row Publishers, 1980. Known by thousands as a master teacher, this book shares many powerful insights on developing the habitual vision of greatness through thinking and studying and teaching. A collection of essays covering many spectrums of life. A book to be read often.

*Turner, James. *Without God, Without Creed.* Baltimore: The Johns Hopkins University Press, 1985. This is a jarring, but on target book, about the origins of unbelief in America. This quote makes it necessary to read the book: " . . . religion caused unbelief. In trying to adapt their religious beliefs to socioeconomic change, to new moral challenges, to novel problems of knowledge, to the tightening standards of science, the defenders of God slowly strangled Him." Turner names big names in the Protestant circle that contributed to this.

*Vitz, Paul C. *Censorship-Evidence of Bias In Our Children's Textbooks*. Ann Arbor: Servant Books, 1986. If parents are concerned, this book will be in their library, but as yet I find few Christian parents who know anything about their children's school textbooks.

*Webster, Douglas D. *A Passion for Christ*. Grand Rapids: Zondervan Publishing House, 1987. One of the finest and most readable works on Christology.

#Whitehead, John W. *The Stealing of America*. Westchester: Crossway Books, 1983. Whitehead, attorney, is the founder and Director of The Rutherford Institute dealing with church/State issues. He is a committed Christian who sees America being stolen right out from under our noses. He knows both fields well: State and church and where Christianity has to fit in if we are to survive.

The End of Man. Westchester: Crossway Books, 1986. In this book Whitehead builds on the ideas stated in *The Second American Revolution* and *The Stealing of America*. Will our moral and spiritual decadence be the end of God's crown of creation-man? He traces modern man's deterioration back to its historical and intellectual roots.

True Christianity. Westchester: Crossway Books, 1989. I know of no better treatment of this topic than this publication. It is short, concise, and challenging. For some it is disturbing if they are satisfied at the level of faith that cannot take on the world.

#Will, George F. "America's Slide Into The Sewer." *Newsweek* July 30, 1990. It is encouraging to read material by a journalist who is not afraid to attack the cultural morality tearing us apart.

*Wuthnow, Robert. *The Struggle for America's Soul*. Grand Rapids: Eerdmans Publishing Company, 1989. A significant study of the struggle in America by evangelicals, liberals, and secularism. It is heavy, but informative.

*   *Rediscovering The Sacred.* Grand Rapids: Eerdmans Publishing Company, 1992. A heavy, but enlightening book on the attempt and evident hunger for something "sacred" in contemporary society. Is the "sacred" being searched for outside the church? The church has to reenter the social center of culture/society.